David Mercer

Plays : One

Where the Differ... ...t,
The Governor's Lady, On... **e Almond
Tree,**...

David Mercer emerged in the... ...n and stage and
this volume represents the firs... ...writing. *Where the Difference Begins*, a
naturalist play, takes as its starting point the recognition of varieties of 'difference' –
between thirties deprivation and fifties affluence and between material prosperity and
its accompanying spiritual and political apathy, as embodied by Wilf, a sixty-year-old
railwayman, and his sons. *A Suitable Case for Treatment* (later made into a film –
Morgan), written in three weeks, demolished much of the received wisdom about the
rules of television drama in its exploration of a man unable to live in the world in a
conforming way. *The Governor's Lady* reflects the freer thinking form and content of
A Suitable Case . . . but here the central character is reactionary. The Kelvin trilogy
(*On the Eve of Publication*, *The Cellar and the Almond Tree* and *Emma's Time*) moves
between Britain and Eastern Europe in a free intercutting between past and present.
One of the strands in *After Haggerty*, Mercer's first major stage success, was a
reassessment of Wilf from *Where the Difference Begins* and Mercer said: 'I think that
the Kelvin trilogy and *After Haggerty* were summing-up plays, gathering together
strands going back into the past, both personally and artistically.'

Mercer Plays: One is published to coincide with the *Days of Vision* an account of
working with David Mercer by Don Taylor.

DAVID MERCER

David Mercer was born in Wakefield, Yorkshire, in 1928. He began his career as a
television playwright with *The Generations* (a trilogy which opened with *Where the
Difference Begins*, 1961) and *A Suitable Case for Treatment* (1962). In 1965, with *The
Governor's Lady*, he began an association with the Royal Shakespeare Company
during which they premièred, among others, *Belcher's Luck*, (1966), *After Haggerty*
(1970), *Duck Song* (1974), *Cousin Vladimir* (1978), *The Monster of Karlovy Vary*
(1979), and *No Limits to Love* (1980). Throughout his life, he continued to work with
television, writing, among many television plays, *On the Eve of Publication*, *The
Cellar and the Almond Tree* and *Emma's Time*. His screenplay, *Providence*, was filmed
by Alain Resnais. David Mercer died in 1980.

DAVID MERCER

PLAYS : ONE

Where the Difference Begins
A Suitable Case for Treatment
The Governor's Lady
On the Eve of Publication
The Cellar and the Almond Tree
Emma's Time
After Haggerty

with an introduction by Stuart Laing

Methuen Drama

METHUEN'S WORLD DRAMATISTS

This edition first published in Great Britain in 1990
by Methuen Drama, Michelin House, 81 Fulham Road, London SW3 6RB
and distributed in the United States of America
by HEB Inc., 361 Hanover Street, Portsmouth, New Hampshire 03801

The painting on the front cover is by Joseph Herman, Boundary Gallery, London.
The photograph of David Mercer on the back cover is © Irving Teitelbaum.

A CIP catalogue record for this book is available from the British Library.
ISBN 0 413 63450 7

Printed and bound in Great Britain by
Cox & Wyman Ltd, Cardiff Road, Reading

CAUTION

All rights whatsoever in these plays are strictly reserved and application
for performance, etc., should be made before rehearsal to Margaret Ramsay Ltd,
14a Goodwin's Court, London WC2. No performance may be given unless a
licence has been obtained

Contents

A Chronology

1926 Born in Wakefield in the West Riding of Yorkshire, the son of an engine-driver.

1942 Left elementary school at the age of 14 and started work as a path laboratory technician.

1945 Volunteered for the Navy and continued laboratory technician work, both on land and at sea.

1948 Left Navy and, after returning to school in Wakefield, entered Durham University to read for a degree in chemistry.

1949 Transferred to King's College, Newcastle-upon-Tyne to study for a B.A. in Fine Art.

1953 Graduated from Newcastle with a degree.

1953–5 Lived in Paris attempting to develop as a painter. Began to write novels.

1957 Teaching English in London Schools; treated at the Tavistock clinic following a nervous breakdown.

1958 Sees Shelagh Delaney's *A Taste of Honey* and thinks he could do better.

1959–60 Writes the first draft of *Where the Difference Begins* (originally entitled *A Death in the Family*. Is taken on by the literary agent Peggy Ramsay, who sends the play to the BBC where it is read by Don Taylor.

1960 Three short stories published in *Stand*, the literary magazine edited by Jon Silkin

1961 Substantially re-written. *Where the Difference Begins* is broadcast on BBC television in December.

1962 *A Climate of Fear* (June) and *A Suitable Case for Treatment* (November) both produced by Don Taylor on BBC establish Mercer's reputation as one of the most innovative television dramatists.

1963 *A Buried Man* (February) broadcast on ATV (this script has never been published). *The Birth of a Private Man* (February) on BBC completed the trilogy of plays *The Generations*. The collaboration with Don Taylor continued with *For Tea on Sunday* (March).

1965 *And Did Those Feet* (June) was the last Mercer/Taylor collaboration. In February *The Governor's Lady* became Mercer's first play to be produced in the theatre (at the Aldwych), followed by *Ride a Cock Horse* (June at the Piccadilly).

1966 *Morgan*, the film version of *A Suitable Case for Treatment*, scripted by Mercer and directed by Karel Reisz, released in April. *Belcher's Luck* produced at the Aldwych (November).

1967 Mercer returns to television with *In Two Minds* (BBC, March) directed by Ken Loach.

1968 *The Parachute* (January) broadcast on BBC1, as are *Let's Murder Vivaldi* (April) and *On The Eve of Publication* (November).

1970 A prolific year for Mercer. The second and third plays in the *On the Eve* trilogy are broadcast on BBC1 – *The Cellar and the Almond Tree* (March) and *Emma's Time* (May). In the theatre *After Haggerty* opens at the Aldwych in February and *Flint* at the Criterion in May.

1972 *Family Life*, the film version of *In Two Minds*, is released, again a collaboration between Mercer and Loach. *The Bankrupt* (November) broadcast on BBC1.

1973 *You and Me and Him* shown on BBC2 (February) and *An Afternoon at the Festival* on Yorkshire TV (May). In July Joseph Losey's film of Ibsen's *A Doll's House*, scripted by Mercer, is released.

1974 *Duck Song* opens at the Aldwych in February. *The Arcata Promise* shown on Yorkshire TV (September).

1976 *Huggy Bear* broadcast on Yorkshire TV (April).

1977 *A Superstition* (August) and *Shooting the Chandelier* (October) are shown on Yorkshire TV. *Providence*, a film directed by Alan Resnais and scripted by Mercer is released.

1978. *The Ragazza* shown on Yorkshire TV (April). *Cousin Vladimir* opens at the Aldwych in the Autumn.

1979. *Then and Now* opens at the Hampstead Theatre in May.

1980. David Mercer dies in Israel in August. *No Limits to Love* opens at the Warehouse Theatre in October. *Rod of Iron* shown on Yorkshire TV.

1988. *A Dinner of Herbs* shown on BBC 1 as part of Mercer retrospective season.

Introduction

David Mercer was born in Wakefield in the West Riding of Yorkshire in 1928. His father was an engine-driver and he was brought up in a solid respectable upper working-class family. Unlike his elder brother he failed to pass the examination to gain entry to grammar school and subsequently left elementary school at fourteen to train and qualify as a pathological laboratory technician. He initially worked in a civilian hospital (attending his first post-mortem at the age of fourteen-and-a-half) and then, from 1945, in the Royal Navy. After leaving the Navy in 1948 he re-entered school and, after a year, went on to Durham University to read for a degree in chemistry. However he soon transferred to King's College, Newcastle-upon-Tyne to a BA course in Fine Art, from which he graduated in 1953. While at Newcastle he published a few stories in the college magazine and after graduating went to Paris, initially to become a painter but subsequently to attempt the writing of novels. By 1957 he was living in London and, following the break-up of his first marriage, was accepted as 'a suitable case for treatment' at the Tavistock clinic. He befriended the poet Jon Silkin, through whom he obtained work as a English teacher and, in 1958, after seeing Shelagh Delaney's play *A Taste of Honey* and feeling that he could do better, he began the following year to write a play (initially entitled *A Death in the Family*) which finally found its way to the play agent Peggy Ramsay and (after unsuccessful attempts to interest theatre promoters) then to Don Taylor, a young producer at the BBC. Taylor worked with Mercer to cut and adapt the play, which re-emerged as *Where the Difference Begins* and was broadcast in December 1961.

Formally *Where The Difference Begins* is a traditional kind of television play. Performed live (apart from a few film and video-tape inserts) it adopted a naturalistic fourth-wall format (being set almost exclusively in a single terraced house in Yorkshire). This reflected the play's origins in Mercer's attempts to out-do *Look Back in Anger* and *A Taste of Honey* and also fitted well with Taylor's position in a very active debate then taking place within the BBC concerning the aesthetics of television drama. Taylor was critical of the experimental Langham Group which saw television as primarily visual, 'a magical paint-box'; rather Taylor emphasised the leading role of language, dialogue, in creating the poetic and analytic effects of television drama. He also held strongly the view that there was a distinctive difference between live television production (with its experience for actors and viewers of continuous performance) and film in which the emphasis was on takes, re-takes and post-production editing. *Where the Difference Begins* proved a fitting vehicle for Taylor's ideas. For the play's setting Mercer employs a device characteristic of the early Sixties – the return of upwardly mobile children to the parental home following a death (both Alun Owen's television play *After the Funeral* and Raymond Williams's novel *Border Country* had appeared in 1960 using a similar pattern). Thematically the play's starting point is the recognition of varieties of 'difference' as they come home (figuratively and literally) to Wilf, the sixty-year-old railway-man – the difference between Thirties deprivation and Fifties affluence and between material prosperity and its accompanying spiritual and political apathy. Most directly the two sons are counterposed – Richard, the 'shagged-out political idealist' and Edgar, a 'solid conservative' scientist. From Wilf's point of view Edgar's self-satisfaction and Richard's aimless (if principled) drifting place them together as beyond connection with him and as traitors to their class of origin and, at one level, Mercer implies an unequivocal endorsement of Wilf's value-system and judgements. The play however also points to worlds beyond the domain of Wilf's traditional working-class home and way of life, as the characters of Richard and, most of all, Margaret begin to define points of development beyond the given.

During the writing of *Where the Difference Begins* Mercer, encouraged by Taylor, formed the idea of further plays to explore these points of development. The second and third plays of the trilogy, *A Climate of Fear* (June 1962) and *The Birth of a Private Man* (February 1963) then trace the progress of new political and personal goals into the third generation, focusing especially on Frances and Colin, the children of the Margaret character (now re-named Frieda). The material here begins to press against the restrictions of the formal and technical possibilities of live, studio-based drama. While the main focus remains on how characters cope with themselves and others within domestic spaces, the extension to the London of CND demonstrations, to Warsaw and Berlin, and the closing scenes of the two plays (Colin imprisoned in a police-van in London and meeting his death while scaling the Berlin Wall) show both Mercer and his characters seeking new freedoms not easily to be achieved.

One route to such freedoms was demonstrated in a play broadcast in October 1962, between the second and third plays of the trilogy. In the quite extraordinary *A Suitable Case for Treatment*, Mercer and Taylor together demolished much of the received wisdom about the rules for television drama. Here the theme of personal breakdown, treated tragically (with Colin's virtual breakdown and, in effect, suicide) in *The Birth of a Private Man*, becomes the comic centre of the play, *both* thematically and formally. While still broadcast live, the use of film-clips (mostly gorillas), of Morgan's dreams, of the associative (rather than necessarily sequential) linking of images as well as the simple naturalistic representation of Morgan's bizarre behaviour – all reflect the intention of offering a play which would allow an audience to share Morgan's view of the world (a world in which 'there just doesn't seem to be anything . . . that comes up to my best fantasies'). While this somewhat limited the implications of the play as an experimental work (because Mercer's innovations could precisely be read-off, and marginalised, as appropriate only to Morgan's abnormality), it also pre-figured a recurrent Sixties motif – the possibility of seeing madness as an authentic response to a mad society. The setting in London (the London of flats, bed sitting-rooms and temporary shifting addresses) is here not coincidental, such an environment being an increasingly significant ingredient of the world of Mercer's Sixties plays. This London is both a place of access to a wider world and the site of the most difficult problems of reconciling British normality to broader, more challenging international political and cultural questions. The attempt of Morgan (ex-Communist and failed writer) to 'carry my art into my life' is figured as a continual disruption of the orderly rooms of naturalistic drama – by appearing at windows, by entering and re-arranging Leonie's room, by letting off smoke-bombs, by listening at key-holes and playing his tape-recorder through them, by making his home in a car, by planting a life-size stuffed gorilla in the middle of his girl-friend's room. While *The Generations* trilogy, with its tragic conclusion and its displacement of British political and cultural problems into the much tougher terrain of Eastern Europe announced the arrival of one of the most original political dramatists of the decade, it was in *A Suitable Case for Treatment* that Mercer cleared the way both for himself and others to begin a different approach to the construction of the television play.

Mercer's collaboration with Don Taylor continued for two further plays. In the first, *For Tea on Sunday* (March 1963), the culminating scene saw a Morgan-like figure chopping-up the furniture of a middle-class London flat with an axe – simultaneously destroying the props of a certain way of life and of a particular television form. It was in *And Did Those Feet* (June 1965), however, that Mercer first began to exploit the possibilities of developing a television play outside the live, studio-based format. Here the life-story of the twin sons of one Lord Fountain (which culminates in their becoming zoo-keepers perched on a trapeze in an abandoned swimming-pool) is told through a script and a production which are based on essentially filmic, rather than live theatrical, principles (the following year was also to see the appearance of the film version of *A Suitable Case for Treatment*, scripted by Mercer and re-titled *Morgan*).

Up to 1965 Mercer was known only as a television dramatist. This was however as much by accident as design. His first play had originally been written with the live theatre in mind and in 1962 he had published the script of a would-be radio play, *The Governor's Lady*, in the small literary magazine, *Stand* (edited by Jon Silkin). A few months before *And Did Those Feet*, this short piece became Mercer's first theatrical production at the Aldwych. Formally *The Governor's Lady* reflects the freer thinking of *A Suitable Case for Treatment* rather than the naturalism of *The Generations* and thematically the two plays are also linked, not only in the re-appearance of the image of the gorilla, but also in the idea of a central character for whom the impossibility of accepting the prevailing political and social reality leads to fantasy and personal breakdown. Mercer, however, by turning to a very different kind of society than that of Britain, is here able to explore this problem within a reactionary (rather than a would-be revolutionary) character. Perhaps the most interesting feature of the play, however, is the central performance of the Governor/gorilla. Here Mercer is able to exploit the clearly unreal quality of live theatre (as against television which gives the illusion of presenting the unmediated real) to produce a more complex image. In the television play *Morgan* may identify himself with the gorilla and project his fantasies into both actions and dreams, however on the stage the actor (Timothy West in the original production) *is* simultaneously the Governor *and* the gorilla even if the play's ending does attempt to re-ground the audience in some primary reality.

During the second half of the Sixties Mercer continued to extend the range of his work within both theatre and television, while retaining certain core political and personal thematic concerns. Two full-length stage plays followed *The Governor's Lady*. *Ride A Cock Horse* (June 1965) was, in part at least, another visit to the terrain of the early television plays, with a writer (this time successful) looking back to, and negatively evaluating, his origins and seeking some new meaning through sexual relationships. *Belcher's Luck* (November 1966), more allegorical in form, recalled *And Did Those Feet* in its analysis of the decline and re-birth of the aristocracy. In television Mercer further developed his exploration of mental breakdown with *In Two Minds* (March 1967), which, in the hands of director Ken Loach, was given a drama-documentary treatment in the tradition of earlier Wednesday Plays such as *Up the Junction* and *Cathy Come Home*. This play constituted Mercer's most sustained attempt to consider both the particular causations and the treatment of schizophrenia (R.D. Laing acted as official consultant on the production), but although Mercer later collaborated with Loach on a film version, *Family Life* (1972), the form was not one which he used again on television. *Let's Murder Vivaldi* (April 1968) used the naturalistic domestic space of earlier television plays in a quite formally counterpointed way leading again to final violence (husband murders wife with a knife in a hi-tech upper middle-class kitchen), while in *The Parachute* (January 1968) Mercer made extensive use of flash-backs in representing the fortunes of an aristocratic family in Germany from 1914 to 1945. *The Parachute* was Mercer's first television play to be set entirely outside Britain and in both method and theme it prefigured the *On the Eve* or Kelvin trilogy of plays which at the end of the decade were to constitute both a new set of formal achievements for Mercer and a significant re-visitation of the political and personal concerns of his first trilogy.

On the Eve of Publication (November 1968) is centrally offered to the viewer through the consciousness of Robert Kelvin, a successful, but ageing writer. Indeed while the play initially purports to be an amalgam of a London literary dinner-party and of flashbacks and voice-overs from Robert's memory, the final scene (a re-writing of time which recalls the close of Golding's novel *Pincher Martin*) suggests the whole play is a product of an imagined future which is closed off by Robert's death. Robert himself is a composite figure bringing together two strands from Mercer's earlier plays – the older man nearing the end of his life and looking through his memories to find a pattern (as does Wilf in *Where the Difference Begins*) and the socialist writer or intellectual suspended between the complacent liberalism of the West and the inhuman bureaucracies of the Eastern European regimes who have usurped the ideals of socialism. It is as though, in Mercer's view, by the end of the Sixties, the earlier three-generational model in his thinking has become overtaken by events – Robert has elements of Wilf, Richard and Colin in his memories, hopes and despairs. There is, however, still a further generation involved. The whole play is in fact Robert's mental letter to Emma, his young mistress – a figure whose apparent lack of strong emotion renders her enigmatic and even one-dimensional. For Robert she represents a further substitute wife, but also the hope – 'now something's afoot – the young' – for both Western and Eastern Europe. The latter is consistently present throughout the play in Robert's memories of Sladek and in his own fantasies of going through the same processes of imprisonment and interrogation. As in a number of earlier plays the viewer experiences an opposition and tension between the attempt to preserve the surface social conventions and harmonious organisation of space and a series of alien and disturbing elements which threaten its stability; however this is represented now not so much by direct confrontation as by the play of fantasy and memory.

The Cellar and the Almond Tree (March 1970) is an altogether harsher and more direct piece in the realities with which it deals, although again much of the surface texture is composed of polite and civilised conversation. While the same fundamental techniques of memory, fantasy and flashbacks are used again, here there are two characters – the Countess and Volubin (whom Robert Kelvin knew as Sladek) – who share the ability of generating such moments for the viewer. Volubin (a figure whose experience of maintaining a socialist faith while opposing Stalinism recalls the figure of Jurek, the husband of Frances in *The Birth of a Private Man*) has memories (including a memory of his meeting with Kelvin in 1939) which fill in the context behind Kelvin's strength of feeling in *On The Eve of Publication*

– a strength of feeling which without this may seem forced and over-dramatised. For Volubin the cellar of the title comes to represent the reality of history of unfreedom under totalitarian regimes (Nazi or Communist). By contrast the almond tree (planted by the Countess when four, now destroyed, but still there in her fantasies) represents the continuing possibility of her aristocratic way of life – a dream as impossible as that of the Governor's wife in Mercer's earlier play, although here the Countess is treated more sympathetically. As the scenes between Volubin and the Countess develop, their memories begin to register parallels and affinities, notably in their shared personal losses (of Kate and the Countess's son) and the play comes to a conclusion when Volubin agrees to indulge her fantasy. The result is that each gains a return to a central scene of their memory – Volubin to the cellar, now as a prisoner of the Communist regime, and the Countess to the banqueting room and to a momentary triumph over the new order.

Emma's Time (May 1970) returns the trilogy to the present in Britain, and to Emma's attempts to come to terms with Robert's legacies, psychological, political and financial. Formally the play draws on the same free intercutting between past and present as in the two earlier plays; however here it is put to different effect. While the first six scenes alternate Emma's response to Robert's death with moments from the beginning of their relationship, the flashbacks here are not explicitly motivated by Emma's memories; rather they stand as scenes in their own right to give some substance to the relationship from which the play is generated. Instead Emma conducts a more direct search for the meaning of her relationship with Robert and for the significance of her lack of strong feeling ('Where's your bloody rage . . . ?' Robert asks) through a number of personal contacts – Mark Lang (the ex-Hungarian television reporter), Robert's mother, his cousin (the elderly 'queen' Charlie) and one of his ex-wives. The final and decisive contact with Sladek (the Volubin of *The Cellar and the Almond Tree*) is pre-figured by the inter-cutting in the middle of the play of extracts from *Ashes and Diamonds*, focusing on the actor Cybulski (motivated in the play by Robert's references to their friendship, although the real source is suggested by Mercer's dedication of the whole published trilogy to him). By the end of the play Emma has rejected the financial legacies and has retreated to a single large white room – analogous to the white cellar of Robert's dreams of interrogation in *On the Eve of Publication* and to the actual cellar of Volubin's torture (he finds her room 'strangely familiar'). Emma's decision to help Sladek to write his true history of the Czech Communist Party then becomes a way of reconnecting to the 'European consciousness' which, according to Mark Lang (a Hungarian refugee from 1956) is embedded in Robert's work and, even in the aftermath of the Soviet crushing of the Prague Spring of 1968, a way of re-affirming socialism and re-joining the central struggle of history. In Emma's decision Mercer returns again to the issues of the close of his first trilogy, of Frances's marriage and Colin's death – and to the idea that it is only by seeing politics in a fully international dimension, by (as a socialist) facing up to the realities of the Stalinist and Soviet deformation of socialism, that any political or personal progress can be made.

Just before the final two plays of the *On the Eve* trilogy were broadcast, Mercer had achieved his first major critical stage success with *After Haggerty*. In an interview in 1973* Mercer said that 'I think that the Kelvin trilogy and *After Haggerty* in its way were summing-up plays, gathering together strands going back into the past, both personally and artistically . . .'. In particular *After Haggerty* contains a fundamental re-assessment of the Wilf character from Mercer's first play – the connection between Wilf and Bernard's father in *After Haggerty* can hardly be missed since Leslie Sands, who played Wilf on television in 1961, also played Mr Link in the first production of *After Haggerty* at the Aldwych in February 1970. It is, however, now the son's London flat, not the traditional working-class terrace that constitutes the central space to be occupied, invaded or defended. The father is now presented not as the custodian of traditional and worthy socialist values, but as the epitome of working-class social and cultural reaction – in his attitudes to mental illness, race, homosexuality, the arts and almost every other topic. The play is also both an intervention in and a commentary on the supposed revolutionary theatre (and culture) of 1968 and after. Bernard's various abortive lectures in Moscow, Havana, Prague and Budapest (the stamping-grounds also of Robert Kelvin) and the dismissal, through parody, of the Living Theatre group show the limitations of theatre as a form of direct politics. Equally however the structure of the play shows Bernard and Claire moving in parallel towards forms of personal liberation through a review of their past and through the deaths (symbolic for Bernard's father) of their respective personal protagonists. In *After Haggerty* Mercer was able for the first time to use live theatre successfully to deal with the full range of concerns which had informed his television plays throughout the Sixties. In Mercer's view, '*Haggerty* and the Kelvin plays do represent the end of about ten years' development of certain themes and autobiographical preoccupations, and what's going to come after is I think going to be much, much more subjective in all kinds of ways',* and certainly to turn to Mercer's plays of the Seventies is to enter a further phase of development, building on the remarkable and original achievements of the first decade of his writing represented in this volume.

Stuart Laing, 1990

* From 'Birth of a Playwriting Man', *Theatre Quarterly* 3, 9, 1973.

Mercer on Mercer

Where The Difference Begins

It was the first play I ever wrote – for the theatre – and a couple of
managers optioned it, but nothing came of the options. Then
Don Taylor got hold of it at the BBC and said he very much
wanted to do it – so I went into television drama by accident. I
wrote the play in total ignorance of the theatre, of television. I
didn't know anything at all. At the time I didn't take television
very seriously. It's a very clumsy, old-fashioned, rather callow
play in all kinds of ways, particularly in television form. The fact
that it went on to television was mainly due to Don Taylor's
enthusiasm and persistence. On the whole it comes within the
naturalistic category. But if you take a very close look at the
dialogue, particularly that of the old engine driver, Wilf, what
comes across as naturalistic sounding is very carefully con-
structed as well . . .

 The play was very important to me because it was a
watershed, both for me personally, and for my efforts to be a
writer, and for my political consciousness and everything.
Previously I'd spent a number of years trying to write novels. I'd
been living in Europe, I was married to a Czechoslovakian wife,
I was deeply identified with the problems of Central Europe,
Communism, the War, Auschwitz, the camps, statelessness,
dispossessed people, and I had spent a number of years trying to
use all this actual historical reality as a sort of metaphor for 'the
condition of man' – probably the phrase I would have used in
those days! The importance of *Where The Difference Begins* was

that I realised that the stateless person, the dispossessed person, the alienated person was myself, in ordinary terms of having come from one particular part of England, one particular period in history, one particular class, and then having the possibility of existing in another, with all the contradictions it entails.

(From an interview with David Mercer by Paul Madden in the National Film Archive programme, April 1975.)

A Suitable Case for Treatment

. . . for me the real breakthrough was *A Suitable Case for Treatment*, because there I had a flash of an idea, and I sat down and wrote it in an absolute kind of trance for three weeks – for me a very short time to write a play in. It broke every rule in the television drama book, and they were all gravely shaking their heads and saying they thought that we'd gone astray this time. It turned out to be a serious creative departure for me in TV, and I'm told by people that it was recognised by others to be a clear development in what people thought television drama could do. It was a great big loosening-up.

Of course, it was extremely well directed by Don Taylor. I think it's his best production of my work, because it was very, very free: idiosyncratic and crazy and odd and quirky with dream and fantasy scenes cut freely into the real action. This kind of thing simply hadn't been on with television drama, because television drama was still oriented more towards theatre than film. So *A Suitable Case for Treatment* was a kind of release for me. . . . Obviously, for me there are very serious undertones to the play – the question of a man unable to live in the world as he experiences it in a conforming way, being beleaguered by images of animals as expressions of a free existence, particularly the gorilla. The gorilla was important because it's one of the most powerful animals in the jungle, but the least aggressive. It's very hard to pick a fight with a gorilla, they tend to go away, and so I think for Morgan the idea of the potential for aggression and the capacity to destroy as symbolized by the gorilla was very important. And then again it goes back too to the bit about the impossibility of being in any formal sense a Communist . . . if you are intellectually and emotionally committed to a particular ideology, as I was and am to theoretical Communism, and yet find no way of becoming active in the world which is consistent with your beliefs, this does create just the kind of split that is dramatized in *A Suitable Case for Treatment*. Morgan, remember, was the son of a Communist working-class family, and perhaps turning the whole thing into a joke and resorting to fantasy was his only way of coping with the situation . . .

(From 'Birth of a Playwriting Man', *Theatre Quarterly* 3, 9, 1973.)

The Kelvin Trilogy

By the time I got around to the group of television plays directed by Alan Bridges (*Let's Murder Vivaldi* and the three plays about Robert Kelvin) I'd been working in films. I'd written *Morgan*, I'd written a draft for *Women in Love*, I'd started *Belcher's Luck* as a film, and had been involved with film directors, and on location and on film sets, and had become involved with the whole technical business of film as cinema – as opposed to television plays, which happen in the studio, are shot with five cameras and controlled from the gallery. I think the juxtaposition of scenes in the work with Alan Bridges and the idea of flashing back, and cutting backwards and forwards, was mostly indicated by me, but developed by Alan during the actual shooting and editing, which is just as it should be. He took a direction of which I might have given him some indication and then contributed things of his own, suggesting ways of cutting it which were a refinement of my ideas. By the time Alan and I had completed *Emma's Time*, we had evolved a really quite sophisticated technique, for television, of using past and present and cut and intercut.

(From 'Birth of a Playwriting Man.')

Marxism and Writing

'Why is this Marxist so concerned with the psychological problems of declassed individualists?' 'Why are the self-styled Marxists in his plays always disenchanted and embittered?' 'Why does he write about the bourgeoisie for the bourgeoisie?' 'Why has he never joined a Marxist organisation?' The answers are that the psychological problems of declassed individuals are revealing about matters of class conflict and alienation; that it would take a Stalinist to be an enchanted and unembittered Marxist; that I do not write for the bourgeoisie – but a bourgeois culture owns the means of production without which my plays cannot be seen; that I have never joined a Marxist organisation because I have not encountered one in my lifetime which I could give my allegiance to without abdicating my critical intelligence . . . I have often and openly declared a contradiction in myself which I have failed to resolve. This is that on the one hand I cannot and do not write programmatically, with conscious objectives: my work is intuitive, and is itself the process by which I discover what I have it in me to say. On the other hand I broadly accept Marx's view that history is a complex of forces, of property and production relationships in a state of ongoing dialectical change. I also accept Lenin's view that a revolutionary party is the necessary expression of this dialectic . . . One could say . . . that my plays do not provoke *Marxist* thought or action; and indeed I would be surprised if an intuitive work of the imagination which by the very nature of this society becomes a product for 'consumption' (or indigestion) could succeed where the steely, rational and incomparable Brecht has failed. Yet one could also say – with Trotsky that all works of art are revolutionary, in the sense that they reflect through the subjective imagination the objective conditions of their time . . . meanwhile I shall continue to adhere to my political positions, to implement them actively whenever and wherever possible, and to try honestly to write plays which derive from my experience and my imagination rather than the crude imperatives of political philistines.

(*The Listener*, 28.5.70.)

Where The Difference Begins

Where The Difference Begins was first broadcast by BBC Television on 15 December 1961 with the following cast:

WILF CROWTHER, an engine driver	*Leslie Sands*
RICHARD	*Barry Foster*
EDGAR	*Nigel Stock*
GILLIAN	*Olive McFarland*
MARGARET	*Pauline Letts*
AUNTY BEATIE	*Hylda Baker*
UNCLE GEORGE	*Beckett Bould*
AUNTY BESSIE	*Jane Eccles*
JANET	*Ellen McIntosh*
WILF'S WIFE	*Rosemary Matthews*
MAN IN BUFFET	*Frank Seton*

Designed by Frederick Knapman
Produced by Don Taylor

Telecine Opening Sequence

Outside the engine sheds in a Yorkshire town. Winter. Late afternoon.

Open on locomotive steam valve and whistle blowing. WILF *is at the cabin window. Coal falling into the tender. The firemen opens the fire door in the cab, lifts fire bars and begins to rake the fire.* WILF *leaves the cab, goes down the line and through the shed. He is a big man in his early sixties, with close-cropped grey hair.*

CUT TO:

WILF *coming up the street behind a row of terrace houses near the railway. He turns into one of the yards and crosses it to the door.*

Scene One

The Crowthers' Living Room and Kitchen.
WILF *enters the kitchen from the back door. He takes off his top coat and hangs it on a hook behind the door. Sits on a stool by the door and begins to unlace his clogs.* RICHARD *comes in from the living room. He is a rather bitter man in his early thirties.*

RICHARD. Hello Dad. How are you?

> WILF *stands up and they shake hands.*

WILF. I'm all right, lad. How's your mother?

> WILF *pulls off his clogs and puts them under the stool.*

RICHARD. I haven't been up yet. Aunt Beatie's with her. She says mother's been sleeping since two. We only got here about an hour ago.

> RICHARD *goes back into the living room followed by his father.* GILLIAN, RICHARD'S *girl, is sitting in an armchair by the fire. She is twenty-three, attractive, gentle, noticeably pregnant.* WILF *looks questioningly at her.*

RICHARD. Dad, this is Gillian. You did get my letter didn't you?

GILLIAN *stands up. All three look awkward.* WILF *goes to her and they shake hands.*

WILF. I did an' all. How d'you do love.

(*Looks at her stomach.*) When you getting married then?

RICHARD. As soon as the divorce is final. It should be through in about a month.

WILF. It's a reight kettle of fish, and no mistake!

GILLIAN. We're both . . . both glad about the baby, Mr. Crowther.

WILF. Why, I should think you are and all love. Tha knows, Margaret – that's his brother's wife – Margaret told me their two were summat as she called a planned family. If them's a planned family, give me a honest to God accident any time on t'year. Sit yourself down love. I'll go and get washed and out on me muck. (GILLIAN *sits down.* WILF *goes up to her.*) Don't fret thisen love. Tha's reight welcome here. Tha's welcome.

He takes a towel which is hanging by the fireplace and goes out into the kitchen, shutting the door.

GILLIAN. I wouldn't have thought he could be as nice as that. (*She puts a hand on her stomach.* RICHARD *sits on the arm of her chair.*) I thought I'd feel ashamed, but I don't.

RICHARD. Well he liked you.

GILLIAN. In a way, I wish I'd known your wife. How can they avoid making comparisons? And it's a bad start, like this. (*Pause.*) Did she get on well with him?

RICHARD. Look Gillian, don't let's start worrying about Janet.

GILLIAN. I wonder what they thought, your marrying a rich and elegant woman like her. That photo of her makes me feel tatty just to look at it.

RICHARD. Does he look the sort of man who'd give a damn whether somebody's rich and elegant? (*Knock on the door.*) That'll be Edgar.

RICHARD *goes to the front door and lets in* EDGAR *and* MARGARET. EDGAR *is stocky and irritable-looking, forty-*

two. MARGARET *is about the same age – a sharp, complex, edgily tired woman.*

EDGAR. Is mother still –

RICHARD. Yes. (*Pause.*) She's asleep at the moment. Aunty Beatie's –

EDGAR. I'll sue that bloody garage one of these days. We had a puncture outside Doncaster. When I got the spare out it was as flat as hell, and –

MARGARET *pushes him into the living room. Puts her case down.*

MARGARET. And I've had a lecture on the idleness of the modern workman for the last twenty miles. (*To* RICHARD, *with a sideglance at* GILLIAN.) How are you darling? Where's father?

RICHARD. He's just getting washed. (*Takes* GILLIAN's *hand. She gets up, looking very anxious.*) Margaret, Edgar, this is Gillian Moore.

MARGARET. Hello Gillian. (*Shakes hands.*) Richard rang me to say he was bringing you with him.

EDGAR (*still at the door*). You didn't tell me he'd said that!

MARGARET. I had no intention of listening to you wittering on about it for five hours in the car.

EDGAR. I told you when Janet started the divorce I'd no intention of meeting your new girl friend. (GILLIAN *sits down.* EDGAR *removes his coat and scarf, speaking angrily.*) What you do with your life's your own affair, but –

MARGARET. But what *you* do with his life is *your* affair, isn't it darling?

EDGAR. You keep out of this Margaret –

MARGARET *flops into a chair and lights a cigarette.*

GILLIAN (*almost crying*). When Richard asked me to come, he told me what you'd say. Now you've said it, I don't mind it as much as I expected. But I think since I am here –

EDGAR. I'm not attacking you personally –

MARGARET. Then who the hell are you attacking?

EDGAR *comes to the fireplace and stands with his back to it.*

RICHARD. How like you to start moralising as soon as you get through the door! Do you think I was going to leave Gillian alone eight months pregnant just because you –

(WILF *enters during* RICHARD'S *speech. He is bare to the waist and is drying himself.*)

WILF. What the bladder of lard's going on in here? Are you fratching afore you've gotten into t'house?

MARGARET. Father – (*Goes to* WILF *and kisses him.*) We were so terribly sorry to hear about mother.

EDGAR (*shakes hands with* WILF). How are you Dad? Just how bad is she?

MARGARET *sits down.*

WILF. As bad as she could be, I'm sorry to have to say lad. Doctor came afore I went to work this morning and –

EDGAR. You mean to say you've been to *work*?

WILF. Why, does ta think I get me brass sitting on me backside surry?

EDGAR. With my mother dangerously ill?

WILF. Don't let it turn thy stomach. I haven't been working for mesen. I've been working for t'tax man.

EDGAR. I give up!

WILF. Nay, tha mun never give up lad! You'll have been introduced to Gillian then? (*Winks at* GILLIAN.) It isn't what you might call planned, but it'll be all reight. (*Turns back to* EDGAR, *who is very angry.*) And what's up with thee, like? Has ta lost a shilling and found a tanner? Or what?

BEATIE *comes in from the stairs.*

BEATIE. Wilf, they'd best come up.

WILF *takes a clean shirt from the oven door, where it has been put to air.*

WILF. You hear what your Aunty Beatie says.

> EDGAR, MARGARET *and* BEATIE *go upstairs. As* RICHARD *is leaving the room he looks at* GILLIAN, *hesitating.*

GILLIAN. I'll stay down here with your dad. (RICHARD *goes out.*) Aunt Beatie said she left you some dinner in the oven. Shall I put it out?

WILF. I don't know as I feel like eating owt love, thank you. It'd nobut stick in me gullet. Is there any tea in t'pot?

GILLIAN (*getting up*). I don't think it'll be hot. I'll make some more anyway, shall I? (*Goes to kitchen.*)

WILF. This'll do me. Don't trouble thisen lass. I'll sup it, as long as it's not stewed.

GILLIAN (*calling from kitchen*). You don't mind my coming up with Richard, do you Mr. Crowther?

> (*She comes back with cup and saucer, puts them on the table and pours the tea.*)

WILF. Mind? Why should I mind? Tha's one on t'family now, int ta?

GILLIAN. Not as far as Edgar is concerned.

WILF. Nay, take no notice on Edgar, Gillian. This is *my* house, tha sees. Not his. If you and Richard's happy, that's all I care about.

GILLIAN. You know, Richard thinks he's been a disappointment to you.

WILF. Gillian, I'll tell you straight love. When him and Janet got married we wondered if they'd make a go on it. They spent their time gadding round t'world on her money. He should have kept his independence from the start.

> WILF *pauses. He looks at the picture over the mantelpiece – a pseudo Van Gogh.*

Then all that painting and writing and nowt come on it.

> *He points at the picture.*

He painted yon picture over t'mantelpiece. One on his first.

GILLIAN. Do you like it?

> GILLIAN *looks up at the picture doubtfully.*

WILF. His mother does. I've never seen flowers like them in nature, mesen. Yon looks like summat t'cat's thrown up.

> WILF *sits down at the table and rolls a cigarette.*

GILLIAN. That's what Richard thinks now.

WILF. Oh aye, *now!* But he thought it were a masterpiece *then.* Don't ask me though. It's his mother has an eye for colour, you know.

GILLIAN. I wish I'd been able to know Mrs. Crowther.

WILF. I wish you had an' all love. But tha's come too late.

GILLIAN. Have you thought about what you'll . . . what you'll do?

WILF. What I shall do?

GILLIAN. I mean, will you stay on here?

WILF. Canst think on any good reason why I shouldn't, love?

GILLIAN. It's just, Richard says you're due to retire in six months.

WILF. Aye, I've been thinking about it. (*Pause.*) Here, would you like to see what British Railways has given me for forty years hard labour?

> WILF *crosses to the sideboard and opens a drawer. He comes to* GILLIAN *with a small white cardboard box.*

GILLIAN. *Forty* years?

WILF. Aye, I went on t'London Midland and Scottish in nineteen twenty.

> WILF *takes a gold watch from the box and gives it to* GILLIAN. *She examines it closely.*

What's ta think on that, then? It's what they give thee instead on a pension, tha sees.

GILLIAN. It's lovely.

WILF. Solid gold silver plated tin. (*He smiles at* GILLIAN.) Has ta seen t'inscription? To Wilf, from Brian.

> WILF *turns the watch over in her hand. There is an inscription on the back.*

GILLIAN. Brian?

WILF. *Sir* Brian! He's gone way of all flesh now.

> *They both laugh and* GILLIAN *hands him the watch back. He stands by her, looking at it.*

There, that copt thee didn't it?

GILLIAN. Do you like being an engine driver?

WILF. Oh aye, being a driver's all reight. It's British Railways as gets up my back.

GILLIAN. But I'd have thought you'd be all *for* nationalisation.

WILF. I am an' all love. It's British Railways sort of nationalisation I'm talking about.

> WILF *puts the watch in its box and goes to put it away.*

Dost know, we getting to have as many bosses as t'parson preached about. And they know as much about the inside of an engine as I know about the inside on Buckingham Palace. Still, t'trouble's on both sides. We don't get sort of young lads firing that we used to. Good ones won't come on t'railway.

GILLIAN. I've always wanted to go on an engine.

> WILF *looks at her, disbelieving but amused.*

WILF. What, on t'footplate? Tha'd change thy mind if tha travelled a few mile tender first. Specially on some of t'old rattlers we have nowadays. (*He sits down at the table.*) Tha knows, they call me t'poet driver down at sheds.

GILLIAN. Why do they call you that?

WILF. Well, when you take an engine back you have to fill a report card in, if there's owt wrong with it, for t'fitters. I always put summat down as'll give them food for thought, like. Take this one last week. Reight shook us insides up it did. So I put on t'card: this engine has square wheels and oval axle boxes. You should've seen t'foreman's face.

They both laugh. BEATIE *comes in from the stairs door. She is crying.*

BEATIE. You'd best go up now Wilf lad.

(WILF *gets up. He is suddenly very old and tired. He stops to look at the two women by the fire as he goes out.*)

Aren't you going as well, love?

She sits down by the fire and cries softly, holding her apron to her face.

GILLIAN. I think I'd better not.

BEATIE. Perhaps it's best. It's no fit thing for a lass in your condition.

GILLIAN. It's not that. But, things being what they are –

BEATIE. Eh love, there's plenty in our family been glad to get to church in time, I can tell you.

BEATIE *dries her eyes and gets up. She collects the cups and saucers on the table.*

I think she's going to go peaceful though, and that's a mercy. What'll become of our Wilf I don't know. He's that stubborn.

(*She carries the crockery into the kitchen,* GILLIAN *opening the door for her.*)

GILLIAN. Do you think he'd come to us?

BEATIE *talks as she fills the kettle and puts it on the fire in the living room.*

BEATIE. He'll go to nobody, Gillian. He's right proud is their father, when it comes to t'bottom on him. That's one on t'things our Edgar and Richard don't understand.

GILLIAN. I think Richard understands.

BEATIE. Maybe he does and maybe he doesn't. It's my honest opinion them lads has gotten above theirsens. An' that's what comes on sending them to t'grammar school.

GILLIAN. But, don't you think Mr. and Mrs. Crowther were doing something worthwhile? Trying to give their children something better than they'd had?

BEATIE. Happen they were. But what I remember is t'way they pinched and scraped to do it. An where's it got them? There isn't one on my three lads making less than fifteen pound a week, without all that education, neither. They look after me, they do, and not one on them lives more than ten minutes walk away. There, they're coming down –

Scene Two

WILF'S *Bedroom.*
Richard, Margaret and Edgar leave the bedroom and go downstairs.
WILF *is in the bedroom looking at his wife's face. Sound of shunted trucks clanking to a standstill. Close up* MRS. CROWTHER'S *face – she is dying.*

Scene Three

Living room, a few minutes later.

EDGAR. What gets me is that you should bring Gillian with you. We could have done without that.

RICHARD. Edgar, lay off will you? Save it.

EDGAR. Save it for when? I've no intention of seeing either of you for a bloody long time, I'll tell you.

RICHARD. Suits me.

BEATIE. Eh, will you both not stop it? With your mother dying upstairs like she is. Y'ought to be ashamed on yersens.

RICHARD. Aunt Beatie, he's my brother. I can't just shut my ears and pretend he's a gibbering puppet, even if he acts like one. He's got to be answered.

MARGARET. Richard, for God's sake –

RICHARD. Do you think I don't care what's going on upstairs? Do you think I don't want to shut my mouth and let her die in a peaceful house?

MARGARET. Well then?

    RICHARD *subsides a little, continuing more quietly.*

RICHARD. You know, she's actually proud of us! That's what cuts me. (*Wearily.*) Proud of all the wrong things, like Edgar making as much in a week as my dad makes in a month.

BEATIE. Now Richard. You've both gotten on, and that's what she wanted.

RICHARD. Haven't we! But what about what we are, apart from what we've got? (*To* EDGAR.) The worst is, Edgar, you don't even care *why* Janet and me had to pack it in. That's a mere detail. Only you know, you do live in a world where people marry the wrong people, and sleep together when they're not married, and all the rest of it.

EDGAR. I do know it's wrong to marry a woman who loves and trusts you, then drink yourself silly and get off with other women, till she can't stand you any more!

BEATIE. Our Edgar!

EDGAR. Ask him. Ask Gillian. I expect she knows as well as I do.

RICHARD. The thing is you see Aunt Beatie, Edgar married a woman who loves and trusts him, and he wouldn't have a divorce even if they were tearing each other's hearts out!

MARGARET. Now just a minute Richard –

RICHARD. I don't suppose you are! I hope you never do either. If you ever had to point out to Edgar that he was driving you round the bend he'd tell you to start learning a foreign language.

MARGARET. I think we've had enough of this –

RICHARD. He's dreaming the great middle class dream, is Edgar –

MARGARET. Stop it!

RICHARD. Well, that's the irony of it. If only my mother and father could have seen it. To educate us, you see, so we'd be richer than them . . . in every sense. And I'm wondering if we haven't become the image of everything they lacked the insight to despise!

> RICHARD *turns away.* EDGAR *has half taken the point. Speaks awkwardly.*

EDGAR. I thought we'd get round to class talk before he'd finished.

RICHARD (*turning*). It's more than that.

EDGAR. Is it? What about the great working class dream? What about all that fame is the spur stuff? That table! I've spent some hours of agony there, I can tell you. And if you let up for a minute, it was: Get on wi' thy work, if tha wants to make owt on thisen! You don't think my father thought he was bringing up two future intellectuals for the Labour Party, do you? It was *brass!* Anyway, the kind of socialism he went in for, it's as dead as the dodo.

Scene Four

WILF *closes his wife's eyes. He crosses her hands on her breast. He stands up, looks down at her. He looks at the framed photograph on the chest of drawers – of two men at an open-air bookstall with posters – 'Join The Left Book Club'. Again he looks at his wife's face – and then back to the photograph.*

Scene Five

Living Room a few minutes later.

EDGAR. You're about twenty-five years out of date Richard. Your so-called working classes want *things*. Just like everybody else. And in those days socialism – you know what it really boiled down to with people like my father? It meant pushing little sods like you and me on to university so's we'd be able to push our noses further down into the feed-bag. So as we'd get to be bosses. You don't think they educated us to be *socialists*? Not on your life! It was to get us out of *this*.

He waves his arm at the room. WILF *appears at the door and comes slowly into the room.*

WILF. Well, tha has gotten out on it, hasn't ta? And so has thy mother.

BEATIE (*crying*). Eh, Wilf, Wilf.

WILF. And I've nobut one question to put to thee, Edgar.

EDGAR. What's that?

WILF. What's ta going to do with thy two lads?

Scene Six

GILLIAN *and* MARGARET'S *bedroom, later the same evening.* GILLIAN *and* MARGARET *are in their bedroom.* GILLIAN *is unpacking,* MARGARET *is sitting at the dressing table, putting pins in her hair.*

MARGARET. I hope you don't mind sharing a bed with me. I snore.

GILLIAN. It's Edgar who's going to mind, isn't it?

MARGARET. Oh, he's long past caring.

GILLIAN. But I meant –

MARGARET. Oh don't mind me darling. It's nice to have a bitch, now and then. Anyway, you'll soon find out about Edgar. When a situation makes him angry, it's usually because it's one he knows he has to accept.

GILLIAN. Have he and Richard always quarrelled like that? Or is it only because of me?

MARGARET. As far as I can make out, they've quarrelled ever since they could spit. But for the last ten years it's mostly been about politics. Mutual insults are all they've got left to show they're still fond of one another.

GILLIAN. Well, if they're both sleeping downstairs to-night, I hope they don't get on to either me or politics.

MARGARET. Believe it or not, Edgar was practically a communist when I first met him. We were both in our first year at college. Still, that was nineteen thirty-eight. In those days, if you weren't on the left it meant you were probably psychotic, or something. He's changed quite a bit, has your future brother-in-law. (*Pause.*) How old are you Gillian?

GILLIAN. Twenty three. I'm afraid I'm not very up in politics, myself.

MARGARET. But you're on Richard's side, aren't you?

GILLIAN. Yes. I am.

MARGARET. I never thought I'd marry so young as I did. I wanted a first in history, and a career. (*Pause.*) Well, I got the first. Then I married Edgar. I was full of ideas about, you know, an intellectual sort of life. Books and plays and music . . . all that. Then there was the war, and the children. I often wonder if it could all have been so important to me, if I could let it go so easily. I make resolutions, you know. I go to the library and get a stack of books out. Never touch them from one day to the next. God, I must be boring your head off!

GILLIAN. Did you come from a – from a working class family?

MARGARET. No. My father was a bank manager. True blue.

GILLIAN. What I don't understand is why Edgar should have changed so *much*. I mean, from the way he talks now –

MARGARET. I understand it, believe me. Wanting a different kind of world requires too much mental effort. You end up with a mortgage, and a seed catalogue, and a suspicion that maybe murderers *ought* to be hanged. We did.

GILLIAN. People like Mr. Crowther don't change.

MARGARET. That's only because they've never had the chance. They stay simple, and – ignorant of how much everything else has changed.

GILLIAN. So you agree with Edgar, really.

MARGARET. I don't know who the hell I agree with! I'm past it darling.

She rubs cream on her face.

You must admit, father *is* just a wee bit how green was my valley, isn't he?

Wipes her fingers on Kleenex. Goes to fireplace and throws Kleenex in. Adjusts a pin in her hair.

I wonder why I've put these in to-night.

GILLIAN. Don't you usually?

MARGARET. Only when I want to scare Edgar away.

Going back to dressing table.

GILLIAN. I thought you said he didn't –

MARGARET. Very rarely, he does. But I'm damned if I'll have it at his convenience. And if you don't see the point of that, it's because you're so wholesome. Never mind, we're *both* as safe as houses tonight.

Glances at window.

Why did they have to go round telling the relations straight away? It's raining like hell too. I can't understand why anybody wants to live in Yorkshire at *all.* (*Rounds on Gillian.*) Doesn't anything ever make you feel vicious? It's always men who get what they want and not what they deserve. With women it's the other way round. (*Controls herself.*) I'm sorry, Gillian. Proper hag, aren't I?

(Sound of door downstairs.)

Scene Seven

The Living Room

WILF *and* RICHARD *come in. Pulling off their raincoats.* WILF *sits down and takes his boots off.*

WILF. I'm barn to take these boots off and just have five minutes. (*He sits.*) When your Aunty Mary gets talking she's like a gramophone with t'needle stuck.

GILLIAN *comes in.*

GILLIAN. I thought I heard the front door. Would you like something to eat?

WILF. Dost know, I think I *could* eat summat. Me stomach thinks me throat's cut. There's some cold ham in t'pantry, let's have a sandwich love.

GILLIAN (*going out to the kitchen*). Margaret's gone to bed.

WILF. Hasn't our Edgar come in yet?

GILLIAN *calls* "No" *from kitchen.*

She seems a reight grand lass, Richard.

Bends to light a spill at the fire. Straightens up facing the Van Gogh.

Nowt seems to have gone reight for thee up till now, lad. One road or another.

RICHARD. Sometime, I'd like to tell you how it went wrong between me and Janet.

WILF. Nay, I'm not asking for explanations. Nobut, it looked as if tha were never going to settle down.

RICHARD. I never wanted to. Still, I'm getting used to the idea, now.

WILF. An' what's become on thy painting and writing?

RICHARD. I've pretty well given it up. I never seem to be able to finish anything.

WILF. It takes time, lad. Like owt that's worth doing.

RICHARD. It isn't that dad. I've no talent. (*Points at the painting.*) You know, it's time we took that bloody thing down. (*Sits down at the table.*)

WILF. Your mother loved that picture.

RICHARD. It ought to come down.

WILF. Not afore your mother's buried.

RICHARD. Did I tell you I've given up supply teaching? I've taken a permanent job in a comprehensive.

WILF. So tha's finally made thy mind up to it.

RICHARD. It's a way of earning a living.

WILF. Is *that* all tha can see in it!

RICHARD. Well I wouldn't exactly say I'd got a vocation.

WILF. Tha's over thirty, lad. If tha'd gotten down to it when tha left college, instead on living on Janet's money, tha'd happen be in a better position today. (*Sits down at the table opposite* RICHARD.)

RICHARD. Well, I've got down to it now.

WILF. I cannot understand why our Edgar's gone one road, and tha's gone another. I can't weigh it up.

RICHARD. I envy Edgar, in a way.

WILF. Tha envies him? What for?

RICHARD. He's a good scientist. He's doing something he wants to do, and he's good at it.

WILF. And is there nowt tha wants to do?

RICHARD. No. Nothing.

WILF. Dost mean to say, if tha can't be some sort on an artist, tha's not playing, like?

RICHARD. Could be.

WILF. Nay, tha wants to pull thy socks up!

RICHARD. You know dad, Edgar and I have opposite views on

just about everything. Only his fit the world as he sees it and mine fit the world as I'd like to see it. That's a big difference. I'm tired. I'm so tired that being an adequate husband and father is about as much as I can reasonably expect of myself now. (*Pause*.) And that, coming from somebody who's never gone hungry, never been worked to exhaustion, never struggled or *had* to – that's the end. I'm ashamed to say it to you dad. (*Rises*.)

WILF. Nay, I know there's more than one kind of struggle, lad, if I know nowt else. (*Pause*.) Everything looked a damn sight different when I were your age. Dost know, when we first came here tha could be out in t'fields in five minutes. On a Sunday night we used to put Edgar in t'push chair and thee in thy pram and walk two or three mile along the canal. It wasn't built up then. You could fair smell t'countryside t'other side on t'pit. If tha goes up there now, tha'll see we've almost joined on to Leeds! It's all gone, all that nature. (*Pause*.) T'sort of life we had, and all, tha doesn't see that no more neither. Many a time ten and fifteen in here on a Sunday for their teas. We used to get on singing hymns when it were all cleared away, like. Mind there were nowt solemn about it. We all enjoyed us sens. T'same folk we never see them from one month to t'next, nowadays. Their sons and daughters comes up in their cars to take them for a drive on a Sunday afternoon. But it's not t'same. (*Broods*.) Now, we've gotten t'telly, tha knows. Nay, when I were thy age I had thee lads, and thy mother, and I thought t'time'd come when we should have a different road of going on in this country. (*Pause*.) By, tha talks about socialism! I were as red as John Penny's eye after a night on t'beer. Socialism had some guts in it in them days. But if it's altered, so has t'working classes. And there's an end on it, for most on them.

RICHARD. It shouldn't be an end of it.

WILF. Eh, what dost expect, if t'sons can nobut turn round and say they tired? Tha grieves me, talking like that. What's up with thee?

RICHARD. You know what your sons are, right enough! One solid conservative and one shagged-out political idealist.

WILF. Tha says tha's gotten different views from Edgar. *Stand* on them then! Dost want it chucked at thee on a plate?

RICHARD. I'm only trying to say –

WILF. That tha's in a reight pickle!

RICHARD. It's a question of where to begin again, dad.

WILF. Tha mun find thy road, same as we had to, Richard. Nobut, tha's an educated man. Tha mun do better than we *could* have done, with all t'will in the world. And happen being educated, tha'll not let them pull t'wool over thy eyes.

He bends down to pick his boots up. GILLIAN *comes in with a tray.*

GILLIAN. There. It's all ready. Will you have it by the fire?

WILF. Eh love, my appetite's gone again. I'll get mesen off to bed, if you don't mind.

GILLIAN. Are you sure?

Quite suddenly WILF *is almost in tears.*

WILF. Ah mun go up, lass.

He looks from one to the other as if appealing to them. GILLIAN *goes to kiss him.*

GILLIAN. Goodnight, father.

He puts his arms round her, still holding his boots.

WILF. Tha's a good lass. Good night, both on you. You'll bank t'fire up, won't you? Keep yoursens warm.

WILF *goes out. He walks upstairs slowly, carrying his boots.*

GILLIAN. You haven't been . . . upsetting him, Richard?

RICHARD. I don't know. I suppose I have. I didn't mean to. We weren't arguing, or anything. I was trying to tell him how I feel about . . . well, you know.

GILLIAN. And what about how he feels?

RICHARD. Yes, I know.

GILLIAN. He's so vulnerable, all of a sudden.

RICHARD. I know.

GILLIAN. He's really expected, hoped for quite a lot from you and Edgar. Hasn't he?

RICHARD. Yes. He has.

GILLIAN. Did you know?

RICHARD. I haven't really talked to him for years, till to-night. (*Pause.*) Hadn't you better be going up to bed yourself?

GILLIAN. I suppose so. The baby's like a lead weight to-night. (*Pause.*) Richard, the room where your dad's sleeping –

RICHARD. What about it?

GILLIAN. Was it yours?

RICHARD. Mine and Edgar's. Why?

GILLIAN. I had to go in for some sheets. I found this.

Lifts up a cushion from the sofa and brings out a worn and shapeless knitted monkey.

You told me about him, remember?

RICHARD (*takes the monkey*). In that chest of drawers? (*She nods.*)

I thought he'd been cremated years ago!

GILLIAN. So I brought him down to keep you company. Make up for me!

They both laugh. RICHARD *sets the monkey on top of the clock on the mantelpiece.*

Well –

RICHARD. Stay in bed in the morning – there's no need to get up early. Beatie's staying next door, so she'll be in about half past eight.

GILLIAN goes to him. They stand with their arms round each other.

GILLIAN. I shall miss you. It's the first time we've slept apart.

RICHARD. And I shall miss you.

GILLIAN. The blankets and things are in the hall. (*Kisses him.*) Good night.

RICHARD. Goodnight love.

GILLIAN. Luv.

> *They kiss again. She leaves.* RICHARD *pours a cup of tea and takes a sandwich. Sits by the fire.* EDGAR *comes in rubbing his hands, and goes to stand in front of fire.*

EDGAR. Everybody in bed?

RICHARD. Yes.

EDGAR. How did my Aunty Mary take it?

RICHARD. Tearfully. Slightly predatory as well. Tea?

EDGAR. Yes please. Why predatory?

RICHARD (*pouring tea*). That ring my grandmother gave my mother. Aunty Mary's been after it for years. Have a sandwich.

EDGAR (*takes a sandwich, bites into it.*) You don't spare anybody, do you?

RICHARD. How did yours go? Uncle George is a bit senile, isn't he?

EDGAR. Hadn't a clue who I was talking about. Still, the poor old sod's nearly seventy-three.

> *For a few seconds they chew, eyeing each other.*

RICHARD. Well?

EDGAR. Well?

RICHARD. Made any nice bombs lately?

EDGAR. I must say, you've managed to turn my mother's death into a memorable occasion.

RICHARD. Which otherwise it wouldn't have been, would it?

EDGAR. Now look here, Richard –

RICHARD. All right, all right. Forget it. Let's have a truce, shall we? An armed truce.

EDGAR. I'm perfectly willing to set aside –

RICHARD. No, don't set anything aside Edgar. Just shut up and help me make the beds.

Richard goes into the hall. Comes back with a pile of blankets, sheets and pillowcases.

Which will you have, a sofa or two chairs?

EDGAR. Which do you prefer?

RICHARD *throws blankets on chair and sofa and gets out his cigarettes.*

RICHARD. Let's have a cigarette and work out the protocol. (*Lights one.*)

EDGAR. You can sleep where the hell you like.

RICHARD. Now, now!

Takes out a coin and spins it.

Call –

EDGAR. Heads.

RICHARD. Heads it is, brother. Which'll you have? The Dorchester or the Ritz?

EDGAR. I'll have the sofa.

RICHARD. All right then. Let's get on with it.

They begin to make up a bed on the sofa.

RICHARD (*throwing blanket*). Come on.

EDGAR. All right, all right.

RICHARD. Come on, nurse Crowther . . .

RICHARD pulls the blanket and EDGAR grabs at it. Tug of war. RICHARD begins to laugh and EDGAR too begins to enjoy it.

Scene Eight

WILF'S *Bedroom.*

WILF *is at the door of the bedroom where his wife is lying. He is wearing rough, striped pyjamas. He goes up to the bed foot and stands looking down. Hesitantly he touches her feet where they make a pyramid under the sheet. Moves to the bedside, rubbing his hand across his face.*

WILF. An' I mun go on? (*Pause.*) Without thee? (*Pause.*) Did they please you, our lads? (*Pause.*) What does it all come to? (*He moves closer to her face.*)

I wish I were dead myself, tonight. (*Pause.*) I've never wished that afore in my life. (*Pause.*) Never. (*Long pause.*) Where are you? (*Pause.*) They frighten me. (*Pause.*) When they get on at one another, they make me shiver. I'd sooner it had been me to go. (*Pause.*) It's worse to lose their mother.

Rain drumming heavily against the windows. He rises. Looks to window, goes to the door. Stands looking at the bed.

Ah mun learn to bide it. (*Pause.*) We all mun.

Scene Nine

The Living Room.

RICHARD *and* EDGAR *are in pyjamas.* RICHARD *is arranging a pillow on the armchair.* EDGAR *gargling in the kitchen.* EDGAR *comes in from the kitchen and goes to poke the fire.* RICHARD *gets into the armchair and pulls the blankets over him.*

RICHARD. Hey, you in the choir!

He sings, imitating boy soprano.

Oh, for the wings, for the wings, of a dove . . . far away, far away would I . . . that time Billy Munt was pumping the organ and he stopped just when you were on top C. You burst into tears and the organ sounded like a dinosaur breaking wind.

EDGAR *lies down on the sofa.*

Bill was killed in Cyprus.

EDGAR. Well, if we'd taken a strong line in Cyprus from the start –

RICHARD. Oh, come off it. He'd just finished at Leeds Art school when he was called up. Because he was an *artist*, see, they set him on painting signs in Greek for the troops to display. Disperse or we fire. Billy was with the Cypriots from the start so he painted the letters as small as he could –

EDGAR. So?

RICHARD. So when they went to break up a demonstration one morning, they couldn't read Billy's writing, it was too small. There was some shooting, and he got killed. The brutal comedies of war, don't y'know.

EDGAR. I thought we were supposed to have a truce?

RICHARD. Don't mind me. I'm passionate. I get carried away. (*Pause.*) Well, I suppose it's all old hat, now.

   EDGAR *catches sight of the knitted monkey.*

EDGAR. What the hell's that?

RICHARD. What?

EDGAR. On the clock.

RICHARD. You ought to know.

EDGAR. What do you mean, *I* ought to know?

RICHARD. It's a monkey.

   He goes to the mantelpiece and takes the monkey off the clock. Goes back to the armchair.

EDGAR. Never seen it before in my life.

RICHARD. As a matter of fact, you had one of the few real relationships that you ever had in your life, with this monkey. (*Pause.*) It was my monkey.

EDGAR (*mimicking*). It was my monkey!

RICHARD. To be exact, it's a knitted monkey. Stuffed with

kapok. You used to amuse yourself by tying knots in its tail, didn't he? (*To the monkey.*) Yes he did. The sadist was well to the fore in your character even in those days.

EDGAR. It stank.

RICHARD. Stank? Every knot in that monkey's tail was a knot in my tail, chum. (*Holds it up, looking at it.*)

EDGAR. It stank because you were an incorrigible bed wetter.

RICHARD. Yes and why? Because I had to share a bed with a torturer. You'd have made a granite statue wet its bed.

   EDGAR *bursts out laughing.* RICHARD *throws a pillow at him.* EDGAR *throws it back. A pillow fight develops, which ends up with them laughing and wrestling on the floor.* MARGARET *appears in the hall doorway in her nightdress.*

MARGARET. Edgar! Richard!

   The two men stare at her, embarrassed.

What the hell do you think you're doing? You were making too much noise to hear it, but your father's crying like a child in his sleep!

   EDGAR *slowly sits up.* RICHARD *and* EDGAR *look at one another helplessly.*

Scene Ten

The Living Room. The following morning. EDGAR *is reading 'The Times' alone at the breakfast table.* MARGARET *comes in wearing a dressing gown, she looks haggard.*

EDGAR. You'll have to make some fresh tea. (*He speaks without looking up from the paper.*)

MARGARET (*weighing the pot*). It's half full.

EDGAR. It's cold.

   MARGARET *goes to the kitchen. Empties tealeaves in sink. Fills and turns on electric kettle.*

MARGARET. Where is everybody?

EDGAR. Richard and Gillian shopping. Aunt Beatie next door. My father's gone to arrange about the funeral.

He turns to the crossword and takes a pen from his pocket. MARGARET comes in and wanders over to the window.

MARGARET. Still raining.

EDGAR. I know.

MARGARET. There's a dead bird in the gutter. Oh Edgar it's *flat*. Flattened out.

EDGAR. Run over.

MARGARET. And a lot you care!

EDGAR puts down his paper in exasperation.

EDGAR. I am not the Lord God Almighty! I do not have the welfare of every little sparrow at heart! What are you going to do, report me to the police?

MARGARET. Oh, go back to your crossword! (EDGAR *carries on reading*.) A room with a view. One goodsyard, a row of tarted up slums and about half a million chimneys. And Aunt Beatie says she wouldn't live anywhere else!

EDGAR. I don't suppose it's the view she's fond of.

MARGARET (*imitating* BEATIE). Ah've had a 'undred and fowerteen bairns an' there int one on 'em makin less ner –

EDGAR (*looking up irritated*). She showed a damn sight more guts raising her family than you'll ever do with yours.

MARGARET. Now don't start prickling with local pride. If you see Aunt Beatie as a sort of provincial corn goddess that's okay by me but don't expect me to keep a straight face.

EDGAR (*going back to his crossword*). I don't even know what a corn goddess is.

MARGARET. No, you wouldn't know, would you? (*She sits down at the table.*) I seemed to spend the whole night having nightmares. And Gillian slept like a baby.

EDGAR. Should have taken one of your pills.

MARGARET. Do you know Edgar, I believe if I woke up one morning and told you I was dying, you'd say I should have taken one of my pills!

EDGAR. There's two things wrong with you Margaret. Anaemia and constipation. Both are amenable to treatment – pills.

MARGARET. I'd better not start telling you what's wrong with you.

The kettle whistles and she goes out into kitchen.

D'you know what Gillian told me last night?

EDGAR. What?

MARGARET. She said before she got big, they did it nearly every night.

EDGAR. Wait till they've been together as long as we have.

MARGARET (*in the kitchen doorway*).

I ought to write one of those articles. (*She comes to the table, carrying a teapot.*) I gave myself to a nuclear physicist by Margaret Crowther. Intimate details of what it means to be married to the men who risk the perils of radiation to make *your* bombs.

EDGAR (*filling in a clue in the crossword*). Overdoses of radiation cause sterility, not impotence.

MARGARET. My God, what's *in* the paper this morning?

Puts on an announcer's voice.

Strontium ninety, up two points. Fission products, a steady fall.

EDGAR. Very funny!

MARGARET (*pouring tea*) Gillian's scared stiff she'll have a baby with two heads. I told her what you said about fall-out hazards being exaggerated. It's odd isn't it, the way some people go on worrying when they've been told everything's perfectly all right. Well, she said Richard said –

EDGAR. Richard is a vacillating idealist. He couldn't tell a neutron from a nappy. It's people like Richard who get mixed up in these marches without knowing a damn thing about radiation except what they read in the weekly papers.

MARGARET. I think Gillian's absolutely all right for Richard. You know, when I met you I thought it was terribly romantic your being a scientist. All those test tubes.

EDGAR. I haven't touched a test tube for years.

MARGARET. Richard's a sort of everything manqué, isn't he?

EDGAR (*he gets up, puts his pen away and goes to sit on sofa*). I gather you want to talk about Richard and Gillian this morning.

MARGARET. I just want to talk. Sooner or later you'll have to realise that there's no point in treating Gillian like a tart. Has it occurred to you that they show every sign of being happy together?

EDGAR. And has it occurred to you that so did Richard and Janet? He can't spend his life getting married and divorced and marrying his mistresses, can he? And don't tell me it's anything to do with being an *artist*. I don't think the work of art exists that was worth ruining anybody's life for.

MARGARET. I wonder how Richard sees us –

EDGAR. I don't give a damn.

MARGARET (*fiercely*). Then you ought to! (*More quietly, to herself.*) Sometimes I feel as if I don't exist.

EDGAR. All I can say is, there's a lot of evidence to the contrary!

MARGARET (*ignoring him*). Something about Richard and Gillian together. They aren't all the things we *are*.

EDGAR. Such as?

MARGARET. Trivial. Stunted. Absurd, really. We're absurd. (*Pause.*) Even you must have your dim suspicions. Over forty, married, two children, three thousand a year. What about *you?*

EDGAR. For heaven's sake what about me?

MARGARET. Oh, it's both of us! I know. I'm wondering if I could have been different. (*Pause.*) What do we care about? What passionately concerns us? You sneer at Richard and the people that go on the bomb marches, but you're a *smaller* man for not even entertaining the idea. Hardly matters if Richard's right or wrong. He and Gillian are a *different kind* from us. I want to know how it is. And why it is. Can't you see what I'm trying to say?

EDGAR. Oh yes! I can! (*Mocking her.*) You and I are trivial, stunted and absurd. You know it and I don't, and in some peculiar way this makes you one up. Richard and Gillian are neither trivial, stunted nor absurd, and this makes *them* one up. Frankly I haven't a clue what it all means. It must be the change of life!

> MARGARET'S *face has slowly contorted as she listened. She bangs her fists on the table suddenly, and upsets the cup of tea. She is crying.*

MARGARET (*crying*). Damn you Edgar! Damn you. Edgar, I'm nearly middle aged. My sons are growing up and I'm empty. I used to be clever . . . interested, when I was young. I was happy then just to lie down in bed beside you. Do you never think about the future at all? Maybe another twenty years, and how am I supposed to spend it? Grovelling in a rock garden and cutting sandwiches?

EDGAR (*goes to her genuinely concerned and upset by her reaction*). Margaret, I honestly didn't know you were so unhappy.

MARGARET. It's something I've never . . . let into my mind, until now.

EDGAR. I wouldn't have said we had so little.

MARGARET. Then why do I *feel* we've got so little?

EDGAR. I expect you'd like the best of both worlds.

MARGARET. What worlds?

EDGAR. Mine . . . and Richard's. I imagine that intelligent women always do.

MARGARET (*harshly*). Don't you *dare* patronise me!

EDGAR (*half smiling*). Oh, Margaret!

MARGARET. Leave me alone – for a bit. Please.

EDGAR (*showing furtive relief.*) Well, I did say I'd pick my father up at the undertaker's.

MARGARET. Yes, all right.

EDGAR. We'll talk about all this again. When we get home, Margaret.

MARGARET. If you want to.

EDGAR. I'm . . . sorry, Margaret.

> *He goes out of the front door.* MARGARET *is left alone at the table. Her face is tense. She is gripping the teacup with both hands.*

Scene Eleven

Old Folk's Club. The same morning.
The 'Old Folk's Shelter' is a small brick building on a vacant lot in the main street. In its one room are a few shabby armchairs, a table and a coal stove. Uncle GEORGE *is a frail old man in his early seventies. He sits at the table playing with dominoes. Aunty* BESSIE *sits near him, knitting.* WILF *passes the window and comes in. He takes out a packet of cigarettes and puts them in front of* GEORGE.

WILF. Now then! I've brought your cigs mesen this week.

BESSIE. Eh, our poor Alice.

GEORGE. You what?

BESSIE (*shouting*). I say, our Alice'll not be bringing your cigs no more. (*To* WILF.) He understands nowt you say. It were good on your Edgar to come and tell us last night. I am sorry, Wilf. Eh, she used to bring him his cigs every Saturday, come sunshine or snow.

WILF. Will you come to t'funeral then?

BESSIE. Nay, he's not fit to take nowhere.

GEORGE. Where's our Alice?

BESSIE (*shaking her head at* WILF). She's passed away, George. Last night. Don't you remember, our Edgar came to tell us?

GEORGE. Aye, they don't care about you when you begin to lose track on yersen. (*He becomes crazily malicious.*) Is it Wilf? Wait till you qualifies for t'old folks club lad. Soon be thy turn. We come here to die, tha knows. Aye, I've seen three on them die in front of yon very fire!

WILF (*to* BESSIE). Not much on a place, is it?

BESSIE. It's not so bad when there's a few on them here. You get a bit of company, you know. He still plays his dominoes.

GEORGE (*fumbling at the cigarettes*). We had your Edgar round last night.

WILF. I know, George, I know.

GEORGE. Like a dog with two tails, yon one.

WILF. Now what d'you mean by that?

GEORGE. Wants some stick, yon one.

BESSIE. He doesn't know half on what he's saying, Wilf. Take no notice lad.

WILF. What's up with our Edgar, then?

GEORGE. Tha wants to take him away from yon school and put him down t'pit! T'other one an' all. Tha's wasting thy time, lad.

WILF. You're thirty year behind t'times George. Our Edgar's a grown up man. So is Richard.

BESSIE. Two lovely lads they are, an' all.

GEORGE. Just thee wait. Tha'll see when tha's sitting here day after day watching folk through yon pane of glass. It won't be long.

BESSIE. I sometimes think it'd be a blessing if he were taken.

What if I go afore him? He can't dress his sen. He can't feed his sen. If he has a cig you've got to watch him or he's on fire.

WILF. I never thought George'd go like that. He were a fine strong feller.

BESSIE. Edgar said Alice went peaceful.

WILF. Aye, she went peaceful. (*Pause.*) I've always hesitated to ask you Bessie, but are you all reight for money? Can you manage?

BESSIE. Eh Wilf, lad, we live on us pension and I've enough put by to bury us you know. Our Keith sends t'rent, when he bethinks his sen. He's a manager now. He has sixty fellers working under him.

WILF. They're all getting on, aren't they?

  GEORGE *is getting a cigarette into his mouth, with great difficulty.* WILF *lights it for him.*

What we trying to tell you George, our Alice has passed on.

GEORGE. Aye, yon lot from Parliament wants to come up here and tell some on t'old folk they well off, like. They do.

  Pause. His mind clears a little.

Three quarters on them that's had families round here, they've watched their bairns grow up into reight Tories.

BESSIE. It's funny, isn't it. For all his mind wanders he can turn owt into politics! (*Pause.*) There's not so many like him and you left, Wilf.

WILF. Happen it's just as well.

BESSIE. He lived and breathed Keir Hardie when he were a young feller. You're going to be lonely Wilf. Why don't you join t'Darby and Joan Club when you retire?

WILF. I prefer fishing.

BESSIE. I suppose you could go to one on t'lads.

WILF. I want to be dependent on nobody. (*Looks round.*) I couldn't bide this place, Bessie.

BESSIE. Well, it's always warm. And you hear all t'gossip.

GEORGE. Don't thee listen to her. We come here to die. Then tha sees, t'muck'll cover us, and it's all ower! I won't say I wouldn't sooner have died in t'pit, but tha's got to die somewhere.

BESSIE. We don't spend all our time here you know, Wilf. We can get into t'pictures for ninepence. Nobut he goes to sleep and many a time I can't wake him. I make t'best on it an watch t'picture round again.

WILF. Does he still take his gill?

BESSIE. Does he! He drinks more free beer than he pays for, down at Fox. But I will say, he's worked hard all his life, he's entitled to his glass of beer.

GEORGE. Young feller come to t'door afore t'last election, he says: I hope we can count on your support, Mr. Ackroyd. He were nobut a little un. A good breath'd have fair blown him ower Ilkley Moor. I says, sitha young feller, tha wants to make thisen scarce, afore I lose my temper. Tha wants to get thisen off to Spain, I says. Fight for them that's making a world fit for t'workers to live in. But ay'm canvassing for the conservative party, he says. Well dost know, I picks up on yon shovel and I has him out on that door like a shot out on a gun!

Wheezes into laughter.

BESSIE. He gets it all mixed up, you know.

WILF. He's not t'only one! (*Pause.*) It grieves me to see him like this, Bessie.

BESSIE. He were as right as rain till he stopped work. An' mind you don't let it take you like that! You'd think there'd be summat else in a man's life besides his work. Folks nowadays, they know how to enjoy theirsens a bit better. (*Pause.*) Well, you've got your bairns, Wilf.

WILF. Nay, when they're grown up there isn't much left on what they were when they were little lads. Nobut I look at them sometimes and it's a reight effort to think on I'm their father. When I hear them talking I sometimes feels as if I were born with my head full of slack coal!

BESSIE. Well you can't expect t'world to stand still, can you?

GEORGE. Alice, did you say? Did you say Alice has passed away?

BESSIE. Yes, owd lad. She has.

GEORGE. Who's going to bring me my cigs then?

BESSIE. Wilf's just given you your cigs! (*To* WILF.) He isn't callous, Wilf. It's –

WILF. Nay, I know. I'll be getting on.

BESSIE. I think we shall sit on here for a bit. Then we'll go and get our dinners. You'll come and see us, won't you Wilf. You an' George were very close, at one time.

WILF. Your fire wants making up.

He takes a skep of coal and shakes some into the stove.

They ought to give you some better coal.

Stands looking round the room.

Tha's better off in your own home, than here, Bessie.

BESSIE. Nay, I like to get out and see what folks is doing. What else is there? (*Pause.*) T'days is long, when you get old, Wilf. You'll see. Eh, you sometimes wonder what it's all been for, don't you?

GEORGE. I can remember t'first day our Alice went into service, dost know. Setting off with her little tin trunk. She were hardly big enough to see over t'table top.

BESSIE. He can remember t'early days all right. But he couldn't remember summat that happened yesterday!

GEORGE. Thirteen year old, she was. Two year afore t'Kaiser war. (*Pause.*) It hasn't been nowt but bloody wars, when you come to look at it. Has it? Still, with a bit of luck we shall be under t'sod afore t'next one. Capitalists has got to go on making wars, tha knows. That's Marx, that is. Karl Marx said that.

BESSIE. I cannot make him understand it isn't like he thinks no more. Our house is a palace compared with what it used to be. We just managed to get it done out afore he give up work.

WILF. I'd best be off.

BESSIE. An' you'll come and see us, Wilf? Our Alice always came round on a Saturday.

WILF *hesitates by the door, looking from one to the other.*

WILF. I'll come an' see you. I'll come round to your house.

BESSIE. Nay, you'll nearly always find us here lad, with t'other old uns.

WILF. Aye. Well I'll be seeing you then. (*He goes.*)

GEORGE. Aye. Tha'll see us if I last.

Scene Twelve

The Kitchen. Later the same morning.
MARGARET *is now dressed. She is waiting for the kettle to boil, and stands reading a brass plaque on the wall, a poem – 'Mother'. The kettle boils and she makes another pot of tea.* WILF *comes in the front door, takes off his coat and comes through to the kitchen.*

MARGARET. Edgar's gone down to the undertakers in the car, to meet you!

WILF. Has he? I thought he wasn't coming so I walked back. I stopped at t'owd folks shelter to give Uncle George his weekly packet of cigs.

MARGARET. Uncle George? Is he still –

WILF. Aye. He's past it. To look at him now, you wouldn't think he were a reight grand speaker. He knew t'history on t'trade union movement backwards. I'll always remember him t'way he used to be. Eh, one Saturday afternoon it's years back now, I heard him heckling somebody speaking for t'Catholic Truth Society, in t'market place. This priest like, he stood it as long as he could, then he turns to George and says: (*Imitates posh voice.*) My dear man, if God did not create the world, perhaps you'd be good enough to tell me what you are standing on at this moment! And George, quick as a flash, dost know what George said?

MARGARET. What?

WILF. Quick as a flash George says – an electromagnetic flux!

They laugh.

But he were a reight un! He were a reader, you know. Lenin, Trotsky – he had a go at the lot. (*Pause.*) He worked till he were seventy, an all. Now he has to be looked after like a baby. (*Pause.*) If that's growing old –

MARGARET. I'm sure you won't go like that! (*Pouring his tea into a cup.*)

WILF. I'd sooner be put to sleep like a bloody dog. Tha's a right good lass nobut can I have my mug?

MARGARET (*gets mug from shelf*). I always forget don't I?

WILF. I've never asked you how t'bairns are, Margaret.

MARGARET. Oh, they're fine. Edgar's talking of sending them to boarding school.

WILF. Nay!

MARGARET. Don't tell him I told you. He's rather touchy about it.

WILF. It's same as t'bloke said –

MARGARET. What?

WILF. Wonderful, wonderful, what'll happen next!

MARGARET. Now don't you start taking the micky out of Edgar! (*Pause.*) I don't know whether I want them to go or not.

WILF. I can see by t'time t'Crowthers gets to t'third generation, we'll have a life peerage in t'family or summat!

MARGARET. Well you started it!

WILF. I'm wondering what I have started!

MARGARET (*hesitating*). Gillian's nice, isn't she?

WILF. I've right taken to her. Where are they, any road?

MARGARET. Shopping, for Aunt Beatie. I never got on with Janet.

WILF. I can't say as I took much notice, love. There wasn't a time when she came here without bringing a few fish hooks, or a trout fly or summat. Mind there's nowt to beat t'flies you make yoursen.

MARGARET. I wonder what it's like to be really rich. (*Going to sink.*)

WILF. Same as being poor, nobut tha's gotten a lot of money!

MARGARET (*slightly resentful*). Whenever I try to talk to you, you always make fun of me.

WILF. What's on thy mind, Margaret?

MARGARET. I can hardly stand this trouble between Edgar and Richard.

They come into the living room and MARGARET *stands in front of the fire.*

WILF. Dost think I can?

MARGARET. At one time you'd have thought Richard and Janet were the ideal couple.

WILF. There isn't any such thing, a man and woman makes theirsens out on some idea on t'future. And a man's got to be strong. He's got to give a woman strength, for all t'strength she's gotten's for her bairns. An t'world that he wants – she wants it, for if she doesn't she can mean nowt to him.

MARGARET (*fiercely*). No! It isn't that. It can't be just that.

WILF. Now what's gotten into thee?

MARGARET. *Nothing's* got into me!

WILF looks at her. He takes his tobacco tin and matches from the mantelpiece and rolls a cigarette.

WILF. Dost know, when Richard came home from college he asked if I could get him set on down at sheds? I'd have looked all reight, wouldn't I? Next thing we heard he were a clown in a circus, then he were a navvy, then we got a telegram saying: Married yesterday, leaving for Berlin to morrow. Our Edgar doesn't know the half of it. His mother and me kept that side on it dark, tha sees.

> RICHARD *and* GILLIAN *come in,* RICHARD *carrying a loaded shopping basket which he puts on the table. They take off their coats.*

There you are then. Have you seen anybody you liked better than yoursens?

RICHARD. I don't reckon much to your new town centre.

WILF. Nay, Gillian, sit thee down love. Take t'weight off your feet.

> GILLIAN *sits down.*

Tha munt let nobody hear thee running down t'new centre. They reight proud on it lad!

GILLIAN. It's awful!

WILF. Would tha prefer t'oed slums then, Richard?

RICHARD. I don't like brand new slums!

WILF. Tha sees, t'feller that built them understands Yorkshire folk. He knows they go round with their eyes on t'pavement looking for tanners.

> BEATIE *comes in and goes to the shopping basket. Begins to unpack it.*

BEATIE. Did you get bread, Gillian love?

GILLIAN. It's on the kitchen table.

> (BEATIE *takes the basket into the kitchen.*)

BEATIE. That's been a reight grand help to me. Mrs. Craven is in a state over Alice. She says they moved in same week as you Wilf and it's just thirty years next week. It's a long time to be neighbours, and never a wrong word neither. (*Feels in her apron pocket and goes back into the living room.*) Eh Richard lad I'm forgetting, I copt telegram lad on his way t'front door. There's one for you love. I hope it's nowt. (*Hands telegram to* RICHARD.) And Wilf, you've not drawn them curtains in t'little bedroom. (RICHARD *reads the telegram. Stands looking stunned.*)

GILLIAN. Richard! What's the matter?

She goes to RICHARD *reads telegram aloud over his shoulder.*

Arriving two p.m. this afternoon – Janet.

BEATIE. Eh, no!

MARGARET. But how did she –

EDGAR *comes in quietly from the kitchen.*

RICHARD. Who told Janet then? Who the hell *told* her?

EDGAR. I did. I asked her to come.

GILLIAN *bursts into tears, puts her hands to her face. After a moment she rushes out, upstairs.* RICHARD *follows her. To* MARGARET.

Well don't look so bloody outraged! (*Pulls his coat off, throws it on a chair.*) You knew Richard was bringing Gillian, but you didn't tell me, did you? Oh no! Why do I have to be kept in ignorance of what's going on in my own family? (*Pause.*) Let me tell you, marrying Janet was the only thing Richard ever did that brought my mother any happiness –

MARGARET. Why are *you* kept in ignorance? Because your insight into human nature is so profound you think making the best of a bad job is the anglo-saxon contribution to civilization!

EDGAR. Margaret, if either you or Richard had told me, do you think I'd have sent for Janet? As a matter of fact I wired her this morning not to come. Not much hope of being in time I knew, but –

MARGARET. Sometimes you make me *sick!* What were you thinking about? A tender reconciliation under Gillian's *nose?*

WILF. Edgar, I don't rightly know what tha's been up to, an' I'm sure tha nobut had best on intentions. But I'm not stopping in this house to watch you at one another's throats. I'm not! One road and another I don't know where to turn between you. An' if you don't care as it's your mother lying dead up in yon middle bedroom, I care as it's *my wife*. She's dead, and nowt'll bring her back, and I've been trying to weigh you all up for t'last twenty-four hours, but I've had enough. You've given me summat to think about between you –

RICHARD *comes in as his father stops speaking.*

MARGARET. How is she?

RICHARD (*to* BEATIE). Will you go up, Aunt Beatie? She's not so good.

BEATIE. You want to make your minds up to stop it. Stop it. All of you. You'll send your father out of his mind.

BEATIE *goes upstairs.* RICHARD *sits wearily in the armchair.*

RICHARD. I'm sorry about it all, Dad.

WILF. I'm off out, I'm barn to your Uncle Jack's and by God you'd better sort yersens out, for I'll have no more!

Goes to hall, puts on cap and reappears in the doorway.

When t'undertaker comes your Aunty Beatie'll show him up. And if Janet turns up, I've no doubt she'll soon see why I'm not at home to see her. I'm leaving you all to it. (*He touches his throat.*) I'm up to here with it.

He goes out. MARGARET *goes to hall door.*

MARGARET. He's not the only one either.

She goes upstairs. Pause.

EDGAR. I wonder what it is about you that inspires Margaret's loyalty! (*He sits on sofa.*)

RICHARD. Maybe she's taken a look at you and come out of the anaesthetic.

EDGAR. And just what do you mean by that?

RICHARD (*both angry and tired*). Oh, Edgar! You still haven't really caught on, have you? You're still wondering what all the fuss is about. It's family life chum. (*Puts on an affected voice.*) It's all so *real*. (*Pause.*) You know they're wasting their time when they make documentaries about East End teds and show them to the jaded middle classes. They ought to film us and inflict it on the teds. (RICHARD *sits at the table.*)

EDGAR (*speaking slowly*). I knew you were living with Gillian, but I didn't know she was pregnant. (*Pause.*) Whether you despise me for this or not, it's the sort of thing that *does* make a difference for me. (*Pause.*) I wanted it to make a difference yesterday. And I couldn't. (*Pause.*) Do you know, I just couldn't.

He goes to RICHARD *and leans on table. He speaks with great difficulty.*

What is it about me you hate so much? (*Pause.*) I'm . . . you know, I'm comfortably off now but – for years I've been too busy struggling to get where I am to allow the luxury of stopping to ask whether it's *right*. (*Pause.*) I'm a fairly good scientist.

He sits down leaning towards RICHARD.

I don't understand you. Nothing about you (*Pause.*) The years between you and me . . . they're more like a generation. Men like me . . . came home in nineteen forty-five, and all we saw was this country had to be picked up. Like what I suppose you'd call the bowler-hatted brigade. Only then it was a question of technology . . . research. (*Pause.*) I'm not a very articulate man, Richard.

He takes out a pipe and begins to scrape out the bowl.

I prefer the motoring monthly to the stuff you go in for. (*Rises to mantelpiece. Pause.*) The reason I'm so concerned about Janet is despite the fact we're brothers, I respect what she's a product of, more than I respect what you stand for. She's decent and she's gentle and she never hurt anybody. Qualities you seem to demand, but you never give. (*Sits.*) If I tell you I desperately wanted you and her to make it up – I hope you'll believe me. Now it's my father we've got to think about. (RICHARD *has been listening neutrally. Now he faces* EDGAR *angrily.*)

RICHARD. And we tell Janet we're awfully sorry but there appears to have been a mistake somewhere.

EDGAR. That's a cruel and ugly way of twisting what I tried to tell you!

RICHARD. It's the cruel and ugly truth! (*Pause.*) I'll go and meet her at the station.

EDGAR. When Margaret came in last night I was ashamed – but, I hardly know how to say this. For half an hour I felt we were brothers. Do we have to behave like kids, to be brothers?

RICHARD. To be absolutely honest, I have no pleasant feelings about you whatsoever. Not a . . . single . . . spark. You're . . . much more dead for me, than my mother is.

EDGAR *sits for a second. Rises and gets coat from sofa.*

EDGAR. And do you really mean to tell me that . . . that right at the heart of this, for both of us, it's a political difference? Simply putting the cross in a different place on a voting slip? Do you?

RICHARD. No, I don't.

EDGAR (*putting on his coat*). Then what?

RICHARD. Anyway, it's very much more than a political difference. It's a difference of choice.

EDGAR *is baffled, miserable, still with a trace of habitual bullying contempt.*

EDGAR. I honestly don't know what you mean.

RICHARD. Then we're exactly where we started, aren't we?

EDGAR. I'm going out for a bit. I love my dad. As much as you
do. But he was wrong.

> EDGAR *goes out.* RICHARD *follows and shouts after him*
> *from the door.*

RICHARD. That's where the difference begins.

Scene Thirteen

TELECINE. *Station, afternoon of the same day.*
(RICHARD *runs up the slope into the forecourt of the station, looking*
at his watch. He gets a platform ticket from the machine. The train
arrives and as he runs up the steps of the footbridge, people from the
train come across the bridge towards him. He pushes through them
and sees JANET. *She is conventionally well-dressed – a smart,*
good-looking woman.

JANET. I'm glad you came to meet me.

RICHARD (*taking her suitcase*). You shouldn't be here.

JANET. How is your mother?

RICHARD. She died last night.

JANET. Oh –

RICHARD. Look, Janet. You can't come to the house.

JANET. Why not?

RICHARD. Let's go to the buffet. We've got to talk.

Scene Fourteen

Railway Station Buffet.
JANET *sits at a table in the buffet.* RICHARD *is at the counter.*

MAN. Egg and chips please, miss.

> RICHARD *brings two cups and puts them down on the table.*

RICHARD. I don't think there's . . . I'll get some sugar.

JANET. For God's sake, Richard. I'm not going to drink it. I don't want it.

RICHARD (*sits down*). I'm surprised you came. For all you were fond of my mother.

JANET. Hadn't you better explain first why we're here and not on the way home?

RICHARD. You were fond of her.

JANET. Yes. I was.

RICHARD. It was cancer.

JANET. I know. She wrote and told me.

RICHARD. Edgar shouldn't have asked you to come.

JANET. I thought it . . . considerate of him.

RICHARD. Despite the circumstances?

JANET. Despite?

RICHARD. Edgar's quite capable of hoping for an eleventh hour reconciliation!

JANET. You can hardly blame your own brother for not wanting to see your marriage break up!

RICHARD. And you?

JANET. I came . . . to be with your mother.

RICHARD. After a day's delay.

JANET. It was impossible to come yesterday.

RICHARD. I wonder what could make it impossible, when she was dying?

JANET. You've still got that habit of interrogating people rather than asking.

RICHARD. Well then, why didn't you come yesterday?

JANET. Edgar's exact words in the telegram were: cannot live more than a few days.

RICHARD. I see. A calculated risk!

JANET. Are you reproaching me for coming, or for not coming? (*Pause.*) What do you want me to do, Richard? Take the next train back to London – or what?

RICHARD. And you got the telegram at your flat?

JANET. I was spending a week with John Miller and his parents. My mother phoned me. She's living with me now.

RICHARD. I heard you'd 'been seen' as they call it, with Miller.

JANET. I don't think it concerns you.

RICHARD. Judging from his maiden speech in Parliament, Miller ought to be the concern of every right-minded citizen. There ought to be a lynch Miller campaign.

JANET. What's all this to do with –

RICHARD. He's a vain and stupid man and he's –

> RICHARD *pauses.* JANET's *assurance is wearing thin, she becomes nervous.*

JANET. He's what?

RICHARD. He's wrong for you.

> JANET *seems to be trying to make a decision. In deciding, she becomes both defiant and vulnerable.*

JANET. I know. (*Pause.*) I see too many people the way you would see them, Richard. (*Pause.*) I was having a violent row with John when my mother telephoned, and – we'd been rowing all week.

RICHARD. I'm very pleased to hear it!

JANET. Don't make fun of me, Richard.

RICHARD. I'm not making fun of you. Any bastard with his ideas should be –

JANET. I don't want him, Richard. I don't want anybody, unless I . . . still . . . want . . . you.

> *The man at their table looks up briefly from his egg and chips.*

RICHARD. *What?*

JANET. Do I have to say it again? It's humiliating enough once!

RICHARD. No. Once is enough for me. You don't really mean to say, at this stage?

JANET. Why not?

RICHARD. Oh, if we ignore everything that's been said and done . . . the mutual thumbscrewing, why not?

JANET. I don't want to ignore anything.

RICHARD. So the marriage is supposed to rise like a phoenix out of its own ruins!

JANET. I don't know what it's supposed to do.

RICHARD. Janet, it was *your* divorce. Your lawyers. Your money. Your revenge. I'm the guilty party, remember? I'm faithless, unreliable, treacherous – and what was it your barrister bloke called me? A morally unscrupulous person. I would have thought that makes me pretty indigestible!

JANET. It does.

RICHARD. Then for heaven's sake!

They look away from each other. RICHARD *fiddles with his cup. We hear the clatter and noise of the cafeteria.*

It's over a year since the final row Janet. I remember very clearly what you said. You said: I simply don't love you any more. I can't love you any more, because I can't love somebody I don't trust. And apart from in court, I haven't seen you since. It's a bit late to come up with this!

Pause.

JANET. It seems to me now that . . . if I hadn't been so obsessed with whether I could trust you, I wouldn't have lost you.

RICHARD. Well, it's finished. You wanted to finish it, and you did.

JANET. Can't we go home? I'd like to see your father.

RICHARD. I brought Gillian Moore home with me. She's going to have a baby. We're getting married. (*Pause.*)

JANET. I see. And does she know . . . all about you and me? About what happened?

RICHARD. She knows the facts and my interpretation of them. I tried to tell her your side of it as well.

JANET. Did you tell her what happened in Majorca?

RICHARD. Yes . . . I told her, one day I simply decided to stop writing. I said I told you, and started to get drunk and you walked out. I told her you came back that night and found me in bed with the Spanish maid. Said you cleared out there and then. (*Pause.*) I must say, it sounded a bit farcical in the retelling. That's the trouble with facts.

JANET. And did you tell her the rest? That you couldn't stand my money, or my friends, or my family? Did you tell her what a phoney puritan you are? (*She becomes hysterical.*) Did you tell her you thrived on my *shame*, for everything I'd had and you hadn't? For all the phoney values I'd swallowed and you'd seen through? Like hell you did! You probably confined yourself to telling her that I couldn't forgive you for not being a success!

RICHARD. Well, that's true, isn't it?

JANET. I just hope you don't wear *her* out expecting her to think that coming from a working class background is some kind of virtue in itself!

> JANET *begins to cry. She cries helplessly, as if she desperately wants not to and is shamed by not being able to control it.*

I'm saying everything I intended not to say! (*Pause.*) How dreadful it all must be for your father –

RICHARD. He probably wishes we were all back where we came from. I don't blame him if he does, either.

> *Pause.* You know how I always felt when you and I went home –

> JANET *stops crying. Dries her eyes.*

JANET. You made a damn sight more fuss about the gulf between you and your parents than I ever did. And that's funny! I was supposed to be the bourgeoise!

RICHARD. Janet – all your life you've been able to share things with your parents. In families like ours the children are alien. They're split right down the middle.

JANET. Anybody'd think you'd have been happier if they'd sent you out to work when you were fourteen!

Pause. RICHARD *pushes away his cup. Leans on the table. Speaks abstractedly.*

RICHARD. One half of me loves my mother as somebody about three feet taller than myself, with big red arms and an apron that smells of new bread . . . hanging the washing out in the yard. And my dad – a giant in overalls that smell of engines and dark shag. And behind *them* . . . the chimneys and soot and mills and the goodsyard. Soapy water running in the gutters and the tealeaves drying on a square yard of soil round a dead rose tree.

He sits back, staring vacantly past JANET.

The other half of me sees them with a sort of aching detachment. My mother worried about her home-made clothes on Edgar's convocation day . . . and saying "Now Wilf!" when my father talked too much after a couple of cocktails at one of Margaret's parties. (*Looks* JANET *in the eyes.*) To watch you being 'nice' to them was like watching a bloody duchess on a district visit!

GILLIAN *comes into the buffet. Dragging a suitcase with difficulty. She looks utterly defeated. She does not see* RICHARD *and* JANET, *but goes to counter.*

GILLIAN. Cup of tea, please.

JANET. Let's stop it, Richard. Let me just go back to London and forget I ever came. I know it's my own fault for coming, but anyway I can't stand any more. Just go, Richard.

They look at each other for a moment, then RICHARD *gets up and walks away. As he goes he sees* GILLIAN *turning from the counter holding a cup of tea. She reaches down for her case and upsets the cup.* RICHARD *goes to her, picks up the cup and puts it and the saucer on the counter. He takes* GILLIAN'S *arm – she is trembling, looking over his shoulder towards* JANET.

RICHARD. Gillian, what are you doing? What do you think you're doing?

JANET *picks up her bag and case. Glances at* RICHARD *and* GILLIAN, *walks out quickly.*

GILLIAN. Janet?

RICHARD. Yes but – why are you . . . What made you leave the house? And your case?

He leads her to a table.

GILLIAN. I was going home.

RICHARD. Home?

GILLIAN. Back to London. Back to your flat, I suppose.

They sit, holding each other's hands across the table.

It all suddenly seems so utterly hopeless.

RICHARD. I *told* you I wouldn't have Janet come to the house –

GILLIAN. I know. When you'd gone, that was what struck me as being so, so *bad*!

RICHARD. I don't know why the hell Beatie didn't stop you –

GILLIAN. She didn't see me. She was getting bathed. And Edgar and Margaret had gone out. Everything Edgar's said, it looked exactly like that to *me*. I felt as if I'd no place there. No right there.

RICHARD. And you imagine you could just walk out? Just get a train and go back? Like that?

GILLIAN. Whatever's happened, Janet has a right to be there – if she wants. (*Pause.*) I suppose she's gone?

RICHARD. You don't really think she would have stayed, do you?

GILLIAN. I was . . . in a panic Richard. (*Pause.*) Don't let's stay here –

RICHARD. I wish you . . . hadn't to face all this, Gillian –

GILLIAN. She's very attractive. Like in that photo. Sort of well-bred, or whatever it is.

RICHARD. Janet always was bred –

They manage to half smile at each other.

GILLIAN. I feel better now. I thought I was going to sick the baby up when I read that telegram. Don't let's stay here.

RICHARD. Come on then –

They get up, and RICHARD *takes her case in one hand,* GILLIAN'S *arm in the other. They slowly walk out of the buffet.*

Scene Fifteen

Living Room – Later in the afternoon.
GILLIAN *is lying on the sofa in her dressing gown, with a travelling rug over her legs.* BEATIE *is tucking the rug in,* RICHARD *is watching.*

BEATIE. Now shall I send for t'doctor?

GILLIAN. I'm all right, honestly.

BEATIE. You want some stick, going out like that. If you lose your baby you *will* have summat to get worked up about.

GILLIAN. But I –

BEATIE. Now that's quite enough for one afternoon. You rest yoursen for a bit, and thank your lucky stars it's no worse.

RICHARD. Can I do anything?

BEATIE (*straightening up.*) You and our Edgar between you, you've done enough I should think! I hope never to see t'like again! Your dad mortally offended, this poor lass next door to a miscarriage, you and Edgar at daggers drawn . . . I wonder what I've come into, I do an' all.

RICHARD. There's no question of a miscarriage –

BEATIE. Oh, and since when have you been an expert, like? Have you had any bairns?

RICHARD. What d'you think I am, a hermaphrodite?

BEATIE (*to* GILLIAN *who is giggling*). What's he say? Summat blue, I've no doubt. (*To* RICHARD.) Now you stop with her, I've got some baking to do.

BEATIE *goes into the kitchen, closing the door behind her.*

GILLIAN. I feel sleepy now.

RICHARD. Try to sleep then.

He sits on the arm of the sofa and she rests her head on his lap.

GILLIAN. When you love somebody, you can love everybody else a bit more, can't you?

RICHARD. What's that supposed to connect with?

GILLIAN. I was just thinking. I was frightened of Janet. (*Pause.*) I know it isn't going to be easy for us, Richard. (*Taking his hand and putting it to her face.*)

RICHARD. Don't be daft.

GILLIAN. But I know it isn't. I want to face it.

RICHARD. Well not now. Try to sleep.

He gets up and goes to the armchair near her.

GILLIAN. Tell me a story.

RICHARD. Why tell you a story?

GILLIAN (*feels the baby*). Tell *it* a story then. You'll have to get into the habit some time.

RICHARD. That's a boorjuice habit.

GILLIAN. I don't care.

RICHARD *makes a performance of settling down in his chair.*

RICHARD. Well then. Let's see, a story. Well it was like this, see. Once upon a time there was a little house –

GILLIAN. By a silver river with frogs sitting on lilypads –

RICHARD. No, as a matter of fact it was by a mucky canal full of dead dogs and illegal sewage.

GILLIAN. Social realism for little tots!

RICHARD. That's it. Well this house by the canal was just at the end of the snicket from the gas works to the slaughterhouse. And in it there lived a little person. A social realist. He was three feet high and he could use a knife and fork, and when the story begins he'd just heard how the world was created . . .

from the big people. They told him: in the beginning was Keir Hardie and Keir Hardie was with God and Keir Hardie practically *was* God. Course he didn't create the world. A devil created the world. A capitalist devil who said: let there be factories and there were factories. Let there be muck and there was muck. Let there be brass and there was brass . . . for some folk.

He gets up, walks to the fire, stares into it. Looks at the Van Gogh.

All the big people had been working for the devil for as long as they could remember. (*He kneels down in front of the fire.*) Mostly for brass, but partly because he was a gentleman and he knew how to run the country. Like all the best devils he had a lot of faces as well. He was on the council, he had a posh office at the pit, he owned the railways, he was on the school board of governors . . . he was a magistrate. And he even went to church and took the collection for the other god, the one in the sky. Both Mam and Grandma had a foot in both camps. They were sort of heretics. They knew the world ought to be like Keir Hardie and Dad wanted it, only when they talked about when they'd been in *service* . . . they made it sound all right. (*Pause.*) All that lovely table linen and silver and everybody knowing his place, even the master. And then when they said that Dad gritted his teeth and told them to wait till t'working classes takes over. We s'll wipe us noses on t'table linen. Dad thrilled and terrified at the same time – Mam and Grandma were just womenfolk. Dad wanted the people to own everything and everybody to have an inside lav. He said that was socialism, in case they didn't know it.

Pokes the fire. Stays silent.

GILLIAN. What happened then?

He stands up with his back to the fire.

RICHARD. The little person gradually worked out Dad's ideas for himself. They had to get the devil out and put Labour in . . . get rid of the old factories and t'muck and share out t'brass. This involved going to college so you could meet the devil on his own terms and so you wouldn't have the sort of life the big people had.

He goes to sit at the table.

Eventually the little person grew up and went away. (*Pause.* RICHARD'S *face is sad and strained.*) And got educated and a lot of other things. What's the use of telling stories to a foetus?

GILLIAN. What's the matter Richard?

Pause.

RICHARD. Nothing. Nowt. It makes a good fairy story. That was part one. Part one's the best because it's the ideological part. In part two the devil changes his spots and everybody gets in a proper muddle. Dad's getting on in years and doesn't quite get the hang of the changes. He sees the slums come down and the rocket sites go up. He gets subsidised teeth, free glasses for reading, and a gold watch for devoted service. The day comes when Mam says well there's no getting away from it we're better off now than we've been for many a long year.

Pause.

And practically all there is left to do is shout where do we go from here? Shout: where do we go when the cities aren't fit to live in, when we all have everything to live with and nothing to live *for*? Where do we go, when all the black men have got their independence, when all the coolies are riding round in mini-cars?

There is a knock at the back door.

When we're all fed and inoculated, where do we go? When the life expectancy's raised to 150, where do we go?

Repeated knocking. BEATIE *opens the living room door.*

When we –

BEATIE. It's the undertaker Richard.

RICHARD. The undertaker. (*Begins to laugh.*) That's it – that's where we go!

Scene Sixteen

Living Room. Late the same evening.
BEATIE *is at the table with her workbasket, darning socks.*
MARGARET *is flicking through a magazine.*

BEATIE. Their Uncle Fred and Aunty Mary'll be coming, that makes five. Then there's Eunice, Jack and his wife, and Aunty Cora from Barnsley. Eh, she's a brave un, is Cora.

MARGARET. What's the matter with Auntie Cora?

BEATIE. She's had everything taken away, you know.

MARGARET. She's what?

BEATIE. Eh, it's wonderful what they can do nowadays, isn't it? She were in Leeds Infirmary ten weeks and if she hadn't gone when she did, she wouldn't have lived. Mind, some of them young doctors nowadays they treat you like muck, don't they. I were saying to –

MARGARET. Just how many *are* coming to tea after the funeral?

BEATIE. Well I make it fourteen love, including t'missis next door.

MARGARET. In here?

BEATIE. Eh, we've had some bigger crushes than that, love.

MARGARET. I'll be glad when it's all over.

BEATIE. Nay, Margaret!

MARGARET. I only mean, if we could have the funeral . . . without having them all back to the house. I think father's had enough to put up with, one way and another. So have I, come to that.

BEATIE (*rolling up a sock*). There. That's t'last. Wilf's easily hurt, for all his manliness. And I will say, Gillian's carrying Richard's baby, she's a right to be treated as one on t'family.

MARGARET. Well she'll soon find out *that* has its drawbacks, as well as its advantages.

BEATIE. My lot's done nowt but bicker ever since they first opened their mouths, but I don't know as they're any worse for it.

MARGARET. I wouldn't call what Richard and Edgar go in for bickering!

BEATIE. Edgar'll change his tune about Gillian, you mark my words.

She gets up and goes to put the workbasket away.

MARGARET. It's something more fundamental than whether he does or he doesn't.

BEATIE. When you get to my age and your family's grown up, you get used to them telling you where to get off.

MARGARET. I'm sure I shan't.

BEATIE. Eh, you'll be wanting to get back to them, aren't you?

MARGARET. If it had been for any other reason, I'd have been glad to get away from them!

BEATIE. You're a cut, and no mistake, Margaret. Where did you say Richard and Gillian is?

MARGARET. Gone to see somebody Richard used to go to school with. Laurie Cobb, or somebody.

BEATIE. Oh aye! I know yon one. He's gotten a beard. What do they want to go having beards for? T'isn't natural.

MARGARET. I suppose you could say that not having beards isn't natural either.

BEATIE. My father had a beard. A red one. He were a regular old devil, an' all. He used to sup enough beer on a Friday night to fill a set pot. Mind, fellers *did* have beards in his day. It's these bohemians as gets up my back. (*Clock chimes.*) Eh, is that a quarter to ten? They'll be wanting their suppers.

MARGARET. I'll put the kettle on.

BEATIE. Yes love, put t'electric one on.

> MARGARET *and* BEATIE *go into the kitchen.* MARGARET *fills the kettle.* RICHARD *comes in at the back door.*

MARGARET. Where's Gillian?

RICHARD. In the fish and chip shop round the corner.

BEATIE. Well didn't you wait for her then? She's just same as I was when I were carrying our Percy. Used to take a fancy to summat and I had to have it there and then. You ought to have waited Richard.

RICHARD. She's only at the fish shop Aunt Beatie, she hasn't entered for the Olympic Games.

BEATIE. You've been in t'knife box and gotten sharp, haven't you!

RICHARD. As a matter of fact she wanted some beer as well. So I went round to the Fox for a couple of bottles. I thought she'd be back by now.

> *Takes beer bottles out of his raincoat pocket and takes off coat.*

I got you a stout, Aunt Beatie.

BEATIE. Well I wouldn't say no.

> *She bustles about preparing for supper.*

RICHARD. Would you like it now?

BEATIE. I think I will love. I wouldn't dare with me fish and chips.

> RICHARD *pours the stout.*

RICHARD. Edgar back?

BEATIE. Here's luck. (*Drinking.*) Nay, I suppose he's still at Mrs. Ramsey's. There's one that's going to miss your mother, an' all. They shared a stall at church bazaar you know.

> RICHARD *goes into livingroom. He sits down and picks up a*

newspaper. EDGAR *comes in back door and into the living room.*

There you are Edgar. How did she take it then?

EDGAR. She knew already. Heard it from Mrs. Brotherton in town this afternoon.

RICHARD. News travels fast in these parts. They beat it out on the dustbins in the back yards.

The sound of WILF *and* GILLIAN'S *voices outside.* WILF *is singing 'Why do the nations' from the Messiah.* GILLIAN *appears at the kitchen door more or less supporting* WILF.

EDGAR. Dad! What the hell have you –

WILF (*to* GILLIAN). What did I tell thee? I told thee he'd be t'first to open his trap.

GILLIAN. Come and sit down.

GILLIAN *helps him to a chair. She is gentle with him; there is much sympathy now between them.* EDGAR *and* RICHARD *watch him closely.*

WILF. What are you all gawpin' at then? You're put out, are you? (*Rising and taking off his coat.*)

EDGAR. You're drunk!

WILF. Aye lad, I've had a few. What you got to say about that? I've no doubt tha's gotten summat to say.

BEATIE (*from kitchen door*). Wilf! What have you been doing?

WILF. Nay, don't get thisen worked up Beatie lass. Let him have his say. Then I'll have mine.

He sits down at the table, turning away.

EDGAR. I can't trust myself to speak!

WILF. Eh, thy mother's dead and thy father's drunk, poor sod. Poor old sod. (*Shakes his head.*) It's noan a reight way to be going on, is it?

EDGAR. What do you think?

WILF (*gets up, goes towards* EDGAR). Dost know Edgar, I don't know as tha's ever asked me what I think in thy life before.

RICHARD. Don't you think you ought to go up to bed Dad?

WILF. Thee an'all? Nay, one at a time surry.

EDGAR. He's not in a fit condition to reason with.

WILF (*in front of* EDGAR). Now that's nobut an excuse for not speaking thy mind.

BEATIE. Now he's not going to speak against his father Wilf.

WILF. Isn't he? He's noan barn to speak for him. Are you? Doesn't know enough about me to speak for me. But I know a lot about thee. Funny, isn't it. I nearly brought thee into t'world with my own two hands. Your mother laboured all night, but when it came to t'point tha were born yawling inside twenty minutes. Tha were a raw lump and no mistake. Tha took one look at me and thought daft devil, and tha's thought so ever since! No bigger than that fist. And look at you now. (*Feels* EDGAR'S *arm.*) We *are* related, tha knows.

EDGAR (*moving back, almost recoiling*). Yes, we're related all right!

WILF (*turning to* RICHARD). And thee. Tha were nowt but skin and bone. When they took thee from thy mother, they took her womb, an' all. Now she's dead, isn't she.

> WILF *goes to the window* – RICHARD *goes and sits in armchair.*

Takes summat to bring families together, doesn't it? I wanted you both to come. It's easy to love a bairn. It's easy tha knows. But when t'bairn's gone.

> *Takes* EDGAR *by the shoulders.*

I've wiped thee up at both ends. I've powdered thy arse. I've putten food in thy mouth. (*Points to* RICHARD.) Thee an'all. I've rocked you to sleep.

> *He sits at the table.*

It's nowt but beer talking, is it? Nowt but beer.

> BEATIE, MARGARET *and* GILLIAN *come in from the kitchen.*

BEATIE. I think it's time I took mesen next door. I'll say goodnight to you all. And if you're not too fuddled with ale to take my advice Wilf, you'll do well to get yoursen upstairs.

WILF. Eh Beatie lass, we shall all live through it tha knows. Stay and have thy fish and a pennorth.

BEATIE. Thank you very much I know my place. I'll see you all in t'morning. (*Goes out through kitchen door.*)

WILF. Your Auntie Beatie's a good woman.

EDGAR (*coming close to* WILF). Dad, will you just tell me why this? Why?

WILF. Why? Why I've gotten in this state with your mother lying dead in t'house? That's a tall order, isn't it lad? But she'd have understood would your mother. Dost think we've been blind, deaf and dumb this last fifteen years? Without feelings? Dost think we noticed *nowt*? Dost think tha can walk into this house t'one time I send for thee and carry on same as tha always has? Both of you? I know tha counts on most on what tha says bouncing off me, like. In at one lugole and out at t'other. Eh, I wonder what I've done. What I've gotten. What you are. What are you? I educated you to get you out on this, did I? Well let me tell you it's a reight home. And it's been a reight home without you. So tha's barking up t'wrong tree there. Aye, I've been weighing form up.

He sits at the table and begins rolling a cigarette.

Ah've been weighing form up. Dost see.

EDGAR. I can see you're drunk, and that's about all. I'm surprised you can brazen it out. (*He sits opposite* WILF *at the table.*)

WILF. Tha doesn't follow me, Edgar lad. How can I explain to you? Can you . . . can you tell me summat I'm fond on, for a start?

EDGAR. Beer?

WILF. Nay lad, tha mustn't get sarky. Dost know owt about me? Tha knows nowt. Except I'm thy dad. I'm ignorant. I've

putten thee somewhere I cannot reach, and tha can't turn
back. Even if tha wanted to, which I hope and suppose tha
doesn't. Now, back on t'kitchen window there's a bit on a
flower bed like. Enough to swing a cat, any road. Thy mother
used to plant a few flowers there. Dost know *what* flowers?
When t'wind's in t'wrong direction tha can't smell them for
t'gasworks, but they come up year after year. They make a
bit of colour. In summer we used to take us chairs out and
enjoy t'sunshine. We never lacked owt to talk about your
mother and me. We had our lads.

Finally lights his cigarette clumsily.

How dost imagine t'sort of life we had? On my spiv day we
took us dinners out to t'reservoy to see a bit of nature, like.
One time tha couldn't show me a flower or a leaf as I couldn't
name. We had us pleasures and we'd have given owt many a
time to have thee both share them. But you never settled with
each other when you did come home. Dost remember how to
make a fishing rod, Edgar?

EDGAR. This is all beside the point dad.

WILF. I showed thee how to make one when tha were ten year
old. Dost know when t'hawthorn comes out Richard?

RICHARD. Did I ever? I don't know Dad.

WILF. I told thee. Tha's both forgotten. Tha's gone thy own
ways. Only I sometimes think as t'other things we had to
give you, you've left them behind. Happen they don't mean
nowt.

EDGAR. Oh it sounds fine, the way you put it! But you forget
what you wanted out of us. And if it's gone wrong, well
you've just got to make the best of it!

WILF. You say that, do you? I'll tell thee, t'best years on my life
was when you were growing up. I could talk to thee both.
Show thee things. Put clothes on thy backs and bread in thy
hands. Oh, I wanted you to grow up different from me I
know. But I got more than I bargained for. I look at you now

and think: them's my sons. Reight proud on you both. Only where you've gotten to I don't know. When you chew t'fat about politics and that afore t'war, dost stop to ask *why* I couldn't weigh it all up reight? At eleven year old I were scrattin' coal for me living. What I made were t'difference between eating an' starving in our family. Sixteen year old I were cleaning out boilers. Come home, get washed, drop into bed and start all over t'next morning. And socialism? Tha's reight. I knew nowt, but in them days you didn't have to be brilliant to know which side tha were on. Tha doesn't have to be educated to be a human being tha knows. But in them days I thought I were a man. And that's what I'm noan so sure either on you two is.

EDGAR. It all depends on what you mean by being a man.

WILF. A man's somebody that can hold his head up. He doesn't bury it down into t'ground. He's a feller that won't accept nowt shoddy not if you held a bloody gun to his head. He doesn't give in. An' if y'ask me . . . you two's given in.

He goes to the sideboard drawer and takes out the watch. Holds it to his ear and shakes it gently. Offers it to GILLIAN.

Gillian love, take it and give it to t'bairn when it's old enough to appreciate it. Go on love, take it. It'll noan bite thee.

GILLIAN. You know I couldn't.

WILF. And why not?

EDGAR. Put it away Dad. It's yours. You know none of us could take it.

WILF *hesitates, still holding out the watch and looking at them. Then he puts it back in the drawer.*

WILF. Tha mun please thisens. I shall nobut give it to t'bairn mesen if I live to see it grow up.

Stands with his hands on the drawer, his back to them.

This'll still be your home. I hope you'll come when you want, same as when your mother were alive. Don't get it into your heads I'm barn to leave it and shove mesen on you.

MARGARET. You mustn't take that attitude father. We were going to ask you if you'd like to come to us when you retire.

WILF. That's very kind on you. Both on you. But can you see it Edgar? Can you Margaret? Sort of life I'm used to, and sort of life you're used to. Ah should feel like a fish out of water, same as you feel when you're up here. (*Pause.*) We've nowt in common. We're strangers. Talk t'hind leg off a donkey and you won't change that. I've had t'blinkers off since yesterday. When I leave this house I shall leave it in a wooden box, and not before. (*Pause.*) Eh, I feel reight dizzy all on a sudden. I mun sit down. Why don't you get your suppers?

He goes to sofa and sits down. EDGAR *goes to him and stands over him.*

EDGAR. Is it my fault if we've nothing in common? Is it Margaret's? We can do just about as much for you as you did for us . . . *provide* for you!

MARGARET. Edgar!

WILF. Nay let him be. He's nobut letting off steam.

EDGAR. You seem to have gotten a damn sight more out of my childhood than I did! All I remember is the bread and fat and the algebra. You're getting to be a sentimental old man, Dad.

WILF. Is that reight? Dost remember nowt good, Edgar? Has tha nowt to look back on?

(*There is a long pause.* EDGAR *sits in the chair by the fire.*)

EDGAR. I don't see any of it the way you do. (*Pause.*) I remember many a day . . . if you want to know . . . when you went to work with meat in your sandwiches; when Richard and me had meat for us dinners, and I know for a fact my mother sat down to potatoes when we'd gone. What about her? She had it rough, God knows. (*Suddenly angry.*) Don't ask me to look back on those years through rose coloured spectacles!

WILF. Aye, and all that meat thy mother didn't have . . . tha wore it round thy neck in t'shape on white poplin shirts when tha went to college! Tha didn't refuse t'shirts, Edgar.

EDGAR. Well, people don't have to do things like that any more, do they? Look at your working classes now. Haven't they got it all? But they're not exactly a testament to the highest achievements of the human race, are they?

WILF. They'll never be no different as long as fellers like thee goes over to t'other side!

EDGAR suddenly fetches his coat and puts it on.

What's ta doing now?

EDGAR. I'm going out, and I'm staying out till you've gone to bed. I'll tell you Dad . . . you're no more plausible when you're drunk than you are when you're sober.

WILF. Nay, take thy coat off. I'll get mesen off upstairs.

EDGAR. When you came lurching in here to-night, I was ashamed and embarrassed to look at you. Not so much because you got drunk but because you got drunk when you did. The one thing you had left as far as I was concerned was your dignity – and now you haven't even got that.

RICHARD (*going up to* EDGAR *angrily*). For God's sake *go* out then. Get out.

EDGAR (*with restrained fury*). Don't you talk like that to me.

RICHARD. Are you going? Or not?

WILF hurls himself out of his chair at them.

WILF. God damn you. God damn you, stop it! Will you shut up? If you go on I'll not bide you in my house. I'll not have you another night. I'll see you in hell first both on you.

He goes to the sideboard where there is a framed snapshot of WILF *in his forties, standing by an engine with two small boys* – EDGAR *and* RICHARD. WILF *picks it up and looks at it bitterly.*

I wouldn't come and live with either on you not if it were t'last place on earth. I've that much dignity left, any road. I'll not forget this you know. Sitha God damn and sod it I'll noan come to you if I'm crippled! You're noan my sons and why –

don't ask me why, noan of you. If it's not class nor education nor growing up, it's past me. Best harm we can do you is to die off and leave you with what you've gotten. For it's nowt to do with us. I grew up t'same road as my father and I've no doubt he grew up t'same as his father, but I'm noan in you two. I'm noan *in* you. (*Still holding the picture he crashes it face down on the table, breaking the glass.*) I've lost you some road no man should lose his children ever. Summat's done. Summat's finished. Summat's gone. I don't know what it is. My way on seeing things, tha talks about. What's thy way? Tha's summat I never were. Tha's no time. No time for nowt, not even for thisens. There's some folks as is content to live. Gillian – dost know what I mean? A woman with a bairn inside her knows summat on t'sort. Living content. And I don't mean daft content, neither. (*Goes to the window and draws the curtain.*) Sitha – t'goodsyard. Work it out for thysen. An average on nigh fifty hour a week for forty year. How much time does that make? I know every siding and signal and permanent way over t'county. I've gotten as far as I can go, and happen I know no more for all that. Canst not think what I wanted for thee two? I'm dumb, but dost think I've never wanted to say owt? My head's gotten nowt in it, but dost think I've never wanted to fill it? And I waited for thee two to grow up and make it reight. (*He looks out.*) Eh, when I were a lad we thought it were a marvel to go fifty mile an hour. Now they're barn to t'moon. It's all come about in fifty year, and it'd take a good un to keep up with that. Tha's left us old uns behind reight enough. (*Pause.*) I can fire an engine and drive it. I can cop a pike with a spinner. My eyesight's going now, but I could nick a rabbit at twenty yard with yon old catapult, from t'footplate. (*Pause.*) But I've gotten that feeling in my bones as summat's finished with thee and me. (*He looks up at the Van Gogh.*) Thy mother were bonny. We were as happy together as t'days were long. If we both had t'same thought in us heads about you two we kept it to us sens. But t'cat's out on t'bag now, isn't it? Happen better so. (*He stands between his two sons, his arms on their shoulders*.) It's noan dignity tha misses Edgar lad. It's knowing I've no place in thy world. If tha's ashamed and embarrassed, it's because there's nowt between us. Dost even know what I like to *eat*? What time I get mesen off to work on a morning? They've putten me in t'old men's link. Dost know what that is? Soft jobs for them as time's nearly up. Dost not know *now* why I went on t'beer to-night? (*Pause*.) Tha's as far away from me lad as if tha'd gotten off in one of them sputniks. Tha were fond on thy mother, I know. (EDGAR *looks away. His anger has gone and he suddenly appears vulnerable*. WILF *looks at* RICHARD.) And thee, lad. I wish tha'd been able to do everything tha wanted to. Nobbut tha's tumbled somewhere between what our Edgar's gotten, an' glory. Haven't you? (*Pause*.) Is there nowt left to paint? Nowt left to write about, like? Or what? Tha munt spend thy life doing summat tha cannot bide. Tha *munt*! (*He looks at* GILLIAN *as if appealing to her, nodding over his shoulder at* RICHARD.) He says last night as being a husband and father's all he's capable on, like. (*Pause*.) Well, that mun be a start – munt it?

GILLIAN *looks up at him. Close up of* WILF *and* GILLIAN.

Credits over Left Book Club photograph.
Music – The Red Flag – solo treble recorder.

A Suitable Case For Treatment

A Suitable Case for Treatment was first broadcast by BBC Television on 21 October 1962 with the following cast:

MORGAN DELT	*Ian Hendry*
LEONIE DELT	*Moira Redmond*
CHARLES NAPIER	*Jack May*
MRS DELT	*Anna Wing*
MR HENDERSON	*Norman Pitt*
MRS HENDERSON	*Helen Goss*
JEAN SKELTON	*Jane Merrow*
POLICEMAN	*John Bennett*
ANALYST	*Hugh Evans*
TICKET COLLECTOR	*David Grahame* (Film only)
MR DELT	*Harry Brunning*

1. Gorilla's Cage at Zoo.

MORGAN *approaches the gorilla's cage and stands looking rather disconsolately at the gorilla. The gorilla looks at* MORGAN. *There appears to be some sort of mutual understanding.* MORGAN *puts on dark glasses and walks away.*

2. Divorce Court.

LEONIE *is giving evidence.*

COUNSEL. Would you tell the Court, Mrs Delt, what your husband did then?

LEONIE (*air of haughty wretchedness*). He shaved the dog in such a way that it had a hammer and sickle on its back.

3. Landing of Leonie's Flat.

MORGAN *is contemplating the nameplate to one side of the door. It says* 'MORGAN *and* LEONIE DELT' – *but the* 'MORGAN' *and the* 'and' *have a single line struck through in ink.* MORGAN *removes the card from its frame, takes another from his pocket and slips it into the frame. It says* 'MORGAN *and* LEONIE DELT'. *He is carrying an L-shaped parcel and a long cylinder. He takes a key and puts it in the lock and turns.*

4. Divorce Court.

COUNSEL. And the er . . . the breed of dog?

LEONIE. A poodle.

COUNSEL. Your husband in fact hated the poor dumb creature?

LEONIE. I wouldn't say that. (*Pause.*) It's me he was getting at.

5. *Leonie's Flat. Bedroom.*

The bedroom is tastefully and expensively furnished, with a feminine emphasis. On the bed is a woolly dog. MORGAN *puts his parcel on the bed beside dog, sits on the bed and begins to unwrap the parcel.*

6. *Interior Taxi.*

LEONIE *and* MR HENDERSON *are sitting in the back of the taxi.*

FATHER. It wasn't too painful, darling, was it? A foregone conclusion of course. (*Pause.*) I never liked Morgan.

LEONIE. I know, father.

FATHER. He's brutal, lazy, dirty, *and* immoral. I've also heard he's a Trot, whatever that may be.

LEONIE. It's a kind of communist, father.

FATHER. Indeed? I wouldn't have said he had the moral fibre for *any* sort of belief.

LEONIE. In any case it's not true. Morgan isn't a Trot. (*Pause.*) He isn't anything.

FATHER. Well – when you get the decree absolute, you'll be free of him. (*Pause.*) Why don't you buy yourself something nice on the way home? Celebrate.

LEONIE. I think I might. You've been terribly good about all this.

FATHER. Thank God none of us will have to put up with him any longer.

7. *Leonie's Flat. Bedroom.*

MORGAN *now has the parcel unwrapped. It is a replica in wood of a gallows, with a noose hanging from the arm.* MORGAN *sets it upright on the floor. Takes the woolly dog, puts it in the noose. Pulls it tight, pushes it and watches it swing. Steadies it. Rises and walks out.* MORGAN *goes through the hall to the living-room. Crosses towards chair and drinks table. As he crosses:*

MORGAN. Hullo Room.

He takes a large roll of paper from chair, crosses to wall above gramophone and pins up a notice . . . 'NAPIER go home'.

MORGAN. Pins . . . wall . . . notice . . . (*turns into camera.*) Have a drink, Morgan? Don't mind if I do.

He goes over to drinks table, pours himself out a tot and sits in the chair. LEONIE *comes in the front door carrying large dress bag, goes across and into bedroom.* LEONIE *comes towards the bed, throws down parcel and coat on seeing dog hanging. Goes towards it. She picks up the gallows and dog and goes back towards the bed. She throws the gallows and dog on bed and walks away quickly towards the hall.*

LEONIE. Morgan. . . .

She stops as she sees him sitting in the living-room. Crosses to him.

LEONIE. Morgan! I told you not to come here. I also asked you for your key. Will you give it to me please.

MORGAN *indicates notice and* LEONIE *turns and sees it. Walks over to it and takes it down.*

LEONIE. I suppose you think that's funny. (*Unpins it and rolls it up.*)

MORGAN. Not at all. I mean what it says.

LEONIE. I divorced you this afternoon.

MORGAN. How did my image come over in court?

LEONIE. Will you *please* go?

MORGAN (*scratching*). Did you see what I did to your woolly dog?

LEONIE. I did.

Pause.

MORGAN. Is Charles Napier living here?

LEONIE. You know perfectly well he isn't. (MORGAN *rises and goes to her.*)

MORGAN. I've been to see a psychiatrist. He was fat, and extremely furry. Furry suit . . . furry hands . . . furry –

LEONIE. If it's money you want, I can let you have twenty pounds.

LEONIE crosses over to desk drawer but changing her mind takes cigarettes.

MORGAN (*shouts*). This is my flat as well, you know!

LEONIE. Not yours, darling. Not now.

MORGAN crosses back to drinks table and sits deliberately in chair.

Pause.

LEONIE. This is tiresome, Morgan –

MORGAN. Tiresome! A human life destroyed? A soul eviscerated?

There is a piano in one corner. MORGAN *goes to it. Sits, picks out a tune: the Red Flag.*

LEONIE (*moves in to drinks table*). I don't think you loved me at all until I asked you to leave.

MORGAN (*singing*). Now Hitler's dead and Stalin's gone –

LEONIE. Will you please go, Morgan.

Crosses to end of couch and sits. She lights a cigarette.

Pause.

MORGAN. I've nowhere *to* go. I've given up dossing on people's floors. Living in their flats when they're away. (*Lights cigarette.*) I live in the car now.

LEONIE. My solicitor is writing to you about that too. I bought it. And I want it back.

MORGAN. I went to see a psychiatrist today.

LEONIE. I won't have you back.

MORGAN. I have fantasies.

LEONIE. Nothing new about that.

MORGAN. I believe my mental condition's extremely illegal.

LEONIE. I'm tired of loving you and keeping you and admiring you. If it turns out that you're a psychopath, I'm sure it's the best thing for all our sakes.

> *She rises and goes up to alcove in window.* MORGAN *drinks up, rises and comes to drinks table. Sets down his glass and sits.* LEONIE *walks quickly down to telephone.*

MORGAN. There are two toothbrushes in the bathroom. And one of them is neither mine nor yours. And when did you start using hair-cream?

LEONIE. Welton, Booth and Welton? Mr Booth, please. Mr Booth? Leonie Delt. Yes, yes it was. But when I got home my husband was here. Yes. Yes. You said something last week about a court injunction. Well, he's here now, he's pretending to be mentally ill. I beg your pardon? Yes, he has a key. Yes. That's terribly kind of you. Thank you. Goodbye – (*She puts the phone down and turns.*) – Perhaps you'll understand now, Morgan, that I –

> MORGAN *has walked out during her conversation.*

8. *Underground Station.*

We see MORGAN, *in dark glasses, coming up the escalator. He hums the National Anthem, peers at the posters. He comes off the escalator and walks up to the ticket collector.*

MORGAN. Have you ever killed a man?

COLLECTOR. Just you watch it.

> MORGAN *walks quickly through the barrier.*

9. Hallway of Charles Napier's Office.

A glass door with the name on. MORGAN *opens it, walks round desk right up to* NAPIER. NAPIER *is seated at his desk. The room is tiny, filled with books. There is a desk, an office chair and an armchair.* NAPIER *is looking at some galley proofs. He looks up. He has an amused air but he is apprehensive.*

NAPIER. Good afternoon, Morgan.

MORGAN. Although you used to be my best friend, I can't allow you to sleep with my wife. I don't like it. It makes me feel funny in the head, and whereas it's a run of the mill job for a shrinker it will still cost me money.

NAPIER. Wife in name only, Morgan –

MORGAN (*smiling*.) I shall stave your ribs in and plant a boot in your guts.

NAPIER. Can't we be civilised about all this?

MORGAN. One of the things I came to tell you is that in future you can't count on me to be civilised. I've lost the thread.

He rises, strolls round and sits on edge of desk.

I should warn you that I am becoming dangerous. This afternoon I hanged a woolly dog. Tomorrow I might hang you. (*Pause.*) I'm getting fed up with symbolic gestures.

Pause.

NAPIER. Why the dark glasses, Morgan?

MORGAN. My eyes hurt. (*Pause.*)

NAPIER. Where are you living nowadays?

MORGAN. I live in a car. My address is now BCD 801.

NAPIER (*rising*). Leonie's car, I believe – whisky?

NAPIER *comes round to* MORGAN. MORGAN *takes knuckledusters from jeans pocket.* NAPIER *continues down to filing cabinet R.*

MORGAN. A small one. And then to brass tacks.

NAPIER *gets the whisky and two glasses. He is nonchalant, but the bottle rattles against the glasses.*

NAPIER. How's your novel coming along?

MORGAN. Have you got a sort of acid taste at the back of your throat?

NAPIER. You have a wonderfully bizarre imagination, Morgan.

MORGAN. I'm conducting a war, I've decided to carry my art into my life. Why should I be driven to psychiatrists by people like you and Leonie? Think of all the people who really need treatment. People with obsessions, phobias, delusions and so on. I'm busting the queue.

NAPIER. You started it. If you hadn't gone to France with that pug-nosed little socialist girl (*He has rejoined* MORGAN.) Leonie would never have turned to me. She's very loyal.

MORGAN. You're after her money – admit it.

NAPIER. I doubt if she makes more than twenty-five hundred a year.

MORGAN (*stands*). Twenty-five hundred and seventy. She married me to achieve insecurity, and when she'd got it she didn't know what to do with it.

NAPIER. Violence will get you nowhere, Morgan.

MORGAN. Where has gentleness got me? Where has love got me? Violence has a kind of dignity in a baffled man. The rich have the law, the poor a simple choice between docility and brutality. I am full of love. I shall punch you with love. Will you have love between the eyes or in the teeth?

He takes NAPIER *by the shirt.*

NAPIER. Now be reasonable, Morgan.

MORGAN. But I am being reasonable. I could stand here and tell you to keep away from my wife till I was blue in the face – but would you?

MORGAN *releases him.* NAPIER *shrugs.* MORGAN *goes R. to drinks and* NAPIER *goes back to the desk.*

MORGAN. I counted four haircream stains on the wallpaper in my flat. Did you think me unobservant?

NAPIER. I don't care what you are, Morgan. I'm very sorry for you and all that, but you don't exactly reach me. Not in the solar plexus. Not where the dark gods are located.

MORGAN. Leonie bites in her sleep. She growls at dawn. Without make-up she looks like a wizened parsnip. Her stomach rumbles when she dreams. Her motto – I bath, therefore I am.

NAPIER (*rising*). This has been a most interesting little chat, Morgan.

He goes to end of desk. MORGAN *comes in to him.*

MORGAN. They tell me you keep yourself in petty cash by robbing drunken writers in Soho drinking clubs.

NAPIER. That is apocryphal, I assure you.

MORGAN. Then I must be off.

NAPIER. And I.

MORGAN. To Leonie?

NAPIER. To the theatre.

MORGAN. With Leonie?

NAPIER. With a client.

MORGAN. Exactly.

NAPIER. Little insinuations please little minds.

MORGAN *goes towards door but stops and comes back to* NAPIER.

MORGAN. I definitely meant to bash you.

NAPIER. Goodbye then, Morgan.

MORGAN. Goodbye –

NAPIER. One day –

MORGAN (*at door*). One day we shall strangle the last publisher with the entrails of the last literary agent.

NAPIER. No hard feelings.

10. Greek Cafe.

A seedy Greek cafe in Charlotte Street where MORGAN *is being given a free meal by his mother who is a waitress there.* MORGAN *finishing his prunes. 'Olympos' in neon is flashing in the background.*

MRS DELT. Your dad was run down by the mounted police in Bristol in nineteen twenty-six. (*Pause.*) That's nothing to be ashamed of. But you! Marry a rich woman, live in luxury on your backside. (*Pause.*) And me slaving away in this dump. Look at me. Those aren't lady's hands –

Holds out hands, which MORGAN *looks at.*

MORGAN. One of these days, Ma, they'll be coming for me with a strait-jacket.

MRS DELT. I thought you was going to write for the telly and make a fortune. (*Pause.*)

MORGAN. You know what a strait-jacket is, don't you?

MRS DELT. Don't I! I've been living in one for years. Son, your dad saw himself waving the red flag on the rubble of Buckingham Palace. Don't ask me when. (*Pause.*) Now look at us. You aren't the militant little lad that tried to set fire to Stepney Police station. Where's he gone?

MORGAN. Things are very dicy just now on the ideological front, Ma.

MRS DELT. Your dad was on to you the day he drowned them kittens. You knew what'd happen to them if he gave them away. But oh, no! Drowning was cruel. He says to me the day after: you've given birth to a bleeding liberal!

MORGAN. It's your afternoon off tomorrow. I thought we might take a trip down the river to Greenwich.

MRS DELT. I was thinking of going to the cemetery with his flowers. Ah son, the mess you've made of your life.

MORGAN. You're a funny old woman, do you know that?

MRS DELT. You wait and see. (*Pause*.) It'll all come crashing down.

She reaches down and massages her legs.

MORGAN. What? (*Pause*.)

MRS DELT. Everything. (*Pause*.) I hope I live to see it all in ruins. Then I shall die happy. (*Pause*.) I'm just the same as I was about religion when I was a girl. I couldn't bear it all to turn out untrue. (*Pause*.) Well, I've still got me self-respect. Which is more than you have I should think.

MORGAN. It's very difficult to retain a coherent view of life.

MRS DELT. Your dad wanted to shoot the Royal Family, abolish marriage and put everybody who'd been to a public school in a chain gang. (*Pause*.) He was an idealist was your dad.

MORGAN. It's time you gave up working in this caff. Why don't I come home and take a job and let you retire in peace?

MRS DELT *is much affected. Sniffs at her tears.*

MRS DELT. Oh I am tired, Morgan –

MORGAN. Now, Ma –

MRS DELT. When I look at you. You've grown into a peculiar sort of a feller –

Pause.

MORGAN. I consulted a trick cyclist yesterday –

MRS DELT. What's that?

MORGAN. A specialist in mental troubles.

MRS DELT. And what did he say?

MORGAN. He said – I'm a suitable case for treatment.

MRS DELT. What sort of treatment? Electric shock and that?

MORGAN. No. You lie on a couch and say whatever comes into your head.

MRS DELT. Well let's hope he makes a man of you. (*Gets up*.) I

never did like your Leonie. (*Pause.*) Ah, I shall never have
peace in this world, Morgan. And I don't believe in the next.

    MORGAN *goes and puts his arm round her.*

MORGAN. I'll call for you at two then?

MRS DELT. All right, Morgan.

MORGAN. We'll go and see the Cutty Sark –

MRS DELT. All right, Morgan.

MORGAN. Cheerio then, Ma –

MRS DELT. Cheerio son.

    She sits on at the table as he leaves her.

11. Morgan's Car in Street.

CUT IN. *Sequence of gorilla film. The gorillas parade through
    sunlit jungle.*

CUT BACK TO. *Car, where* MORGAN'S *Mickey Mouse alarm
    clock is ringing on the dashboard.* MORGAN *wakes up. With hot
    water from a thermos he begins to shave in the driving mirror.*

MORGAN (*singing*). Don't ask me why I'm dreaming . . . don't
ask me why.

    A POLICEMAN *comes along the street – stops and stares at*
    MORGAN. *He comes to the offside door and crouches at the
    window.* MORGAN *dabs a blob of shaving soap on the*
    POLICEMAN's *nose. The* POLICEMAN *takes out his hand-
    kerchief and wipes it off.*

POLICEMAN. That's an assault, technically speaking –

MORGAN. Is there anything which is not, technically speaking,
an assault? Birth. School. Work. Sex. Life. Consciousness.
Death –

POLICEMAN. This your car?

MORGAN. No.

    The POLICEMAN *takes out a notebook.*

POLICEMAN. Begged, borrowed or stolen?

MORGAN. Property of wife.

POLICEMAN. Got any proof of identity?

MORGAN. No. Have you?

POLICEMAN. I'm asking the questions.

MORGAN. You were until just now. Now, *I'm* asking them as well. That's an indisputable fact.

POLICEMAN. It's funny how many of you think that's an original line. Address?

MORGAN. How do I know you're a real policeman?

POLICEMAN. You'll just have to take me on trust.

MORGAN. Haven't you got a little card with your photo on it? And an official stamp?

POLICEMAN. No.

MORGAN. If I was Prince Philip, do you know what you'd do?

POLICEMAN. What?

MORGAN. You'd . . . (*Peering.*) have you got a forelock? Well, you'd pull your forelock and straighten your helmet and back the hell out of it. Confess.

POLICEMAN. Do you usually shave in this vehicle of a morning?

MORGAN. Is it against the law?

POLICEMAN. I shouldn't think so.

MORGAN. Then what's all the fuss about?

POLICEMAN. You're the one that's making the fuss –

MORGAN (*singing*). Come into the garden Maud . . . for the black bat night hath flown.

POLICEMAN. I'm asking you to show legitimate right of usage of this vehicle.

MORGAN. You could always ring my wife.

The POLICEMAN *wanders round the car and copies down the number.*

POLICEMAN (*states car number*).

POLICEMAN. You want to watch it –

MORGAN. I know. But where *is* it?

> *The* POLICEMAN *eyes* MORGAN *for a moment then goes off down the street.* MORGAN *wipes his face with a towel and switches on the radio. We hear the fat stock prices.*
> MORGAN *opens a packet of sandwiches, and from a second thermos pours a coup of coffee and settles back in seat to eat them.* JEAN *comes along the street. She stops by car and she and* MORGAN *stare at each other. She goes and leans on window.*

JEAN. I *wish* you'd go away.

MORGAN. You shouldn't have changed the lock. I would go away. But I can't drive.

> JEAN *is fiddling with door handle. She gets into the car.*

JEAN. That copper seemed very interested in you.

MORGAN. Just passing the time of day.

JEAN. Do you love me, Morgan?

MORGAN. Yes.

JEAN. This won't be much fun when it's winter, you know –

MORGAN. They'll have come for me before winter.

JEAN. They don't put neurotics in mental hospitals. Only psychotics and psychopaths.

MORGAN. But I'm not a bit neurotic. I'm happy . . . integrated . . . friendly . . . tractable . . . and I'm extremely loving.

JEAN. Your sunflower's very high now. Nearly as tall as me.

MORGAN. It must be nice to have a bit of garden. Fill it with sunflowers . . . babies . . . empty whisky bottles . . . copies of *The Observer* –

JEAN. I wish you'd get a divorce.

MORGAN. Will you have some breakfast?

JEAN. I love you such a lot. That's why I have to keep you out of the flat.

MORGAN. That's what they call a *non sequitur*.

JEAN. I know.

MORGAN (*singing*). Girls . . . were made to love and kiss . . . and who am I to interfere with this. . . .

JEAN. I'd better go in. I'm tired. I'm going to give up this telephone job.

MORGAN. I wonder how much I could get for this car.

JEAN. You could try working –

MORGAN. Yes. Got to pay for this mental medication. Got to get the mind working. Supple.

JEAN. How's your mother?

MORGAN. She refuses to de-Stalinise.

JEAN *yawns and stretches her arms.*

JEAN. Oh, I love her. (*Cuddles to his shoulder.*)

MORGAN. I'm a bad son. Is it the chromosomes, or is it England?

JEAN. It's your wife.

MORGAN. It all started in the pram with me.

JEAN. What?

MORGAN. I used to lie there gurgling in the sun. Innocent. Laughing at the rabbits and bears on my blue blanket. My mother'd leave me outside the shops chewing a piece of coal or something else for the teeth. Somebody would park a pram with a girl in it next to mine. Then boarding stations. It's been boarding stations for me ever since.

JEAN. Leonie's been good to you.

MORGAN. Yes. I attract people who are good to me. It's my burden. I wish I was eighteen months again, cooing at the butterflies.

JEAN. You can't have me *and* Leonie, that's all. That's what I've decided. I'm monogamous. What are you going to do about it?

MORGAN. What I'd really like is to go to Africa and build hospitals for picaninnies.

JEAN. About Leonie and *me*.

MORGAN. Oh, yes –

JEAN. Yes what?

MORGAN. I mean, I think I can guarantee the Minister's full and careful attention to the problem.

JEAN. You infuriate me. I shall find somebody else – you see. I'm not going to hang about waiting for you to make your mind up.

MORGAN. Is it degrading?

JEAN. Is *what* degrading?

MORGAN. Hanging about waiting for me to –

JEAN *gets out of the car and bangs the door.*

JEAN. You owe me six pounds ten, by the way.

MORGAN. Impossible.

JEAN. Oh no it isn't. My landlady saw the rug. The one you shaved the hammer and sickle on. I've had to pay for it *and* she thinks I'm a communist now, as well as a tart.

MORGAN. You could have told her it was the Turkish national flag.

JEAN. Oh, Morgan, please leave Leonie. I'll have you back if we can be together properly. We can live on my money till you've finished your book.

MORGAN. I'm surprised at you – wanting to be the agent of another woman's unhappiness.

JEAN *bursts into tears. She rushes across the pavement and into the house.* MORGAN *stands up.*

MORGAN. You can't kill the idea –

12. Leonie's Flat.

MORGAN *comes out of the living-room where he has been fixing some wires on the radiogram. He opens the closet door and goes in.*

MORGAN (*singing*). Morgan is sad today, sadder than yesterday
. . .

> *He picks up a small attache case (a tape recorder) opens it and picks up microphone. He begins to recite into the microphone.*

MORGAN. They fought all that night neath the pale Tartar moon,
The din it was heard from afar.
And the bravest of all
Was that wily kelmuk –
Morgan, Skavinsky-Skavar.

> MORGAN'S *voice stops.*

> *A variety of loud jungle noises – screams, squawks and roars are emitted. These stop and are replaced by several bars of* PURCELL'S *Trumpet Voluntary.* MORGAN *scuttles into the living-room. Looks at gram and smiles.*

MORGAN. All shall be well and all manner of *thing* shall be well. Thing. Thing. Thing thing thing. (*Sings.*) Morgan is sad today. (*Speaks.*) Very sad. Sad man.

> *Goes to a large flat brown paper bag leaning in the chair. Takes from a bag a huge blow-up of a gorilla's face, and goes up into dining alcove, to Picasso, which he removes. Hangs the picture, setting it straight and stepping back to dig the effect. Collects carrier bag etc. Puts the Picasso into the bag. And goes quietly away.*

13. Leonie's Flat.

The room has been returned to its normal state. The radiogram is playing softly the M.J.Q. NAPIER *and* LEONIE *are at the table. They clink their champagne glasses.*

NAPIER. Cheers, darling.

LEONIE. Cheers.

> MORGAN *and stepladder appear outside the window.*
> NAPIER *and* LEONIE *lean back in their chairs. Dinner has
> been very satisfactory.* MORGAN *has his dark glasses on as
> usual.* NAPIER *and* LEONIE *are absorbed in each other and
> unaware of* MORGAN.

LEONIE. Fruit, darling.

> NAPIER *takes grapes – begins to peel one.* MORGAN *pushes
> back his dark glasses.*

CUT IN. *Film of gorilla eating grapes.*

> MORGAN'S *glasses drop over his eyes and he climbs down
> ladder.*

NAPIER. Do you know darling, I wouldn't have met you if it
hadn't been for Morgan.

LEONIE. Poor Morgan.

NAPIER. Don't waste your pity on him.

LEONIE. I don't pity him.

NAPIER. One of society's throwouts I'm afraid.

LEONIE. Can he write, Charles?

NAPIER. Oh yes. He can write. He's very talented. Never get
him published though.

LEONIE. But why? Why does everybody say the same thing?

NAPIER (*lighting his cigar*). The man's aberrated. Bonkers. No
sense of structure. I can't understand why you ever married
him –

LEONIE. I adored Morgan. In the beginning.

NAPIER. He's a parasite.

LEONIE. I learned a lot from Morgan. It's no use ignoring his –
his positive side.

NAPIER. I don't really want to talk about Morgan.

LEONIE. We've got to be good, Charles.

NAPIER. What do you mean?

LEONIE. The proctors.

NAPIER. Proctors?

LEONIE. My solicitor definitely said something about discretion, and proctors.

NAPIER. Really, we do live in an archaic society, don't we? In some respects. (*Puffs at cigar.*) You know, I feel rather guilty about old Morgan sometimes.

LEONIE. Why? You never even touched me, before he ran off with that nasty little thing with the stringy hair.

NAPIER. I was waiting to pounce though. I knew Morgan would go too far one day. So I simply waited.

LEONIE. It made it easier to send him packing. Morgan has no sense of values at all. (*Touches his hand.*) I feel secure for the first time in years now.

> *They look at each other.*
> MORGAN *in the hall is sitting listening at the keyhole. He sits up in a Buddha position and lights a joss stick.*

LEONIE. I wouldn't say Morgan is exactly immoral. No. He never meant to hurt me. There are some men who help women to mature, whilst remaining adolescents themselves. Morgan's one of those, poor darling.

NAPIER. Let's dance. (*He rises and goes to her. Escorts her down into the main room by the radiogram.*)

LEONIE. I'm sure the only dancing Morgan would have approved of is negro fertility rites –

NAPIER. I notice you still haven't had the lock changed.

LEONIE. No. I suppose it's terribly Freudian. You know, by leaving that picture of a gorilla on the wall I think Morgan was trying to tell me something.

NAPIER. A postcard would be more efficient.

LEONIE. He had an awful childhood you know. That blowsy old mother. And his father working in the sewers.

NAPIER. Is that what Morgan told you?

LEONIE. Yes . . . well didn't he?

NAPIER. He once told me his father worked in a gasworks.

LEONIE. He's an awful liar of course. (*Breaking away from him.*) Do you think I'm bourgeois, Charles?

NAPIER. Darling, of course not. (*They kiss.*)

In the hall MORGAN *is dancing with* LEONIE'S *coat.*

MORGAN. Do you think I'm bourgeois, coat?

In the living-room NAPIER *and* LEONIE *have sat down on the sofa.*

LEONIE. I think you'd better not go on being his agent.

NAPIER. It hardly matters. He'll never finish anything.

LEONIE. Oh it has been nerve-wracking these past few years. One gives and gives. I feel desiccated.

NAPIER. Poor Leonie . . .

LEONIE. You do love me, Charles – ? (*She turns to him.*)

We see MORGAN *at the keyhole. He gets up and goes to the closet.* NAPIER *is about to kiss* LEONIE. MORGAN *opens the tape recorder and turns the switch. As* NAPIER's *lips touch* LEONIE's *the record keeps turning but there is silence.* NAPIER *and* LEONIE *are frozen with surprise. We now hear an American rocket count-down.*

VOICE. Six, five, four, three, two, one, zero.

This is followed by a loud recording of a rocket launching. NAPIER *and* LEONIE *spring apart.*

LEONIE. Morgan!

NAPIER. Where?

They cross to gram and turn the record off then go out into hall. LEONIE *goes into dark bedroom and switches on light. Goes out to hall. And goes to closet door.*

LEONIE. He's in there . . . I know he is . . .

> *She opens door.* MORGAN *stands there holding his tape machine. He turns switch. He turns to the light.*

MORGAN. Ten years' searching for the substance of art – misled by abstraction, fooled by the lure of style. In fact, I ignored the concrete. Working it out, assuming twelve pounds ten per week for my keep, I have cost you three thousand and seventy-five pounds. A bad investment.

NAPIER (*moving in*). I think we've had about enough of this.

> LEONIE *cries.* MORGAN *turns switch. Star-Spangled Banner booms out.* LEONIE *rushes into bedroom and* NAPIER *follows.* MORGAN *switches off.*

MORGAN. I may be sad – but I'm loving. I constitute a case for life, growth . . . fond of flowers, animals and little children. I even help old policemen across the road. What more do you want?

14. Morgan's Dream.

Clip from old Tarzan film – JANE *is captured by the apes and Tarzan rescues her. Music.*

(1) Bassoon theme from Britten/Purcell
(2) USSR Anthem
(3) Bring in Vivaldi's 'Autumn'
(4) Fade Vivaldi
Mix from Vivaldi to USSR Anthem loud.

We now see a table and two chairs. Behind them is a big blowup of Stalin. MRS DELT *sits at the table sipping Russian tea and looking at a dossier on the table. She takes out and looks at a photograph of* MORGAN *prison-style with number BCD 801 along the bottom.* MRS DELT *takes a pen and starts to write in dossier.* JEAN *and* MORGAN *approach.* JEAN *has a carbine over her shoulder and* MORGAN'S *hands are tied. They come up to table and* MORGAN *goes to stand in front of it.*

MRS DELT. Hullo son.

MORGAN. Hullo Ma.

MRS DELT (*brandishing dossier*). Not what you'd call thirty-five glorious years!

MORGAN. No Ma.

She opens dossier.

MORGAN. Can I sit down?

She motions him to do so.

MRS DELT. How do you feel about it then?

MORGAN. Very sad.

MRS DELT. Is that all?

MORGAN. It's a brutal old world, Ma.

MRS DELT. You started off with every advantage! Born into a decent, working-class family. Good secondary modern education. Nice steady job in a canning factory. (*Pause.*) Then you went off the tracks. (*Pause.*) Suddenly. For no reason.

She scrabbles among the dossier pages.

MORGAN. I'm looking for a niche, Ma. (*Pause.*) I've got symptoms to feed.

MRS DELT. What symptoms?

MORGAN. Anxiety, vertigo, agoraphobia, dandruff, hallucinations, pains in the spinal column, violent impulses, despair, depression, passion –

Pause.

MRS DELT. You'll never get yourself put away at this rate.

MORGAN. It isn't that I *want* to get myself put away, Ma –

MRS DELT. What *do* you want then?

MORGAN. Or who –

MRS DELT. It comes to the same thing.

MORGAN (*to his* MOTHER). It's my distinct impression that you gave me a rough time in nineteen twenty-seven. Aren't you ashamed? (*Pause.*) A little, totty, helpless infant. (*Pause.*) Still, I suppose you were ignorant. You lacked a theory of the human personality. (*Pause.*) There I was. (*Pause.*) A small, roaring bundle of sensations in a world of flickering lights and shadows. (*Pause.*) What it is to inhabit a universe where there are no toes – only tootsy-wootsies. (*Pause.*) And faces hanging over the cot like imbecilic moons. (*Pause.*) It's an outrage.

MRS DELT. It's no use blaming me, Morgan.

MORGAN. I've already conceded your ignorance.

MRS DELT. That's not a very nice thing to say, either. (*Pause.*) You're ungrateful. Your father used to read Mayakovsky over your cot – there can't be many babies grew up with that sort of advantage.

MORGAN. You know what happened to Mayakovsky don't you?

MORGAN *closes his eyes.*

MORGAN. I have a distaste for the absolute. Ma. If I've let you down – blame that.

MRS DELT. You don't know what it is – a mother's anguish.

JEAN. You two are getting on my nerves.

MRS DELT. I wish I was dead. I wish it was all true about heaven and I would go to join your dad, Morgan. (*Pause.*) You was such a gay little boy. (*Pause.*) What have they done to you?

MORGAN. I don't know. Whatever it is, it's very insidious. (*Turns to* JEAN.) What have they done to me?

JEAN (*coming round to him*). It's time you took a hold of yourself.

MORGAN. I see. You want me to turn into a babbling extrovert –

JEAN. I want you to be a man.

MORGAN. Meaning?

JEAN. Stop messing about.

MORGAN. Meaning?

JEAN. Well you're just nothing the way you are.

MORGAN. This is very unjust. You're as bad as Leonie. Always inviting me to step into life – but for *me* it's like stepping off a precipice. (*Pause.*) And put a skirt on.

MRS DELT. Well I can't see us getting any further than this today. Take him away.

JEAN. Do you love me Morgan?

MORGAN. Yes.

JEAN. Then *do* something!

She cuts MORGAN'S *hands apart and escorts him out.*

15. Psychoanalyst's Consulting Room.

MORGAN *is lying on the Analyst's couch.*

ANALYST'S VOICE. Have you been asleep?

MORGAN. Have I?

ANALYST. You've had your eyes closed for a long time.

MORGAN. I had a dream about my Ma, and a girl I know. (*Pause.*) I bet you're tickled to bits to hear that!

    Pause.

ANALYST. Why do you say so?

MORGAN. Dunno.

    Long pause.

You're a very *dull* psychoanalyst.

ANALYST. Why am I dull?

MORGAN. I expect it's me that's dull.

    Pause.

ANALYST. Then why are *you* dull?

    Pause.

MORGAN. I could sing something?

Pause.

ANALYST. You're not singing, are you?

MORGAN. It's very boring here.

ANALYST. What would you like to do?

Pause.

MORGAN. Don't you want to hear about my dream?

ANALYST. Do you want to tell me?

Pause.

MORGAN. You know, you drive me up the wall.

Pause.

Well?

ANALYST. Well what? (MORGAN *sits up.*)

MORGAN. Did you hear about the woman and the analyst?

ANALYST. What about them?

MORGAN. She said: Doctor, doctor kiss me!

ANALYST. Yes?

MORGAN (*brightening*). And he said. Kiss you! I shouldn't even be here on the couch with you. Ha Ha. Huh?

Silence. No response from the ANALYST. MORGAN *looks very dejected. Long pause.*

You can't get *me*! (*Pause.*) I absolutely refuse to do things here instead of (*Pointing a finger at the wall.*) out there.

ANALYST. Have I asked you to do anything here?

Pause.

MORGAN. No.

ANALYST. Then.

MORGAN (*irritably.*) Then I'm skewered? Eh?

ANALYST. Skewered?

MORGAN. You're a terrible one for the old symbols, aren't you?

ANALYST. Do you think so?

MORGAN. All right, all right! *I* am then. (*Pause.*) It's all right for you sitting there. (*Pause.*) I've got to get up and go out amongst those Anglo-Saxons. (*Pause.*) Is it time?

ANALYST. Nearly.

MORGAN. I'm the one that's exposed to these English. Not you. You're healthy. Healthy mind in a healthy body. Eh? A good match for those types out there. I'm too sensitive for this vale of tears. And then there are the purely technical problems of bread and roof. Women. Marauding policemen. National Health Payments. (*Rises.*) Well, cheerio then. See you tomorrow. (ANALYST *gets up.*) Got cramp have you? Try banging your foot on the floor. You shouldn't sit with your legs crossed.

> MORGAN *goes out – door slams.*
> ANALYST *turns to look after him lighting a fag.*

16. Leonie's Flat. Night.

It is 2.00 a.m. LEONIE *and her mother are just coming in from the theatre. We hear voices:*

MOTHER. I enjoyed that thoroughy . . . so well acted.

LEONIE. I'm so glad you liked it. etc. etc. (*She opens the living-room door.* LEONIE *turns the light on as they enter. Shuts door.*)

MOTHER. It's so good of you to have me, darling. I'd have hated to go back to Maidstone without spending the whole evening with you and Charles.

LEONIE. Do you like him?

MOTHER. He's charming. (*Pause.*) The sort of man you should have married in the first place.

LEONIE. Oh, Mother!

MOTHER. I know you're still loyal to Morgan in some way I simply can't understand, but –

LEONIE. I don't want you to compare them, that's all. (*They cross towards the sofa and sit.*)

MOTHER (*sharply*). There *is* no comparison of course. Charles has breeding.

Pauses. Smiles.

He tells me he went to Winchester.

LEONIE. Yes.

Pause.

MOTHER. It's all been *most* harrowing, Leonie. (*Pause.*) Thank goodness there aren't any children. (*Pause.*) One shudders at the idea of Morgan having progeny.

Pause.

LEONIE. Morgan *loves* children.

MOTHER. He may love them. I'm not saying the man's a monster. What chills me is the thought that you might have perpetuated the Delt family. (*Pause. Speaks rather cruelly.*) I wonder why you didn't?

Pause.

LEONIE. We hoped he'd get somewhere with his writing first.

MOTHER. I always found him *quite* illiterate. He once told me the only person he'd read was Wyndham Lewis. (*Pause.*) Your Uncle Seaton knew Wyndham Lewis before the war and thought him a detestable person.

LEONIE. None of which has anything to do with whether or not Morgan can write.

MOTHER. You know, I've never been able to tell you this before, Leonie but the one and only time you both slept in my house, do you know what I found inked onto the bedspread the day you left?

LEONIE. A hammer and sickle.

MOTHER (*taken aback*). Oh, so you knew about it!

LEONIE. No.

MOTHER. Then how did you guess that he –

LEONIE. He's got a thing about hammers and sickles.

MOTHER. Well it's a very silly thing to have a thing about! I'm all for social mobility, or whatever they call it. But if some of these people can't accept one's standards! (*Pause. Goes to* LEONIE.) My poor darling, I do admire you for having taken him on, only please don't think about him any more.

LEONIE (*rising*). Would you like something to eat?

She crosses towards the door. MOTHER *follows her.*

MOTHER. I'd rather go straight to bed. I'm so sorry darling. I'm both garrulous and insensitive. I don't know what it is about Morgan . . . he does rather set one off, doesn't he?

LEONIE (*laughing*). Yes.

CUT TO:

Bedroom in darkness except for street light through window. MORGAN *is climbing in the window, a small square box in one hand. He plants his foot on a box which scrunches under him. His feet knock powder, bottles, etc. to the floor. He looks at his watch and sets a pointer on the bomb he is carrying. Then hears voices from the hall. He crawls under the bed.*

MOTHER. I think I'll take the early train down tomorrow, dear. I have people coming for lunch.

LEONIE. All right, Mother, etc. etc.

She opens the bedroom door. They enter and LEONIE *switches on light. Sees wreckage by dressing table.*

LEONIE. Oh, no! (*She crosses to it.*)

MOTHER. Oh.

LEONIE. Morgan!

MOTHER. I thought you'd had him stopped coming here.

LEONIE. I have. In theory.

She looks round the room. And at clock.

LEONIE. It's well after two. I think he's mad.

She goes out to the hall and opens closet door. Mother is picking up the wreckage. She has an idea and goes over to the bed and peers under it.

MOTHER. Morgan! Come out –

MORGAN *crawls out and stands up, leaving the bomb undetected.* MORGAN *stands facing* MOTHER *as* LEONIE *re-enters after her search.*

LEONIE. Oh Morgan –

MOTHER. Don't you think you are being rather tiresome?

MORGAN. Yes. (*To* LEONIE.) Where's Napier?

MOTHER. You surely didn't expect to find Charles here?

MORGAN. Why not?

He moves down L. MOTHER *following.*

MOTHER. Why not? Do you imagine that Charles and Leonie ?

MORGAN. Yes. That's what I imagine.

LEONIE *crosses and sits wearily on stool at dressing table.* MOTHER *moves in on* MORGAN.

MOTHER. It's a mistake to judge others by one's own standards of conduct, Morgan.

MORGAN *puts his face close to hers.*

MORGAN. You've got real insight! (*Turns away.*) I wish I were black.

He turns and goes to sit on bed.

MOTHER. I beg your pardon.

MORGAN. I'm tired of being white.

MOTHER. Spare us Morgan.

MORGAN. I'm all for negritude.

MOTHER. He's raving.

MORGAN. It's the usual ontological problem.

MOTHER. Will you go, Morgan? Or shall I ring the police?

MORGAN. Silly woman.

LEONIE. Morgan.

MORGAN. I can't help it. I didn't decide to say it. It just came out. I sometimes doubt whether I'm free at all. (*He stretches out on the bed.*) I'll bet your brains are seething. Both of you. Wondering how to get rid of me. I get lonely you know. I have to have a bit of company.

> MOTHER *has moved round the end of the bed. She is going towards the door.*

MOTHER. We were about to go to bed.

MORGAN. It's cold on Parliament Hill. And I get frightened. I need lights. Music. Women.

> MOTHER *looks scandalised.*

MORGAN. *Young* women.

LEONIE. What's happened to Jean then? Has she kicked you out as well?

> MORGAN *sits up.*

MORGAN. Shall we have a cup of cocoa? Get the dressing gowns on. Tell stories about giants, and little chaps in liripipe hats?

LEONIE. Can't you just leave me alone Morgan? Why do you come? You're making me hate you.

MORGAN. It's entirely your fault that you and I aren't tucked up nice and snug in this bed at this very minute. Man and wife.

MOTHER. I know you, Morgan. You're all bluff. And behind the bluff – a cringing, dependent lout.

MORGAN. First prize to the lady with the hammer nose and the sickle-shaped mouth.

> MOTHER *stares at him in outraged disbelief. She goes to telephone on bedside table and begins to dial.*

LEONIE. *No* mother!

MOTHER *hesitates – puts down receiver.*

MOTHER. No? Then you can deal with him yourself.

She goes out.

LEONIE. Were you ever happy with me? I don't think so. I think you wanted it to break up. But you hadn't the guts to do it yourself. I can understand men wanting other women besides their wives. What I can't understand is how a man can make a woman suffer then turn round and say that the actions which caused her to suffer aren't important to him.

MORGAN. Yes. It's abominable.

LEONIE *gets up and crosses to him.*

LEONIE. Is ordinary decency so contemptible?

MORGAN. Perhaps it's time we tried something else. Maybe we should let people steal from us, betray us, wreak havoc in general. Learn to yield, to lose, to dispense with judgment.

LEONIE. You make my head ache. You always did. When I first got to know you I thought you had a kind of dignity. Something I'd never seen before in a man.

MORGAN *looks remote. He closes his eyes.*

CUT IN. *Still of gorilla looking dignified.*

MORGAN *smiles a little.*

MORGAN. Dignity?

LEONIE (*quietly*). How do you manage to live now?

MORGAN. Same as before. The heart pumps, the legs jog along, the kidneys distil, the bowels churn.

LEONIE. Don't make fun of me. I mean are you all right?

MORGAN. Sound in wind and limb. (*Pause.*) Free meals off Ma at the Greek caff. Comfortable back seat in BCD 801. On the whole, tickety boo.

Pause.

LEONIE. I wonder what you'll be like when you're sixty.

Pause.

MORGAN. Pretty squalid, I should think. However, there's a quarter of a century to get things straightened out.

LEONIE. And there's always Jean.

MORGAN. Yes.

LEONIE. Do you love her?

MORGAN. Yes.

LEONIE. Yet you say you love me!

MORGAN. Yes. No one can say I lack the capacity, even if I'm equivocal about the focus. (*Pause.*) I also love a wide variety of fauna and flora, e.g. voles, gum trees, dolphins, dandelions, human babies, anthropoids, of all kinds. And certain types of building. Aztec temples, kraals, igloos, wigwams, bronze-age earthworks. (*Pause.*) But I can't stand the pyramids. (*Pause. Looks at wristwatch.*) I think that's just about all I had to say.

LEONIE. I'll never have you back. But I'm glad I had you.

MORGAN. I'm glad I was had.

Pause.

LEONIE. I have to have stability.

MORGAN. I know.

LEONIE. Would you like to give me a goodbye kiss?

MORGAN. Why? Am I going?

LEONIE. I've got to be up for work.

Pause.

MORGAN. There's just the matter of this anti-Napier device under the bed.

LEONIE. The what?

MORGAN. A sort of wee bomb. (*Door opens.*) More of a thunderflash really.

LEONIE'S *mother bursts into the room in her dressing gown, unable to contain her anger.*

MOTHER. Morgan, will you leave this house?

MORGAN (*to* LEONIE). It has a time fuse. Made it myself.

They take no notice of MOTHER.

MOTHER. If you both propose to ignore me, I shall call the police.

MORGAN *gets up, goes to* LEONIE'S *mother.*

MORGAN. Mrs Henderson, you are a grotesque bourgeois lady and the police will get you nowhere. I meant to tell you this several years ago, but I forgot. To invoke the forces of law and order is a very negative attitude. What are we to do then? Shut our eyes and bellow: Constable, arrest that man? Think how bitterness and rancour will shrivel his heart in the loneliness of a prison cell! (*Pause.*) No, madam! You must love the wretch. Fatten him up on compassion till his pelt ruptures in gratitude. (*Hisses amiably into her face.*) Or he'll blow you sky-high.

MOTHER (*to* LEONIE). Surely it's possible to have him certified.

LEONIE (*gently*). Come on Morgan. I'll come to the door with you.

LEONIE *crosses towards door.* MORGAN *wags his forefinger at* LEONIE'S *mother like a metronome.*

MORGAN. Tick tock, poor old Mom. You are standing on a bomb.

They go out, the door closing behind them. LEONIE'S *mother stares after them for a few seconds, stunned by* MORGAN.

MOTHER (*venomously*). Ridiculous!

She sits on the bed to wait for LEONIE. *Suddenly there is a flash, a bang, and the room is filled with black smoke.* MRS HENDERSON *shrieks – disappears, enveloped in sooty clouds.* LEONIE *comes into the hall and dashes to bedroom door, which opens. Her mother appears, grim, stark, black-faced*

and dishevelled, smoke billowing out round her. LEONIE'S
*face twitches, she is almost laughing. Puts up her hand to hide
her expression.*

LEONIE. Mother! Are you all right?

MRS HENDERSON *pauses.*

MOTHER (*acidly*). Are you amused?

17. Morgan's Dream.

CLOSE UP. *A still of* MORGAN'S *face with dark glasses. It begins
to spin faster and fatster. This turns to a glowing screen in a dark
room where* MORGAN *enters with his hands tied. We hear drums
and music – the USSR Anthem fades up and on the screen – a
Tarzan film.* MORGAN *watches, smiling. The film changes to the
execution scene from Eisenstein's 'Potemkin'. This changes to a still
of a bullet-scarred wall in Spain.* MORGAN *is frightened. Drums
beat and* MORGAN *turns as a firing squad approaches consisting of*
LEONIE, JEAN, MR *and* MRS HENDERSON, NAPIER *and*
MRS DELT. *We track along their faces. A* POLICEMAN *enters. He
ties a black handkerchief over* MORGAN'S *eyes. The drums fade.*

POLICEMAN. Got anything you want to say then?

MORGAN. Yes.

A long pause.

POLICEMAN. Either I've gone deaf, or you're not saying it.

MORGAN. It's all gone.

POLICEMAN. We'd better get on then.

MORGAN. Wait a minute. It's coming back. Yes. I've got it.

POLICEMAN. Come on then.

MORGAN (*clearing his throat*). Constant revolutionising of
production, uninterrupted disturbance of all social conditions, everlasting uncertainty and agitation, distinguish the
bourgeois epoch from all earlier ones. All that is solid melts

into the air. All that is holy is profaned, and man is at last
compelled to face with sober senses his real conditions of life
. . . and his relations with his kind.

    A long pause.

POLICEMAN. Is that all?

MORGAN. No.

POLICEMAN. It's a rare old mouthful, and quite enough I
should have thought.

    Pause.

MORGAN. Has it clouded over yet?

POLICEMAN. No. It's still a bright blue day.

MORGAN. I planted some sunflowers in a girl's garden.

POLICEMAN. Did you now!

MORGAN. Am I getting on your nerves?

POLICEMAN. I wouldn't say that.

MORGAN. I do get on people's nerves.

POLICEMAN. It's only human.

MORGAN. When I was twenty-three, I wanted to marry a
beautiful girl and live on a Greek island. (*Pause.*) Watch the
kids browning in the sun. Lie beside the honey-brown girl at
night with moths banging round the lamp. (*Pause.*) I was
very wistful, at twenty-three.

    Pause.

POLICEMAN. Have you finished?

MORGAN. I don't want to finish.

POLICEMAN. Nobody wants to finish. Always trying to put it
off. But the event *will* take place, young man.

MORGAN. Do you love life, constable?

POLICEMAN. I think I can say I do.

MORGAN. I'd sing . . . but my throat's dry. (*Pause.*) I like
singing.

POLICEMAN. We could allow a hymn, possibly. A little hymn.

MORGAN *shakes his head.*

MORGAN. It's very quiet. Are they still there?

POLICEMAN. They're waiting.

MORGAN. Have you ever heard cicadas?

POLICEMAN. Once. (*In a surprised tone.*) That was in a foxhole in southern Italy. A summer night. (*Pause.*) Would you like a cigarette, son?

MORGAN. Yes please.

> The POLICEMAN *puts a cigarette in* MORGAN'S *mouth and lights it.*

Have you ever put your cheek against your wife's nose when she's asleep. Felt her breath?

POLICEMAN. Never.

MORGAN. As warm and light as the darkness!

POLICEMAN. Maybe – when you're young!

> *Pause.*

MORGAN. Is the sun high?

POLICEMAN. Straight above.

MORGAN. I can feel it on the top of my head. (*Pause.*) I like the smell of hair that's hot with sun. The scalp moist. Tiny rivulets of sweat behind the ears. (*Pause.*) I get quite nostalgic over these concrete physical things. (*Pause.*) Men should throw shadows in history – not offstage, so to speak.

> *Pause.*

POLICEMAN. You do run on, Mr Delt!

MORGAN. Am I holding things up?

POLICEMAN. Well, they'll be wanting to get away for their dinners –

MORGAN. And I shall be rotting when they are digesting –

POLICEMAN. Now you mustn't get morbid –

MORGAN. Oh, no!

Pause.

POLICEMAN. Now then?

MORGAN. All right.

> POLICEMAN *takes cigarette. He walks across to firing squad and raises his hand. The firing squad comes to attention. He lifts his hand higher – they take up firing positions.*
>
> CUT IN. *Odessa steps sequence from 'Potemkin' as the squad fires at* MORGAN.
>
> CUT TO. MORGAN'S *bloodstained face. A series of stills of* MORGAN'S *face as a corpse. Mix to a coffin on trestles with three candles burning on it. Music: Vivaldi's 'Autumn'.* MR DELT – *an old working man in flat cap and muffler – enters. Slowly, he snuffs the candles. Superimpose still of* MORGAN *dead, and mix to:*

18. Jean's Room.

MORGAN *is in bed asleep, tossing and being restless. It is a bedsit., with screened kitchen in one corner, an armchair, dressing table, etc. A large stuffed gorilla stands in the centre of the room. It has a large notice pinned on it saying:–*
'Jean happy birthday, with love from MORGAN
Enclosed one Anthropoid.'
JEAN *comes in door – home from her night shift on the exchange. She tosses coat and bag on chair. Sees gorilla and goes over to him. She hugs him as she reads the note . . . then sees* MORGAN *asleep on the bed. She goes over to him. He turns restlessly. She kneels beside him. Touches his face softly.*

JEAN. Morgan. Poor Morgan.

> MORGAN *wakes confused.*

JEAN. You were crying, love. Why cry?

MORGAN. What time is it?

JEAN. Nearly six. I've just got back from work. Tears.

MORGAN. Is it sunny?

JEAN. I think it's autumn. The air's sharp. Nearly frosty. Would you like some coffee?

MORGAN. I dreamt I was executed by a firing squad. Then I was looking into a room where my own coffin stood on trestles. It had candles on, and my old man came with a snuffer and put them out.

> JEAN *looks at him – kisses his cheek. Stands and goes across to the kitchen corner and switches on kettle.*

JEAN. It's been a rotten summer. I hate London. I hate this rotten telephonist job.

> *Puts coffee in cups.*

MORGAN (*sitting up*). You don't reckon much to me, either.

JEAN. It isn't that. I want to think I'll arrive somewhere . . . at something. If you'd have me I'd be happy. I'd love everything. But you won't. I'm quite realistic, you know.

> JEAN *is busy pouring out the water and making coffee.*

JEAN. There's a man wants to marry me.

MORGAN. William?

JEAN. No.

MORGAN. Peter!

JEAN. No.

MORGAN. You must have a pretty seething sort of life when I'm not around.

JEAN. I don't think so. But in any case you're not around very often are you? (*She goes over to him.*) God knows what you do with your time.

> (*She sits on the bed.*)

MORGAN. You haven't said thanks for your birthday present.

> JEAN *looks at gorilla and smiles.*

JEAN. Thanks for my birthday present.

MORGAN. They're not easily come by you know, stuffed gorillas.

JEAN. I don't suppose they are.

MORGAN. Well – I thought you'd be hysterical with pleasure.

Pause.

JEAN. You're a fool, Morgan –

MORGAN. I know.

Pause.

JEAN. Other men I know, I can say they're like this or like that – but I can never say what you're like.

MORGAN. I wonder if I've got a brain tumour? (*Pause.*) I've had head X-rays and nobody saw anything. (*Pause.*) Imagine a little black tumour growing there – dislocating the whole set-up!

JEAN goes to the sink with her mug. Rinses it.

JEAN. I think I'm going to marry this man, Morgan.

MORGAN. I've always been a hypochondriac. (*Pause.*) You know those Victorian glass bells that they used to cover wax fruit with? I sometimes feel as if I've had one put down over me.

JEAN. Morgan, somebody wants me. Somebody wants to marry me. Hasn't it sunk in? And I think I nearly love him as well. I wouldn't if you'd behaved differently, but I nearly do. I want to know what you have to say about it –

MORGAN. It's extremely complicated.

JEAN. Come on.

She gets up and goes across to the fire which she lights and sits in front of it on the floor. MORGAN *sits on edge of bed. Then crosses to door and puts his trousers on.*

MORGAN. There just doesn't seem to be anything in this life that comes up to my best fantasies. (*Pause.*) Man is an inventive creature – ingenious, industrious, shaping the natural world. Then why the chasm? It beats me. (*Pause.*) Have you ever dreamt you were dead? (*Sits beside her.*)

JEAN. Millions of times.

MORGAN. Well I didn't like it! I do care, Jean.

JEAN. Convince me.

MORGAN. I'm entombed in love. (*Pause.*) I'm essentially outward-directed you know – but I think I'm a bit short in the reach.

> *Pause.*

JEAN. I think you're essentially a hole in space, when it comes to love!

MORGAN. That's because you interpret me incorrectly. People frequently do. (*Finds his sneakers and puts them on.*) Otherwise I'd be swinging –

JEAN. Where are you off to?

MORGAN (*coming over to the fire*). I've got a crowded day before me. Got a cig?

> JEAN *silently hands him a packet of cigarettes and a box of matches which have been lying on the corner of the fender.*

JEAN. If I could think of any way to keep you – I'd keep you.

> *Pause.*

MORGAN. What would you do with me?

> *Pause.*

JEAN. I don't know. (*She laughs suddenly.*) Hug you –

> MORGAN *rises.*

MORGAN. Autumn's gone. It's still summer. (*Pause.*) There are great shafts of sun – all down the street. (*Pause.*) When I was ten, I wanted to be a milkman. (*Pause.*) Wanted a striped apron and one of those crates. (*Pause.*) I used to think of occupations as if they were little cubicles . . . hundreds of them, waiting for me to choose one and step in. Shut the door. Walk out to the other side a butcher, pilot, doctor, actor, but I never imagined one that was a canning factory.

(*To window and opens it.*) Perhaps I was under the impression that fruit and vegetables grew in cans. On can trees. (*Pause.*) Yes. Life is a great struggle to defy categories. (*Pause.*) You've got to equip yourself my father used to say. But for what? Yes. Life became baffling as soon as it became comprehensible. (*Pause.*) A sort of invisible fog began to emanate from objects when I got to that stage. It stopped my ears, my eyes – it percolated. (JEAN *comes over. Pause.*) I complained of this to one of my tutors, and he assured me it was the ontological experience. (*Pause.*) People thought me very callow and engaging. I sat over my books at night with a corrugated brow – grappling with the enigmas of those things which are for themselves and those which are in themselves.

JEAN. I don't know why you can't simply make up your mind –

MORGAN. There has to be a period of mourning –

JEAN. Mourning *her*!

   MORGAN *goes back to the bed and sits.*

MORGAN. I have my ritualistic side. I deplore the modern tendency to accept things without making a fuss.

JEAN (*stalking away*). Oh, save it for your analyst or whatever he is! (*Leans on bed. Pause.*) You're incredible. It isn't therapy *you* need – it's lobotomy!

MORGAN. You shouldn't be flippant about these things –

JEAN. I know. I'm sorry. (*Pause.*) I wish you'd stayed in your flipping canning factory.

MORGAN. There are times when I have a twitch of nostalgia for it myself.

   MORGAN *goes over to the gorilla, grabs hold of it. Sings.*
     Lovely to look at –
     And lovely to hold –
     And heaven to kiss.
     Can there be –
   Stops suddenly. Peers into the gorilla's face. Makes a gorilla face at it.

MORGAN. I'll bet you had fun in life. Lolloping through the jungle. Eating bananas. Standing on dead animals' chests and yodelling away there –

JEAN. It's time something was decided one way or the other, Morgan.

Pause.

MORGAN. How do I know what I'm going to decide until I've done it?

JEAN. You didn't tell me Leonie has already divorced you.

MORGAN. It doesn't simplify matters at all. (*Pause.*) In fact it complicates them.

JEAN. How?

MORGAN. I regard that marriage as unfinished business. You can't liquidate a human being with a decree nisi. (*Pause.*) Perhaps I should insist on a re-trial. Do they have them? (*Pause.*) Then there's also the question of Charles Napier – physically loathsome, mentally retarded and I should think genetically unsound. He uses hair cream – what do you make of that?

JEAN. Your treatment of Leonie shrieked out for a divorce!

MORGAN. What? (*Crosses to bed.*)

JEAN. Oh, I know all about it. She rang me and told me I was a digit in an infinite series –

MORGAN. I wouldn't have thought Leonie could formulate such a wry metaphor!

JEAN. It's an expression I've heard you use any number of times. You're the *guilty party* Morgan.

MORGAN. Putatively – the country's boiling with matrimonial deceit. (*Pause.*) That's one thing I never did. I never actually *deceived* Leonie. Whereas Napier slid into our lives like a boa constrictor. You've never seen him with her – he undulates. Turned my back one day and he gulped her down like a rabbit.

JEAN. I wish I could have fallen in love with somebody who was integrated –

MORGAN (*dejectedly*). Perhaps I'm not fit for life at all –

JEAN *goes to the door. Opens it.*

JEAN. Twenty-four hours, Morgan. To get things sorted out once and for all.

MORGAN (*tapping his head*). It's very peculiar and lonely in here. I don't think I'm equipped. (*Rises*) I wonder why people are always showing me the door? Is there no place in the world for the Delt Syndrome?

He slinks past JEAN, *pauses in the doorway, turns round.*

JEAN. Oh, Morgan!

MORGAN. If I'd been planted in the womb of an orang-outang, none of this would ever have happened –

JEAN. Please –

MORGAN. Man lacks continuity with Nature –

JEAN. I'm closing the door now.

MORGAN. I'd be sitting in some cosy place all hairy, and primordial, and –

JEAN *firmly closes the door in his face.*

19. Psychoanalyst's Room.

The ANALYST *is sitting in his chair by the head of the divan, alone. He looks at his watch.* MORGAN *comes in. Closes the door. Stands defensively. Points at the divan.*

MORGAN. I'm fed up with coming in and lying there. (*Pause.*) I don't think I shall, today.

ANALYST. Why do you feel like that?

Pause. MORGAN *goes to the window.*

MORGAN. I like the dusk. (*Pause.*) There's a (*sniffs*) a smell of woodsmoke –

ANALYST. They're burning the leaves in the square –

> *Pause.*

MORGAN. I'm very tired. (*Pause.*) Do you think you and I'll be together for long?

ANALYST. How long do you visualise?

> *Pause.* MORGAN *rubs his hand across his face*

MORGAN. Oh, I don't know. (*Pause.*) I suddenly wondered if I'd see all the seasons through this window. (*Pause.*) Sun . . . wind . . . rain, fog . . . snow. (*Pause.*) I've decided to go and live with Jean.

> *Pause.*

ANALYST. Are you happy about it?

> *Pause.*

MORGAN. She's alive.

> *Pause.*

ANALYST. In what sense alive?

MORGAN (*gestures impatiently*). Ah, lay off it for today will you? (*Pause. Walks up to* ANALYST.) Don't think you'll get me to conform! Not to anything –

> *Pause.*

ANALYST. Perhaps you'll become sufficiently free to decide for yourself – whether you'll conform or not.

MORGAN. I think I'll go now.

> *But he stands waiting. The* ANALYST *stands, comes forward. They look at each other.*

Did you hear what the white rat said to the other white rat?

ANALYST. What?

MORGAN. I've got that psychologist so well trained that every time I ring this bell he brings me something to eat –

> ANALYST *smiles and* MORGAN *smiles back.*

MORGAN. Well, goodnight then.

ANALYST. Goodnight.

20. Jean's Room.

JEAN *in sweater and slacks is washing a jersey at the sink. Knock at the door. She goes over to answer it.* MORGAN *is standing there.*

MORGAN. Hullo.

JEAN. You've come then.

MORGAN *shrugs.*

JEAN. Are you going to be good?

MORGAN. I'm a very disassociated person, basically. I think it's that. Yes.

JEAN. Will you love me?

MORGAN. Yes. You know, when I was four I wanted to be a pirate. I wonder if I have regressive tendencies? Would that diagnosis be compatible with the facts?

JEAN. Oh, Morgan.

MORGAN (*sings*). Wanting you, all my life I've been wanting you . . .

JEAN. Come in then. (*She goes to sink.*)

MORGAN. Hullo room.

He closes the door.

As the door closes we see it from the hall. It is covered with a huge portrait of Lenin. The hall is crowded with MORGAN-*type possessions: – A duffel bag; typewriter; machine gun; vase of flowers; Mickey Mouse alarm clock, etc. Credits over film of Guy – the gorilla at London Zoo.*

The Governor's Lady

The Governor's Lady was first staged in London at the Aldwych Theatre on 4 February, 1965 in a programme of short plays entitled *Expeditions Two* with the following cast:

LADY HARRIET BOSCOE	*Patience Collier*
AMOLO, a native servant	*Chris Konyils*
CHARMIAN MAUDSLEY	*Elizabeth Spriggs*
SIR GILBERT BOSCOE	*Timothy West*
JOHN MAUDSLEY	*Morgan Sheppard*
POLICE SERGEANT	*Mark Jones*

Directed by David Jones
Designed by John Collins
Lighting by David Reed

The play is in one continuous act punctuated by blackouts or fades.

Exterior and Interior of a bungalow in Africa surrounded by jungle.

The main stage is a composite set with the sitting room right with a round tea-table and two upright chairs.

On the left of the stage is the bedroom area with a large double-bed covered with a white mosquito set.

On the left of the bed is a very high tall cupboard.

The forestage is a verandah area on which are two rush chairs and a drinks table.

On the right the jungle encroaches and from one of the tall trees hangs a swing.

Scene One

Afternoon before tea.
African music.

HARRIET *is seated at the tea-table. She is writing in her diary.*

HARRIET. May 15th . . . I cannot resist the temptation to anticipate Charmian's visit this afternoon, for the pleasure of writing my insights now and feeling them vindicated when she has gone.

> *Pause.*

Some women should not live in Africa, and Charmian is one of them. The heat withers her skin and the boredom withers her spirit . . . yet she still inspires in me that weary affection which passes for a bond between old women.

> *Pause.*

I wonder . . . I have no doubt she and John consider it eccentric of us to take this house on the plateau . . . what was it John said? Practically the jungle.

> *Pause.*

She will drive herself here in that ghastly what is it? Jeep?

> *Pause.*

And harass me with her inanities for two hours or more . . .

AMOLO. Mrs Maudsley, Madam –

HARRIET. Surely not! What time is it?

CHARMIAN. Harriet, darling . . . I know I'm too early –

HARRIET. Of course not. How nice to see you. Such a wretched drive out here in the middle of the afternoon. Let's have tea at once, shall we? Amolo – tea. And you're just the person to help me, Charmian.

CHARMIAN. Help you?

HARRIET. I can't find Gilbert's gun.

CHARMIAN. I can't think why you should want Gilbert's gun.

Are you going to attack somebody, or are you expecting to *be* attacked? Anyway, how should I know where it is?

Pause.

I came for tea, darling, since you invited me for tea.

HARRIET. You know you've always had a flair for finding Gilbert's things when he loses them –

CHARMIAN. That is true. But it is a flair of no practical value in the circumstances.

HARRIET. Circumstances?

CHARMIAN. Harriet, how could Gilbert lose *anything*, when Gilbert is dead?

Pause.

HARRIET. Did I ask Amolo to bring in the tea? I am a good shot, you know, Charmian. And I feel safer when I have the means to protect myself. There *was* a time when a white woman in this colony could dispense with such vulgarities. Now, however –

CHARMIAN. One doesn't say 'this colony' any longer, Harriet. Times have changed, my dear. Since they won their precious freedom you have to be careful what you say.

HARRIET. I have always thought . . . and I always shall think . . . that the natives are children. I know I am an old-fashioned woman, a stubborn old woman –

CHARMIAN. But you want to die in full possession of all your prejudices?

HARRIET. What's that, Charmian?

CHARMIAN. I said –

HARRIET. But I fail to see why they should wish to exchange their simplicity and innocence for *our* vices and machines.

Pause.

Leave the trolley, Amolo . . . I shall not need you.

AMOLO. Yes, Madam.

HARRIET. I agree with Gilbert. Independence at this stage would mean anarchy.

Pause.

Lemon?

CHARMIAN. Please.

Pause.

Dear Harriet!

HARRIET. Why Charmian . . . you are almost in tears!

CHARMIAN. Listen darling. You're quite sure you know when and where you are?

HARRIET. But why on earth shouldn't I?

CHARMIAN. Harriet, it is one year since this colony became independent. And six months since Gilbert died. Harriet, you are not the Governor's wife . . . You are the ex-Governor's widow.

Pause.

I've . . . I can't go on pretending I don't notice that your mind is . . . wandering. There, I've said it. I've tried and tried to think of a kinder way of putting it. But there isn't one. Harriet, John and I think . . . we think you should consider going home. Have you seen a doctor?

HARRIET. My dear Charmian, I *am* at home. And I am perfectly well, thank you.

Pause.

I think the drive must have tired you out.

Pause.

And yet, it is so lovely up here. It has its compensations. Gilbert says that it is always five degrees cooler up here than anywhere else in the colony.

Pause.

CHARMIAN. I meant – London, Harriet.

HARRIET. You don't know what you are saying, my dear. Leave Karalinga now?

Pause.

You know, Charmian, Gilbert feels – and I couldn't agree with him more – that it is precisely now when they need us most. When they have to choose between *us* and those awful little demagogues of theirs with a degree from Manchester or wherever it is.

CHARMIAN. You can quote Gilbert till you're blue in the face, darling, but it won't do me a bit of good. And it makes *them* fractious.

Pause.

Peter says they've got us by the short and curlies –

HARRIET. By the *what*?

CHARMIAN. It does sound ghastly, doesn't it. Children are so mature nowadays. John says when he was Peter's age he spent all his time reading Shelley and worrying about self-abuse. Thank God we only have one grandchild. I'd be prostrate by now if Tim and Mary had any more like Peter.

HARRIET. Short and curly indeed! A boy of sixteen –

CHARMIAN. Curlies, Harriet.

HARRIET. Well, I ask you!

CHARMIAN. It has a certain crude vigour, as dormitory language goes –

HARRIET. My dear Charmian, a boy who can be as facetious as that at sixteen can be a socialist at twenty-one!

CHARMIAN. I don't *quite* see the connection –

HARRIET. From the moment they came to power in 1945 Gilbert noticed the prevailing tone in their dealings with him was one of disrespect . . . a, a want of feeling and discretion.

CHARMIAN. Well, darling, you remember what the Permanent Under Secretary said at the time –

HARRIET. I don't believe I do.

CHARMIAN. Uneasy lies the Red that wears a crown!

Laughs.

No, Harriet, it won't do. Gilbert failed to adapt, and people who fail to adapt – especially in colonial matters – are, as I have no doubt Peter would say, sitting ducks.

HARRIET. I shall never understand you, Charmian. You talk as though it is all over and done with.

CHARMIAN. But isn't it?

Pause.

HARRIET. So long as Gilbert is Governor of Karalinga, it is the *colony* that must learn to adapt.

CHARMIAN. Harriet –

HARRIET. Will you have some more tea?

CHARMIAN. Harriet –

HARRIET (*petulantly*). Now what is it?

CHARMIAN. Gilbert is dead.

HARRIET. Then I have nothing more to say on the subject. We all have our, our idiosyncracies, Charmian. You must cling to yours, and I must cling to mine.

CHARMIAN. I would hardly call it an idiosyncracy, to ignore the fact that Gilbert caught pneumonia, and died, and has been buried nearly six months.

Pause.

HARRIET *I* was speaking of the subtleties of colonial adminis-tration, Charmian.

Pause.

CHARMIAN. Look, darling, why not let John and me come and help you pack? Have everything sent off by sea, and book you an air passage to London?

Pause.

This house is too lonely, Harriet. Anything could happen to you out here, and none of us would know.

Pause.

Living out here with two or three native servants . . . not even a telephone . . . must you, Harriet? At least, come and stay with us for a while –

HARRIET (*sharply*). Do *not* insist on treating me as if I were mentally infirm, Charmian.

Pause.

Amolo can reach the town on his bicycle in forty minutes. Should I need you in any way during Gilbert's absence, I am grateful to think you would come if I sent for you.

Pause.

CHARMIAN. Well, if you will insist on being indomitable –

Pause.

HARRIET. Not indomitable, Charmian. Independent.

CHARMIAN (*jungle noises start*). Well, it's nice to know you're not entirely without faith in independence!

Pause.

I think I'd better be going. Come out and see what I did to the jeep thing on the way up here –

Both go off. Blackout.

Scene Two

Morning: breakfast.
Fade-in Mozart Piano Concerto.

AMOLO *is serving breakfast.* HARRIET *enters.*

HARRIET. Good morning, Amolo. No, leave it . . . I'll see to it myself. You can go now.

AMOLO. Yes, Madam.

HARRIET. Amolo –

AMOLO. Yes, Madam?

HARRIET. Where is that music coming from?

AMOLO. My nephew, Madam. He is visiting. Has gramophone.

HARRIET. I see. Your nephew is fond of Mozart?

AMOLO. Fond of all music, Madam.

With pride.

He is a student.

HARRIET. A music student?

AMOLO. Go for engineer, Madam.

HARRIET. Ah! At Manchester College I suppose –

AMOLO. No, madam.

Pause.

Moscow.

Pause.

HARRIET. That will be all, Amolo.

AMOLO. Yes, Madam.

HARRIET (*peevishly*). And ask him to turn the gramophone down, will you?

AMOLO. Yes, Madam.

AMOLO *goes out. The music stops.*

HARRIET. Absurd. Poor Charmian.

Pours tea.

She does not understand that they are . . . how can one put it? Biologically remote from us. Charmian will ramble. She rambles and rambles which always infuriated Gilbert. I remember once during a lull at a Memorial Service in Westminster, she brayed out 'when are you going to get that paunch of yours knighted, Gilbert?' So cruel! So unjust!

She slices at an egg.

The way a person slices an egg can be most revealing. There. Poor little embryo. I wonder if I –

Jungle noises as GILBERT *enters. He is in full Governor's regalia.*

GILBERT. Morning, Harriet.

HARRIET. Why, Gilbert! What time did you get back last night? I didn't hear you.

GILBERT. Small hours. No reason to wake you. Slept in the dressing room.

HARRIET. Will you have an egg?

GILBERT. I think, a banana.

HARRIET. A fresh egg –

GILBERT (*picks up an egg*). Frankly, I've always considered eggs to be messy things.

Smashes it on the table.

All that sog inside. No more eggs.

HARRIET. Did you have a good trip?

GILBERT. Arrived in Bonda just after a ritual murder. And in Kadun too early for the trials. All this rushing round from one province to another, ridiculous. A Governor, should be . . . remote. Pass the bananas, will you, Harriet?

HARRIET *passes the bananas. Noisy eating punctuated by snorts and grunts.*

HARRIET. You must be very hungry, Gilbert.

GILBERT (*a growling belch*).

HARRIET. Really! Let me give you some tea.

She pours the tea.

GILBERT (*slurping*). They've actually asked me to let them have a report on the colony's fitness for self-government. Thoughtful of them, isn't it? Especially when they'll go straight ahead with it whatever I say.

Pause.

HARRIET. Charmian was here yesterday. For tea,

GILBERT *knocks a cup off the table clumsily – it breaks.*

Gilbert! What an extraordinary thing to do. That was one of my mother's breakfast cups. Gilbert, you deliberately broke it. Amolo!

GILBERT. Very odd, that. Had a sort of . . . impulse.

HARRIET. And a very cruel one, if I may say so.

GILBERT. Now, Harriet –

HARRIET. My mother bought those cups in –

GILBERT. Oh, damn your mother's cups.

HARRIET. Gilbert!

GILBERT. You loathe those cups. You've said so before.

HARRIET. Civilisation, Gilbert, is the art of tolerating what we loathe.

GILBERT. Prissy old devil.

HARRIET. I think I shall go to my room and write some letters. You must have been out in the sun. We shall say no more about it.

GILBERT *knocks off another cup.*

GILBERT. Oh, God! Now, that *was* an accident –

HARRIET. Was it, Gilbert?

Pause.

Where *is* Amolo?

Pause.

It has suddenly gone very quiet –

GILBERT. I've never liked that boy. Imagine . . . imagine Amolo voting. Can you? Ridiculous.

HARRIET *is uneasy.*

HARRIET. It's so quiet, Gilbert.

GILBERT. Subhuman. Subhuman, the lot of them. Can't help it, but no use ignoring. It's a matter of evolution, Harriet. Brainpan's too small.

Pause.

Ever seen one?

HARRIET *goes to the door.*

HARRIET. I believe . . . I believe there's no one there, Gilbert.

GILBERT. Now, what's the weight of the average human brain? In ounces. A *white* human brain.

HARRIET. Is there such a thing as a *black* human brain?

GILBERT. Ho-ho, you old liberal, you!

HARRIET *comes back to him.*

HARRIET. Gilbert, do not be jocose. I am trying to tell you that the servants, the servants have all disappeared.

GILBERT. Damn good riddance.

HARRIET. I don't know what it is, but I have the distinct impression that you are not yourself today. And what are we going to do for servants?

GILBERT. Get some more, Harriet. Get some more.

HARRIET. If it were not nine o'clock in the morning, I should say you had been drinking.

GILBERT. How like a woman!

HARRIET. We are too old for scenes, Gilbert.

GILBERT. Too old for too many things, if one listened to you!

HARRIET. I hope you are not going to raise *that* subject again.

GILBERT. What subject?

HARRIET. That subject.

GILBERT. You know, I sometimes wonder if you aren't getting just a bit senile Harriet.

HARRIET. I shall go to my room. I will not listen to this.

GILBERT. And the servants?

HARRIET. I have managed your domestic affairs efficiently for forty years, Gilbert . . . I am not a spiteful woman, but what would you like me to do? Chase into the bush after them?

GILBERT. Don't think of it, Harriet. Don't think of it.

> *Pause.*

The proper setting for a colonial administrator's wife is, of course, a garden. Where everything is pruned . .. and sprayed . . . kept under control.

> *Pause.*

So stick to the garden, won't you? Stick to the garden, there's a good woman.

HARRIET. Your mind is wandering, Gilbert. You ought to see a doctor.

> *Pause.*

Do stop scratching! It's hardly . . . Take a bath or whatever you like, but do not scratch, Gilbert!

GILBERT. It's that damned headman in Bonda. The feller's crawling. Now you run along and write your letters, m'dear.

HARRIET. Perhaps by lunchtime you will be more yourself.

GILBERT. I hope so, Harriet. If that will please you. I hope so.

> *Fadeout.*

Scene Three

Evening.
Fade-in Nocturnal jungle sounds.
HARRIET *at the table writing.*

HARRIET. May 16th. The situation is maddening. The servants ran away this morning, for some inexplicable reason, and nothing will induce Gilbert to take the matter seriously.

> *Pause.*

An extraordinary change has come over my husband. He seems . . . coarsened. Almost brutal, at times. It is perhaps one of the inevitable trials of old age that human dignity should prove so vulnerable to the malfunctionings of the body and mind.

Pause.

Gilbert is waging a struggle with himself in which I can take no part, except insofar as I can, and must, share his humiliations.

Pause.

How one longs for white servants at moments like these; and despite one's love for Africa, there is always that sense of emergence from the primordial . . . that nostalgia for reason and order, which these poor people cannot achieve – no, not in a hundred years.

Pause. Creaking. Silence. Creaking. Silence. Creaking. Silence.

Gilbert . . .

Louder.

Gilbert – Gilbert, where are you?

Sound as of some kind of ring being thrown on to a post.

GILBERT *on the wardrobe.*

GILBERT. Now where the devil would you *expect* me to be?

Pause.

HARRIET. *Not* on top of the wardrobe! And *not* rifling my jewel case!

Pause.

What are my necklaces doing on this bedpost, might I ask?

Creak. GILBERT *is throwing necklaces on to the bedpost.*

Gilbert, come down here at once! Give me my jewel case. Come along. Give it to me.

Creak. Rattle.

GILBERT (*irritated*). Nearly missed that time! Go away, Harriet. Go away and write your blessed diary.

HARRIET. Not until you come down off that wardrobe and . . .

Crying.

Oh, Gilbert!

GILBERT. Harriet, you are trivialising our relationship –

HARRIET. Won't you come down? Just for me?

GILBERT. I can't imagine why you should think *you* are any sort of temptation!

HARRIET. Come down, my dear –

GILBERT. Ha! *My dear* now, are we?

HARRIET. Oh, this is futile.

GILBERT. You're not the woman I married, Harriet.

HARRIET. I am not indeed! I should like to think that nearly half a century had brought a little wisdom. Common sense, at least.

GILBERT. Who the devil wants wisdom in a woman? What about your woman's instincts, eh? What about them?

HARRIET. I have noticed before, that when you begin to talk like a character out of a Russian novel, it is best to leave you to your own devices.

GILBERT. A Russian novel? Me? I've never read one of those damned things in me life! All those vitches and ovnas . . . ukins and inskys.

HARRIET. It is your loss.

GILBERT. But, you wouldn't say I'm an *uncultured* man, would you, Harriet?

HARRIET. Until recently – no.

GILBERT. Now, they can say what they like but these people . . . these wretched natives . . . they're *all* instinct. Primitive.

Pause.

I can admire instinct in a white woman of gentle birth. We have, we have centuries of slow, painful refinement behind us. But oh, my God, the unadulterated thing! The *thing* itself! Chaos! Absolute chaos!

Pause.

If they knew what I really think about this situation . . . why, they'd have me out. Have me out, Harriet.

HARRIET. Gilbert . . . I do believe . . .

GILBERT. What's that? What?

HARRIET. Gilbert, are you –

GILBERT. Am I *what*?

HARRIET. A trick of the light.

GILBERT. Trick?

HARRIET. I had the distinct impression you were . . . salivating.

GILBERT. Salivating? What the devil do you think I am? *Animals* salivate, Harriet. Human beings spit. There's a world of difference.

HARRIET. Well, are you?

GILBERT. Or drool, I suppose.

HARRIET. There has never been the slightest confusion in *my* mind. A person who drools is not a person.

Pause.

Which are *you* doing, Gilbert?

Pause.

GILBERT. I'm spitting, Harriet. I'm spitting. I spit when I get carried away.

HARRIET. Then be good enough to regain control of yourself.

GILBERT. You know, there's something bloody odd about you this evening.

HARRIET. I have never known you lose control of yourself in forty years of Government service.

GILBERT. There's a difference between losing control and getting carried away.

Pause.

In any case, the point is an academic one since I am not prone to either, when publicly fulfilling my obligations as a servant of Her Majesty's Government.

Pause.

HARRIET. What *resonance* there was in that phrase . . . once.

GILBERT. Oh, the *resonance* has gone, right enough!

HARRIET. When there was order in the world –

GILBERT. Law and order. Nowadays it's all, wha'do they call it? Pragmatism. Oh, there are people who regard me as a sort of living fossil! I know. I'm an enemy of pragmatism, you see. And it doesn't do these days, Harriet. It doesn't do.

HARRIET. It is satisfying to think that our kind have always acted . . . disinterestedly. That the instincts have been . . . sublimated.

GILBERT. You always were a clever woman, Harriet.

HARRIET. Do come down, my dear –

GILBERT. What about a night cap?

HARRIET. On the balcony? As we . . . used to?

GILBERT. Right. I'm coming down then.

HARRIET. It's a lovely night –

Pause.

Let me help you down, my dear!

Chattering of monkeys. GILBERT *pours drinks.*

GILBERT. It's a long time since we did this.

Pause.

Life's too long, really. Ought to be cut off in the prime.

He goes down to the verandah in front.

HARRIET. I am not sure that a woman knows what . . . or when . . . her prime is.

GILBERT. Different for a woman.

HARRIET. That was how my father explained away a great deal in his declining years. Everything was . . . different for a woman. But he never mentioned his prime.

GILBERT. Great diplomat, your father.

Pause.

The middle classes can run the Empire, he used to say, but it takes an aristocrat to run the middle classes.

Pause.

Wouldn't recognize things as they are today.

HARRIET. I remember . . . at a week-end house-party once, he encountered that Lawrence person –

GILBERT. T. E.?

HARRIET. David Herbert –

GILBERT. Ugh!

HARRIET. We were strolling in the garden before dinner. Someone was talking about the Weimar Republic. Lawrence was being most tiresome, and my father said to him: Mister Lawrence, you stick to your solar plexus and leave Germany to the politicians –

GILBERT. Oh, splendid!

Pause.

HARRIET. Lawrence was a venomous little man, you know. He despised people like my father. He despised what we all stood for. But he lacked wit –

GILBERT. Worlds apart –

HARRIET. His reply must have been unexceptional, because I can't remember what it was.

GILBERT. Your father was in his prime then.

Chattering of monkeys outside.

HARRIET. He was not a bigoted man.

Pause.

GILBERT. These young men *now* . . . They talk about the first war marking the end of an epoch . . . They've no real idea what there, what there *was*.

Pause.

HARRIET. And yet . . . I sometimes think, Europe was besotted with sex after 1919.

GILBERT. Europe was in its prime, just before the First World War.

HARRIET. Well, we enjoyed some of the last of it, Gilbert –

Pause.

GILBERT. That's a pretty bowl –

HARRIET. Really! We have had that bowl for over twenty years.

GILBERT. Oh, it's pretty all right!

HARRIET. You gave it to me yourself.

GILBERT. Did I now? Did I?

HARRIET. You have always had exquisite taste, Gilbert.

GILBERT. Curious . . . don't remember it.

HARRIET. We have so many fine things.

Pause.

I sometimes . . . even after all these years I still think how it would have been to have had children. Someone to pass these things on to. The sense of . . . continuity. It becomes more important as one grows older.

Pause.

I don't like to think it might be . . . as if we had never existed.

GILBERT. Getting morbid, Harriet.

HARRIET. And these things will pass into the world after we are gone, and they will be . . . anonymous.

GILBERT. Morbid!

HARRIET. Oh, our lives have been rich, and full. I am grateful for that.

Pause.

GILBERT. Well, who mentioned not having children? Did I?

Did I say anything about it? No. You raised the subject.

Pause.

There's something . . . obscene about an old woman maundering over her sterility.

HARRIET. The question of whose incapacity was involved was never settled.

GILBERT. And why not? What in God's name is science *for*, then?

HARRIET. I have often put the same question to myself. Science illuminates, but it fails to explain. I believe that was the gist of *your* refusal to undergo a medical examination.

GILBERT. All this beating about the bush –

HARRIET. Gilbert, since you came home yesterday, I have had a strangely . . . cut off feeling. Almost . . . almost the sensation that you wish to do me harm, Gilbert. Or to put it another way, that you wish harm might come to me.

   Pause.

Everything was perfectly normal when you went away –

GILBERT. Everything is perfectly normal now, Harriet. Perfectly normal.

HARRIET. But, we don't appear to have quite the relationship that we had before.

   Pause.

The relationship that we have enjoyed since we were young people.

GILBERT. You mustn't allow yourself to feel guilty, Harriet. One has to adjust, as one gets older.

HARRIET. Guilty?

GILBERT. A more passionate woman might have . . . so to speak, disturbed the balance.

   Pause.

HARRIET. You are spitting again, Gilbert. Wipe your chin.

GILBERT. I'm going to shave this damned beard off. It gets . . . matted.

HARRIET. It is very distinguished.

>*Pause.*

You didn't tell me that you intended to grow one whilst you were away.

>*Pause.*

An imperial suits you.

GILBERT. It compensates somewhat for the waning authority of the Crown, don't you think? If Queen Victoria had had a beard the Empire would have lasted for a thousand years!

>*Pause.*

Still, they do . . . tend . . . to get . . . matted.

HARRIET. Never mind. It will photograph so much better than a . . . what does one say? A *naked* face? A bare face?

GILBERT. Nude face?

HARRIET. Most certainly not.

GILBERT. There, that's the last of the whisky.

HARRIET. Surely not? There was . . . surely, half a bottle?

GILBERT. Then Amolo must have been at it.

HARRIET. *Not* the sort of behaviour that goes with political maturity!

GILBERT. Ought to get back up the trees, where they belong.

HARRIET. Oh!

GILBERT. Now you're shocked.

HARRIET. I *am* shocked.

GILBERT. I can just tolerate the hypothesis that Amolo and I have a common ancestor in the lemur. Where I diverge from enlightened opinion is in the crass assertion that Amolo and I are the same beneath the skin. My remark was an attempt to be graphic about the divergence.

HARRIET. Nonetheless, it was the sort of remark one hears from gutter racialists –

GILBERT. Admirably put, Hariet, but you know me better than that.

HARRIET. I know you are not a racialist, Gilbert.

Pause.

That I could *not* bear.

GILBERT. But you women . . . *you* know there's . . . something different about them. Now don't you? Something . . . attractive.

Pause.

HARRIET. Attractive?

GILBERT. What do you mean, 'attractive'?

HARRIET. You said: something attractive.

GILBERT. I said repellent, Harriet.

HARRIET. I heard you distinctly. You said: attractive.

GILBERT. And equally distinctly, I heard myself say repellent.

HARRIET. That must be what you intended to say.

GILBERT. Dammit, *I* know what I said!

HARRIET. Then we cannot profitably discuss the matter any further.

GILBERT. I *intended* to say attractive, and I *said* attractive.

Pause.

HARRIET. There you go again!

Pause.

GILBERT. You know, Harriet, it's just possible . . . it's just possible that *you* find them attractive!

HARRIET. I find them repellent.

GILBERT. Ah!

HARRIET. You needn't sound so pleased about it.

GILBERT (*shouting*). I am *not* pleased.

HARRIET. Oh? Aren't you?

GILBERT. I mean . . . I don't know where the devil all this is leading –

HARRIET. In my case – to bed. In your case, Gilbert, perhaps . . . up on the wardrobe, where you belong?

Monkeys. Fadeout.

Scene Four

Fade-in HARRIET.

HARRIET. March 18th. I must force myself to put it down in writing: Gilbert is going insane. The evidence is overwhelming. He is gratuitously violent – so far, thank heaven, directed elsewhere, than at my own person. He has wilfully broken every bowl and vase in the house, and most of the cups. He appears to be losing control of his bodily functions and has also evolved the distressing habit of vomiting forth his bananas, then eating his vomit! In my last entry I spoke of sharing his humiliations! I see now that I was trying to conceal the truth from myself, for Gilbert and I are beyond sharing . . . He has gone where I cannot reach him, and is so far in this that I cannot, I dare not hope for his return.

Pause.

Yet, such is the resilience of human nature that I have already taken certain practical steps.

Pause.

My poor Gilbert! I have unearthed the picnic basket which Charmian gave us last year, and I propose from now on to serve him his meals on plastic plates and his tea and coffee in a plastic beaker.

Pause.

I found a set of clean dungarees in Amolo's room which, after

some persuasion and cajoling, Gilbert consented to wear . . .
until I can have his ruined suits cleaned and pressed. When I
look at Gilbert, my whole instinct is to weep and weep.

> *Pause.*

This must be conquered like any other.

> *Fadeout* HARRIET. *A long drawn out yell. Fade-up into
> Bedroom area.* GILBERT, *in semi-darkness – a great hulking
> figure in dungarees. He is strangling* AMOLO. *The body thuds
> on to the stage.* GILBERT *scuttles off.* HARRIET *enters,
> frightened. Enter* GILBERT *humming 'The Teddy Bears'
> Picnic'. He now has gorilla hands.*

GILBERT. What's this?

HARRIET. Amolo . . . I think . . . I think his neck is broken.

GILBERT. Good God!

> *Pause.*

Dead as mutton.

HARRIET. His *neck* is broken.

GILBERT. Came sneaking back for the rest of the whisky, I
suppose.

HARRIET. And broke his own neck?

GILBERT. One of the others did –

HARRIET. But why? Why?

GILBERT. This damned colony's seething. *Seething.* Tribal
feuds . . . politics . . . communist agitators –

HARRIET. Not *Amolo* –

GILBERT. I shall declare a state of emergency throughout the
province.

HARRIET. But –

GILBERT. Arrest the ringleaders . . . declare a curfew . . . soon
put a stop to all *this*.

HARRIET. But Amolo –

GILBERT. What's that?

HARRIET. Wasn't mixed up in anything like that, Gilbert.

GILBERT. My dear Harriet, they are *all* mixed up in things like that.

HARRIET. What are we going to do . . . with Amolo's . . . body?

GILBERT. Have to be buried immediately, of course. Be stinking within twelve hours, poor fellow.

Pause.

HARRIET. Do *you* intend to bury him, Gilbert?

GILBERT. *I?*

HARRIET. There is no one else –

GILBERT. I think I'll have a little swing, and think about it.

HARRIET. A swing?

GILBERT. You know what a *swing* is, Harriet! A wooden seat suspended by two ropes from a –

HARRIET. Yes . . . I know what a swing is.

GILBERT. Then what are you looking so vacant about?

HARRIET. Nothing . . . nothing.

GILBERT. Nothing in that tone of voice means *something*.

Pause.

This is not the time to be perversely feminine!

HARRIET. I think we had better go out into the garden. Amolo's body –

GILBERT. I've never thought of you as a *squeamish* woman, Harriet! The garden –

She goes out fast to the garden and swings. GILBERT *follows and sits on the swing.* GILBERT *on the swing, pushed by* HARRIET.

GILBERT. Come on, Harriet, push me. Harder, Harriet! Push harder –

HARRIET. This is ridiculous –

GILBERT. Push, Harriet –

HARRIET. I am exhausted.

GILBERT. Feeble old woman!

HARRIET. I can bear no more.

GILBERT. Why, Harriet! Come now, I'll *stop* swinging – if you like.

HARRIET. Yes – do. For goodness sake stop.

GILBERT. Didn't *you* ever like to swing?

HARRIET. Oh, yes! I liked to swing. Nearly sixty years ago!

GILBERT. In the privacy of one's own garden, Harriet . . . there are no limits.

Pause.

HARRIET. I think it is time you pulled yourself together and faced reality, Gilbert. The situation is intolerable. First the servants run away, then Amolo is killed – and you do nothing. Nothing.

Pause.

For all we know, we are completely cut off. And once the killing begins –

GILBERT. They can tear themselves to pieces for all I care.

HARRIET. And what if they should tear *us* to pieces?

GILBERT. They wouldn't dare to lay a finger on us.

HARRIET. Revenge takes no account of the consequences.

GILBERT. Revenge? Good God, woman, what have we done to them except bring them a . . . a civilisation? Schools, roads, hospitals, technicians . . . government, Harriet.

Pause.

If they remain savages, as they very obviously do – despite their gramophones and briefcases – then it is not a question of revenge, but of blind, gratuitous violence. And I know how to deal with that!

HARRIET. *Do* you, Gilbert?

GILBERT. Haven't I dealt with it before?

HARRIET. You have certainly shown that you know how to *eliminate* it.

Pause.

Whether you have *dealt* with it, except in a very limited sense of the word . . . I don't know.

(*Pause. Distant sound of drums.*)

Listen –

Pause.

GILBERT. Listen to what? Can't hear a thing.

HARRIET. Surely . . . drums?

GILBERT. Nonsense.

HARRIET. I can hear drums –

Drumming stepped up slightly.

GILBERT. Blood pressure, more likely!

HARRIET. If I were the sort of person who hears things, Gilbert, I would know it!

GILBERT. Drums!

HARRIET. You *must* hear them.

GILBERT. But . . . I don't.

Pause. Drumming.

HARRIET. I am going into the house –

GILBERT. Well, then you'd better be the one to bury Amolo . . . because I'm going for a walk.

HARRIET. I? Dig a *grave*? Bury *Amolo*?

Pause.

How *can* you!

GILBERT. Harriet, you know perfectly well that I can't touch dead things. It's one of my, one of my . . . phobias.

Pause.

On the other hand, you could simply let him rot –

HARRIET. Gilbert!

GILBERT. Leave him to the ants –

HARRIET. But . . . but Amolo is a *Christian*!

GILBERT. I shouldn't think the ants will mind, Harriet. Besides, being a Christian doesn't logically entitle anyone to a burial, now does it?

> *Pause.*

HARRIET. *We* are Christian, too.

GILBERT. Come now. Not *really* Christians. Eh?

> *Pause.*

There are other things besides being a Christian, you know.

HARRIET. Are you no longer a Christian, Gilbert?

GILBERT. Oh, come come come. I really thought we were more sophisticated than that, Harriet!

> *Pause.*

Just a minute. What's that? Listen?

> *Pause. Silence.*

HARRIET. Why . . . the drums have stopped.

GILBERT. Your drums may have stopped.

> *Pause.*

Mine have just started –

HARRIET. But . . . it's perfectly *quiet*!

> *Pause.*

GILBERT. I think you'd better get started on that grave. On that *Christian's* grave.

HARRIET. I am sorry, Gilbert . . . I will not do such a thing. How can you seem to . . . to expect –

GILBERT. You've had the poor devil at your beck and call for the last eight years . . . the least you can do is to bury him!

HARRIET (*moaning*). Gilbert . . . Gilbert . . . I won't, I can't –

GILBERT. I wish they'd stop those bloody drums.

Pause.

Now Harriet, I'll find you a nice spade. I tell you what, I'll find some big stones as well. To put on top. If you don't, the hyenas'll get him, you know.

HARRIET *sobbing quietly.*

Come along . . . that's right give me your arm . . . must get it done before sundown –

Fadeout HARRIET *crying.*

Scene Five

Late.
Fade-in HARRIET *reading her diary. Muted drumming.*

HARRIET. For what sin has my awful punishment been devised?

Pause.

And what woman, grown old and experienced in the world, has had to take pen and record such vile assault on her whole being as I have endured today?

Pause.

And Gilbert . . . Gilbert stood over me whilst I dug a grave. Under the hot sun, I took a spade, and measured the ground . . . and dug a grave for Amolo, whilst Gilbert watched . . . half smiling.

Pause.

I half dragged, half carried the body to the grave, wrapped in a sheet. I read from the Book of Common Prayer (I cannot remember what) and lowered Amolo in, as gently as I could.

Pause.

I was drenched with perspiration – and trembling . . . almost ready to die *then*, and have Gilbert bury *me*.

Pause.

We came back to the house, and have not spoken since . . . I feel . . . fanciful though it might be . . . that in burying that poor native boy, I have buried some angry devouring thing in my husband.

Pause.

Now I must go to bed, for I ache both in body and heart . . . and the drumming out there in the hills is like the beat of evil itself.

Pause.

Perhaps . . . we should give them their country and go.

Pause.

I can write no more.

Pause.

God bring us peace with the morning light.

Gets into bed.

Fadeout.

Scene Six

Fade-up bed in semi-darkness. Low muted drumming. A clock strikes three. There is a scream, and we see GILBERT *trying to climb into a bed. He does so and* HARRIET *pleads with him.*

HARRIET (*in bed; mosquito net over bed*). What are you doing?

Pause.

Gilbert? Is that you?

Creaking springs.

What are you . . . no, no . . . go back to your own bed and go to sleep.

Pause. Silence.

Gilbert?

Pause. Creaking springs.

Gilbert . . . we are old people . . . this is . . . it is . . . you *shall* not!

Pause.

Please . . . please, Gilbert –

GILBERT *grunts several times.*

How dare you, dare you attempt this disgusting behaviour!

Pause.

Gilbert?

Pause.

Be good enough to return to your own bed, and molest me no further.

Pause.

It was . . . it was beastliness when we were young . . . and it would be . . . degraded beastliness now. Gilbert? You cannot. You must not. It was . . . *always* loathesome. There was never any response in me. You know that, don't you?

Pause.

Never in me. *That* was not in me.

Pause.

Gilbert?

Pause.

Gilbert, I shall get up, and cross the room, and go out through that door . . . and lock it. I shall lock you up. Lock you in.

Pause.

Lock you in alone with yourself, where you belong.

Pause.

And perhaps tomorrow . . . if you are good . . . I shall let you out . . . and we shall say no more about it? Shall we? Not another word.

Massive jungle cacophony. Fadeout on bed.

Scene Seven

Next morning. Breakfast.
Long pause. Fade-up HARRIET *at breakfast. She has a rifle by her chair. Enter* GILBERT.

GILBERT. Morning, Harriet.

> *Pause.*

I said Good morning, Harriet –

HARRIET. Yes, I heard you.

GILBERT. Well then?

HARRIET. You will understand if I find it difficult to engage in pleasantries this morning!

> *Pause.*

GILBERT. Dammit, you unlocked the door, didn't you?

HARRIET. As your presence at breakfast testifies!

GILBERT. Then we'll say no more about it.

HARRIET *You* say that!

> *Pause.*

If it will reassure you . . . I do not propose to make an issue of what happened last night.

GILBERT. How are your drums?

HARRIET. I . . . I can't hear them this morning.

GILBERT. Mine have stopped, too.

> *Pause.*

It's a bit . . . ominous, isn't it?

> *Pause.*

The calm before the . . . attack . . . and all that.

HARRIET. Gilbert, why are you trying to frighten me?

> *Pause.*

What are you trying to do to me?

> *Pause.*

What have you become, Gilbert?

GILBERT. Now, Harriet, you unlocked the door of your own free will!

HARRIET. I unlocked the door . . . out of respect for *your* free will –

GILBERT. And why should *I* wish to frighten *you*?

HARRIET. If I knew . . . *I* would know how to help you –

GILBERT. The truth is, of course, that you are a cold, arrogant woman, Harriet. Something disturbs you . . . you find its source in me. And yet, when it comes to the natives you are . . . equivocal. If I were to put them down ruthlessly you would applaud me. Yet secretly, you know that to have what you really want is an act of aggression against yourself.

Pause.

I hope I am being lucid?

Pause.

HARRIET. I . . . do not know you . . . any longer, Gilbert.

GILBERT. Which is why, I suppose, you are carrying that gun!

Pause.

HARRIET. I . . . I am so tired of all this.

Pause.

Do you remember what we were when we first came out here? Do you think I have not the pride of knowing that a few great families in one small country held out as long as they did?

Pause.

Our motives have always been . . . beyond reproach. And to suggest that we were moved by the hungers and lusts which characterise *these* people is to put yourself . . . on the wrong side of the boundary of sanity.

Pause.

GILBERT. A . . . few . . . great . . . families! What a felicitous way of understanding fifty years' precarious authority!

Pause.

Isn't it time we did what we really want for a change?

Pause.

Since we are virtually an extinct class . . . since we've let the *merchants* and *managers* and *technicians* capture the roost . . . we might as *well* go out with a bang!

Pause.

And admit . . . that we are grateful . . . for the modest privilege of . . . destroying . . . each other!

GILBERT *goes off.*

HARRIET. Where are you going?

Pause.

Come *back*, Gilbert!

Pause.

It's no use running off into the bush, you know – they'll catch you and tear you to pieces! You are behaving in a ridiculous manner, Gilbert.

Pause.

You cannot possibly climb that tree.

Pause.

Come down at once. Very well, then. If you will not –

GILBERT. There are some fine coconuts up here, Harriet . . . try one.

Pause . . . Crash of breaking coconut.

HARRIET. I warn you, Gilbert –

GILBERT. Try another –

Coconut.

HARRIET. Oh, I wish they could all see you now . . . in your tree, Gilbert. Like the beast you are.

Coconuts thick and fast.

Like the ugly, monstrous creature you always have been. That is what I have lived with all these years, a monster! I have the gun, Gilbert.

Pause.

Come down, or I shall shoot . . . oh, I've *wanted* to, you

know. I've wanted to. *Wanted* to shoot you. *Will* you come down or must I . . .

She fires. Loud crash. Scream from HARRIET.

Blackout.

Scene Eight

Later the same evening.
Chattering monkeys. Fade-in. Breakfast things still there. Fade-up sound of jeep. We hear it stop – its lights swing across the stage and come to rest. In half shadow there is a tree with the body of a huge gorilla lying beneath it. Voices off: CHARMIAN, JOHN (*her husband*) *and a* NATIVE POLICEMAN.

CHARMIAN (*off*). The place looks deserted.

JOHN (*off*). You take the back, sergeant. I'll take the front.

(*They enter; the* POLICEMAN *first, carrying an electric torch, then* JOHN *and* CHARMIAN *together.*)

POLICEMAN. Mr Maudsley – *you* will take the back.

JOHN (*irritated*). It's hardly an occasion for quibbling about protocol –

CHARMIAN (*frightened*). Poor Harriet –

JOHN. What do you mean? How do we know? She's probably in bed and asleep.

POLICEMAN. In Karalinga, Mrs Maudsley, bad things no longer happen. We are not savages. Know how to behave. I am afraid, sir, this was not always the same with your own people.

JOHN. Oh, let's get on with it!

JOHN *goes off. The* POLICEMAN *comes downstage flashing his torch, followed by* CHARMIAN. *He is near the tree.*

CHARMIAN. I'm sure something's happened –

POLICEMAN. These men from the place of Lady Boscoe – good

men, Mrs Maudsley. Not liars. Thieves. They didn't have to
come to me. Good cook, good houseboy.

> JOHN *enters. He takes* CHARMIAN'S *arm. The* POLICE-
> MAN *is wandering near the tree with his torch.*

JOHN. She's on the verandah. Dead.

> *With a gasp,* CHARMIAN *makes to go towards the verandah.*
> JOHN *holds her back. Nods at the* POLICEMAN.

Best let him go first. His self-esteem and all that. It's nothing
violent. A heart attack, I should say.

> *The* POLICEMAN *has at last trained his torch on the gorilla.*

POLICEMAN. Mr Maudsley –

> JOHN *goes to him, followed by* CHARMIAN – *they look, and*
> CHARMIAN *screams.*

JOHN. My God!

POLICEMAN. I have heard it said many times, Mr Maudsley,
they are the most intelligent, cunning of creatures.

> *Pause.*

And is it not known, sir, by your Darwin that they are our
forefathers? Ancestors of black and white, red and yellow.

CHARMIAN. It's *huge*!

JOHN. And Harriet alone –

POLICEMAN (*slyly*). Perhaps he was a friendly fellow, sir –

JOHN. That's quite enough, sergeant! Don't you realise what
might have happened. Good God! Come away, Charmian.
Ugly brute.

> *Pause.*

Gilbert told me himself . . . ages ago . . . the last, the last
gorilla shot in these parts it was . . . surely it was before
independence, wasn't it?

On the Eve of Publication

To the memory of Zbigniew Cybulski

On the Eve of Publication was first broadcast by BBC Television on 27 November 1968 with the following cast:

ROBERT KELVIN	*Leo McKern*
EMMA	*Michele Dotrice*
JANE	*Pauline Devaney*
HOLLAND	*Thorley Walters*
BARBARA	*Rosalind Knight*
RUTH	*Kay Newman*
DINNER GUESTS	*Geraldine Gwyther*
	Mischa de la Motte
	Winifred Hill
	John Roden
	Hira Talfrey
	Nova Sainte-Clair
	Alfred Hoffman
	Mervyn Prior

Directed by Alan Bridges

The following parts, in the rehearsal script and full copy, were cut from the final recording because of over run:

FATHER	*Alan Cullen*
GRANDFATHER	*Bob Wallace*
MOTHER	*Rose Howlett*

1. Interior. Carlton Terrace Club

A dinner is being held for ROBERT KELVIN *by his publishers.* SIX MEN *and* SIX WOMEN *at a circular table. Open on* KELVIN – *a thin, gaunt man of sixty or so. He is watching* EMMA, *an attractive woman in her early twenties. She is talking animatedly to the man on her right, but we hear no sound in the room.* KELVIN *watches her fixedly, scoring the tablecloth with a fork. The "voice" throughout the play is* KELVIN'S.

VOICE. Dearest Emma ... I'm writing you this letter because ... because ... my God, look at Holland's face. The man is entirely *in* his face, isn't he?

> *Close up* HOLLAND, KELVIN'S *publisher, in his fifties. A plump, sleek face ... glasses, an overripe mouth smirking to itself.*
>
> *Close-up* EMMA: *Listening.*

VOICE You have a certain expertise with these people. Oh yes. A terrible way of animating yourself for them. Why? Because I'm sour? Because what's always easier for me is to withdraw? (*Pause.*) You rob me even of my own silence, tumbling over yourself to fill it. (*Pause.*) My bloody back hurts. Like someone pulling a hot wire through my spine. (*Pause.*) You see ... Emma ...

> *Close-up* HOLLAND *speaking to the* WOMAN *on his left. We hear only his voice – no other sound.*

HOLLAND. Yes. I do think it's Robert's best book. I'm certain. (*Close-up* ROBERT KELVIN.) It's drily passionate ... without, you know, without being dried up! (*Close-up* HOLLAND, *whose smile congratulates himself for the idea.*)

VOICE. I'm writing this letter ... more, sort of ... a journal ... I can't be angry with you. Can't mock you, or deflate you. (*Pause.*) I'm a unique case in one respect. This disease is supposed to double you up well before sixty ... supposed to pull your head down to your chest, and hold it riveted there. And there's some kind of metal contraption to deal with the problem (*Pause.*) Holland is so *fastidiously* sly! It can be disarming. *The Last Days of Buster Crook* ISN'T my best novel. (*Pause.*) It's more what I know than what I feel. (*Pause.*) But I like Buster. Yes. Just as you do, Emma. (*Pause.*) I want a brandy. And a piss. (*Pause.*) I want you. (*Close-up* KELVIN.) I've been writing to you inside my head for days, now –

> *The woman on* KELVIN'S *right,* BARBARA, *turns to him. As throughout, the convention is that when someone speaks, all other sound is blotted out.*

BARBARA. How are the children, Robert?

KELVIN. Their various mothers are not too scrupulous about letting me know. (*Pause.*) Laurie starts at the Lycee next week. Gerald's got a part in somebody's new play. Paula's got a dutch cap and doesn't like it. Do you know where the lavatory is?

EMMA. Down the corridor, second door right.

KELVIN (*rising*). Emma always knows where it is. Where things are.

> *Pause. He stands looking at her.*

Don't you?

> *Pause.*

EMMA. I'm sorry, Robert.

> KELVIN *makes for the door.*

2. Interior. Corridor.

KELVIN *makes his way down the corridor and opens a door.*

3. Interior. Lavatory.

KELVIN *washing his hands. He dries them, looking into a mirror over the washbasin.*

4. Interior. Cheap photographer's studio: 1920.

KELVIN'S GRANDFATHER, FATHER and MOTHER *are being*

photographed. The two men are miners, uncomfortable in suits, collars and ties. They pose, and two pictures are taken.

FATHER. What do we want to be doing this for? Bloody nonsense.

MOTHER. Nay, we want some pictures.

GRANDFATHER. I'm choking.

EMMA strays on to the scene, mini-dressed.

VOICE. Grandad's choking, Emma.

FATHER. Our Robert, come ower 'ere and get thy picture ta'en, lad.

EMMA joins the group and has her picture taken with them. The FATHER makes a clenched fist salute.

FATHER. Up the revolution! Eh? Eh, mother?

5. *Stock film: Storming of Winter Palace.*

We see Soviet workers storming the gates of the Winter Palace in St. Petersberg. Music: 'The Internationale', very loud.

6. *Interior. Photographer's studio.*

EMMA sits alone, by the fluted half column and the potted fern.

VOICE (*as EMMA adopts different poses, and pictures are taken*). My father was a shy man, really (*Flash*). Down the pit, he was known as 'Soft Billy' (*Flash*). I used to ride pit ponies in the fields. Listen, Emma . . . (*Flash*). Listen – (*Flash*). Listen, darling –

EMMA (*blankly*). Viva Che, Viva Che, Viva Che –

VOICE. Shut up, you silly bitch!

For a moment, the screen goes dark.

7. *Interior. Lavatory.*

KELVIN, with his back to the mirror.

VOICE: The book comes out tomorrow. Holland suggests a 'little dinner' in this bloody awful place. You're delighted. You see my mouth turn down at the corners. Dutifully, you take my point. It is boring and pointless, and you realize that that was what you felt in the first place. (*Pause.*) Then you realise that in any case, I shall come. (*Pause.*) I'm inconsistent. Yes. (*Pause.*) But then I tend to think to myself: you never know what you might do. Perhaps a fat cigar in Holland's ear? Or touch Wendy Holland's crutch with a skirling finger under the table? Only to provoke, to test a little. To raise a yelp, or a pitying smile. (*Pause.*) Emma, you fill me with rage.

Exit KELVIN, *into the corridor.*

8. *Interior. Corridor.*

He meanders, abstracted, to the dining room.

9. *Interior. Dining room.*

KELVIN *opens the door and stands within. There is a loud babble of voices in conversation, but the chairs round the table are empty. He closes his eyes. The babble stops. He opens his eyes. The scene is as he left it, and he resumes his place.*

KELVIN. My father was a shy man, really.

Close-up EMMA'S *face, talking. No sound.*

VOICE. I shall get drunk again. And you'll have to help me undress. And you'll be maddeningly gentle, of course. (*Pause.*) Like last night.

10. *Interior. Staircase: Kelvin's house.*

It is the preceding night. EMMA *helps* KELVIN *upstairs.*

KELVIN (*stumbling*). You remember that bit of James Joyce? 'Oh, my back, my back . . . I'd want to go to Aix le pains —'

EMMA *holds him firmly by the elbow until he steadies, and they go up.*

11. Interior. study.

EMMA *brings* KELVIN *into the study, sits him down.*

KELVIN. I think . . . a large Scotch and water.

EMMA. If you want one, Robert.

> *She goes to the drinks table and pours a Scotch. She takes a water jug and goes out of the room.*

KELVIN. I'd want to go to Aix le pains.

VOICE. Emma, if anyone asked me what you are like – I wouldn't know. People define themselves in opposition to each other. What about a bit of opposition?

> EMMA *comes in with the water jug and pours some water into the Scotch, handing it to him.*

KELVIN. Your face is quite expressionless, Emma. Is that good for you?

EMMA. I don't mind how much you drink.

KELVIN. No.

EMMA. I only worry about your health.

KELVIN. Yes.

EMMA. I love you.

KELVIN. Oh, dear –

EMMA. I don't mind anything you do.

KELVIN. What a pity.

EMMA. Why?

KELVIN. Well, my needs are getting to be rudimentary.

EMMA. Do you want to go bed?

KELVIN. No.

EMMA. Shall I put a record on?

KELVIN. Who stole my old record of 'The Internationale'? Who stole it? I bought that record in nineteen thirty-eight.

EMMA. I've put all the records in alphabetical order. It'll be under the I's.

KELVIN. I must think up something that'll *make* you mind –

EMMA. I think I'm going to bed, love –

KELVIN. Aren't I supposed to ring one of my ex-wives?

EMMA. Yes.

KELVIN. Which one?

EMMA. Ruth. She wants to discuss Paula.

KELVIN. Ah.

EMMA. She thinks Paula's got some sort of phobia about her cap.
(*Pause.*) And apparently Ruth's analyst said –

KELVIN. Poor old Ruth. Still at it. (*Pause.*) One couldn't even fart
without old Ruth coming up with some psycho-analytical interpretation.

> EMMA *gets the telephone and brings it to a small table beside*
> KELVIN. *She kisses him.*

EMMA. Why don't you ring her now? I'm going to bed.

KELVIN. Emma, are you quite sure you wouldn't like to stick
knitting needles into Ruth's eyes?

EMMA. Quite sure. (*She goes to the desk.*) I've typed everything
you've written this week.

KELVIN. I've told you . . . why do I pay a bloody secretary?
(*Pause.*) Anyway, those two chapters are rubbish.

EMMA. I thought they were very moving. And funny as well,
somehow.

KELVIN. Oh God.

> EMMA *goes to the door.*

EMMA. I'll leave the bedroom light on.

KELVIN. It'll keep you awake.

> *Pause.*

EMMA. I want to be awake when you come to bed.

> EMMA *goes out.* KELVIN *sips his drink.*

KELVIN. No escape. Won't even shut her damned eyes and let
me have a bit of peace. (*Pause.*) Young. Strong. Healthy. Dedi-
cated. (*Pause.*) Deferential. (*Pause.*) One night I shall creep in
there and clonk her with my shillelagh. On the head. Clonk.
(*Pause.*) And undress at leisure, attempt a few exercises in
grateful privacy.

> KELVIN *picks up the telephone and dials. A woman's voice
> answers.*

Ruth? It's Robert.

12. Interior. Bedroom.

RUTH *is in bed, with the telephone on the pillow beside her. She is talking. No sound.*

VOICE. I feel uneasy about your getting on so well with Ruth, Emma. Because I never listen to her. (*Pause.*) I bought that record of 'The Internationale' in Moscow in nineteen thirty-eight. (*Pause.*) I visited Chekhov's grave. (*Pause.*) Terrible days. People disappearing. Friends. Writers. (*Pause.*) That was six years before you were born, Emm. Can't you see that well . . . the age thing . . . I'm burdened and irritated by it. (*Pause.*) Furious, sometimes. (*Pause.*) Apart from the back, there's occasional cystitis . . . a touch of deafness . . . a trifling but shaming incontinence now and then . . . joints are stiffer . . . mind fumbles at things, misfires and then picks up again, but one remembers. One notes the increasing tremors. As if death were a gentle earthquake of the system, gathering force over the years. (*Pause.*) It was sad, at Chekhov's grave.

13. Interior. Study

KELVIN *puts the phone down on the table, with* RUTH *still talking. He lights a cigarette.*

VOICE. In the spring, Leningrad is full of light. The streets are wide. The air sings.

Pause. KELVIN *picks up the phone.*

KELVIN. Ruth, it is folly to provide a girl of sixteen with contraception. (*Pause.*) On the other hand, it is folly not to.

He puts the phone down. Pours himself another whisky and drinks it quickly. He is dizzy, and lies on the couch. It is very quiet, then we hear some night sounds: voices in the street, the siren of a police car, a dog. Then silence.

VOICE. In Prague, a summer's evening. The long benches under the trees. The brass band. The pints of black beer. The smells: that filthy rotten petrol, but something familiar and acrid as well . . . that catches the throat and the memory. A kind of woodsmoke . . . and pines . . . and sausages. (*Pause.*) Emma, the revolution has been dead everywhere in Central Europe . . . the Soviet Union. Yes, the revolution died. (*Pause.*) But now, something's afoot. Yes. The young. (*Pause.*) One is grateful for the young. (*Pause.*) Let's hope they take . . . everything . . . between their teeth . . . and shake it . . . like a dog with a rat. (*Pause.*) Everywhere. (*Pause.*) On some lake outside Budapest, calm and milky red in the evening . . . such peach trees (*Pause.*) We bit into the peaches. The juice spurted. We kissed, and trickled the sharp juice in and out of each other's mouths. (*Pause.*) I was forty-two then, Emma. (*Pause.*) She asked me: Do you know how bad it is in Hungary? Yes, I said. I know how bad it is. (*Pause.*) And she flung a half-eaten peach into the water.

EMMA *comes into the study with a blanket. At once,* KELVIN *closes his eyes. She removes his tie, his jacket, his shoes. Now she gently arranges the blanket over him. Leaving one lamp lit in the corner, she goes out quietly.* KELVIN'S *eyes snap open, glaring.*

14. Stock film.

The street of a northern or midlands mining village in the thirties. Unemployed miners lounge at doors, squat with their backs against walls.

15. Interior. Dining room.

Close-up KELVIN *glaring at* EMMA, *who is speaking.*

EMMA. Yes. It was in Cambridge. My finals year. (*Pause.*) Robert came to give a lecture about China and Maoism. He'd just come back from Peking.

KELVIN (*snappily*). Hanoi.

EMMA. Yes. He came back via Hanoi. And well . . . he gave this lecture . . . and everyone was very impressed. (*Pause.*) There was a party the following evening in King's College –

KELVIN. I might as well tell you she found me grovelling on my knees being sick into the bloody river.

EMMA. There was a terrible thunderstorm.

KELVIN. I'm too old for all that sort of bloody nonsense.

BARBARA. Then . . . why?

KELVIN. Ugh!

BARBARA. Why, my dear Robert?

KELVIN. Oh, shut up!

EMMA. Robert!

KELVIN. There you are. There you are, you see. No doubt one's vanity is inexhaustible. (*Pause.*) The place should be blown up. As for the students, most of them have the political sophistication of a child of ten.

EMMA. The Backs were lovely, that evening –

KELVIN. Oh, I'll grant you! Very moving, etcetera. And the back of one's head drumming with that filthy music. (*Pause.*) And an extraordinary number of fat girls. Why so many fat girls? I thought the twin ideal nowadays was vacancy of the expression and emaciation of the body? All I can say is they aren't toeing the line in Cambridge.

BARBARA (*to* EMMA). What did you do with him after he was sick?

EMMA. We just . . . sort of . . . stood there. For a bit.

Close-up BARBARA *smiling.*

VOICE. Didn't we just? Didn't we just?

KELVIN. I noted, perhaps by way of distracting myself, that she was neither fat nor emaciated.

Close up EMMA *talking.*

VOICE. One early spring, in an expensive sanitorium on a wooded mountainside overhanging Geneva, so it seemed . . . one of my wives had an abortion. (*Pause.*) I sat in a café that afternoon. I had forgotten it was Christmas Eve.

Close-up KELVIN'S *face. Pause.*

Must my daughter begin at sixteen? (*Pause.*) Young, to love and suffer. And look around to love again. And again. (*Pause.*) Emma, you must speak about those things to Ruth. (*Pause.*) I was . . . in agonies with my own lust. (*Pause.*) At fourteen. (*Pause.*) That year . . . proud, bitter, maimed ex-servicemen still on the streets. (*Pause.*) In Nottingham, was it? (*Pause.*) Nineteen twenty-four? Was it?

Close-up BARBARA *talking.*

KELVIN. In Havana —

BARBARA. I beg your pardon, Robert?

He looks down at the table. She goes on talking.

VOICE. At four p.m. as instructed, I approached the sanitorium. I met the doctor in the lift and he shook my hand. (*Pause.*) Congratulations, he said. (*Pause.*) In her room, she slept. And high up the mountain, the snow glimmered red and the sun was a low orange disc.

Close-up EMMA.

EMMA. That was last summer. I got my degree. And since . . . well I . . . I look after Robert.

BARBARA. I don't envy you.

KELVIN. My old friends often display a weakness for letting people know they can insult me and get away with it. (*Pause.*) Or think they can.

BARBARA. Come, come, darling —

HOLLAND *rises to his feet with his glass.*

HOLLAND. I only want to say . . . here's to Robert. And all success for *The Last Days of Buster Crook.*

They are murmuring 'Cheers' etc and drinking to ROBERT *but we hear nothing. Close-up* HOLLAND, *who goes on speaking.*

VOICE. When we were in Havana, Emm . . . Emma darling . . . Emma love. (*Pause.*) I disliked Hemingway's house extremely. I thought the way you trotted round with that soft pious face on was disgusting. (*Pause.*) I had a pain in my bladder, a sharp twinge in the left shoulder, a violent headache. Really, Holland is a toad. But I should find another word because I like toads. And how much have you made out of me, jolly old Ralph? (*Pause.*) We stick together. He sticks to me — I get stuck to. (*Pause.*) Now, Emma, if you'd only *think* a bit more about Hemingway. And anyway, all those damned animals' heads . . .

antlers . . . horns . . . guns . . . copies of the *New Yorker* . . . bottles and not a sign of the man. Of him. One has to work hard in Hemingway's house to catch a whiff of anything but vanity. (*Pause.*) All those damned animals' heads . . . horns . . . antlers. (*Pause.*) I had thought before . . . maybe there would be a hint . . . a note . . . of isolation. (*Pause.*) Hasta la victoria siempre! (*Pause.*) He cared nothing for Cuba.

> HOLLAND *is still talking.* KELVIN *rises.* HOLLAND *shuts his mouth.*

KELVIN. Ralph, I have just decided . . . inside my head. I have decided that I will no longer go on comparing you . . . inside my head . . . with a toad.

> HOLLAND *flings back his head and laughs. We hear nothing. Everyone laughs,* EMMA *rather nervously.* KELVIN *sits down and* HOLLAND *goes on with his speech.*

VOICE. I sat by the window, Emma, and watched the sunset on the mountain. There was a smell of pine needles. (*Pause.*) But near the bedside, anaesthetic. (*Pause.*) Jane stirred . . . opened her eyes. Smiled. She said: Look behind that picture on the wall. It was a nativity. Reproduction. Quattrocento rubbish. I turned it round. On the back – her temperature chart. (*Pause.*) God knows why . . . we went from there to Salzburg.

16. Exterior. Train.

The train roars through a night landscape.

17. Interior. Train.

In a compartment otherwise empty: KELVIN, *and in the opposite corner* JANE, *huddled in a fur coat.*

KELVIN. You're in pain –

JANE. Yes.

KELVIN. Why did we do it?

JANE. I shall need to see a doctor when we get to Salzburg.

KELVIN. Why did we do it?

JANE. I'm bleeding.

KELVIN. What can I do?

JANE. What did you ever do?

    KELVIN *looks out of the window.*

VOICE. What did I ever do?

18. Exterior. Door.

The door opens.

19. Interior. Room.

From the doorway, we see Kelvin's FATHER *lying dead in bed. Fade.*

20. Interior. Room.

Fade in the same scene, except that it is now Kelvin's dead MOTHER. *Fade.*

21. Interior. Train.

KELVIN *turns away from the window. It is* EMMA *sitting opposite.*

KELVIN. I'm dying.

EMMA. No you aren't, Robert.

KELVIN. Why do *you* have to lie . . . when I don't need to?

EMMA. I don't lie.

KELVIN. I'm tired of explaining –

EMMA. You hardly ever speak to me.

KELVIN. Should I?

EMMA. You don't have to calculate your relationship with me.

KELVIN. Have I got one?

EMMA. Try and get some sleep, Robert.

KELVIN. Did I ever tell you about that curious day in the sanatorium? In Switzerland?

EMMA. Yes. You did.

KELVIN. Have I told you everything?

EMMA. Not yet.

KELVIN. Are you *bored* yet?

EMMA. I'm never bored, Robert.

KELVIN. I don't *like* Salzburg in the winter!

EMMA. Then let's go somewhere else.

KELVIN. Where would you like to go?

EMMA. Anywhere.

> *Exasperated, he looks out of the window. When he looks back, it is* JANE *once more but unconscious, her head lolling.*

KELVIN. Jane! Jane!

> *He kneels on the floor and takes her in his arms.*

Jane! Jane!

22. *Interior. Dining room.*

Close-up KELVIN'S *face. The sound of the train very loud. It fades. A waiter is filling* KELVIN'S *glass. Through half closed eyes,* KELVIN *looks round the table: the animated, silent, clacking heads.*

KELVIN. Er . . . Er –

> *Immediately, everyone is attentive.*

On the question of violence, what I am compelled to say is –

> *The room goes almost completely dark. There is the glimmer of light on a face, a glass, someone's eyes – but it is as if we are in some dark half world of Kelvin's.*

On the question of violence . . . and the young –

> *Now the room is brilliant once more.* HOLLAND *leans solicitously to* EMMA.

HOLLAND. Poor Robert's pretty far gone –

BARBARA. *I* think he's *ill.*

KELVIN. On the question of the *tragic* outcome of the Soviet Revolution . . . and the *justifiable* contempt of students for the stultifying bureaucracies of both systems . . . I mean, when I speak of the needs and hopes of the young. Of that incoherent mythology compounded of Guevara and others –

> *His head drops on to his chest as he mumbles into silence.*

HOLLAND. Emma – shouldn't we get him away, don't you think?

EMMA. It would be a mistake to try. He'd like that. In one second he'd be on his feet calling for another drink and talking brilliantly. It's happened before often enough. I'm not taken in now.

BARBARA. Well. That's remarkably cool of you! I was under the impression that I knew Robert rather well, and –

EMMA. I'm sure you know him very well.

BARBARA. So – we do nothing?

EMMA. He's listening. Waiting. He wants a row.

KELVIN'S *head jerks upright. His eyes open. He gazes round the table.*

KELVIN. Which one of you pinched my bloody record of 'The Internationale'?

BARBARA. He *is* gaga –

EMMA. No.

KELVIN. They raise our hopes. They fill us with respect. What did we ever place in their hands but cynicism and pessimism? (*Pause.*) Our joints creak. Our heads wag. (*Pause.*) Our words . . . our words –

Blackout.

23. *Interior. Room.*

A bare, ill-lit room. KELVIN, *naked, sits on a high stool hugging himself to keep warm.*

VOICE. For instance, Emma . . . my veins are a sluggish blue . . . bulging . . . knotted. Yours . . . delicate. (*Pause.*) My skin flakes. (*Pause.*) Pulling on my trousers this morning I noticed . . . my knees were shaking. (*Pause.*) White hairs grow in my ears . . . my nose. (*Pause.*)

24. *Interior. Dining room.*

KELVIN *watches and maybe listens, whilst* BARBARA *listens to* EMMA.

EMMA. He isn't fastidious, not in any way. He doesn't notice things, I mean what food . . . or drink . . . or the colour of a wall. (*Pause.*) He's always – preoccupied. I don't think it's his back, though of course he has a lot of pain. (*Pause.*) The accountant said we should change the car. I asked Robert. He said: why not? And then forgot about it. (*Pause.*) Well, there was one of those supplements all about cars . . . and I picked one. They brought it round and took the other away. The next day Robert had to go somewhere, and he didn't notice. About the car. What's that, he said? New car! Is it? (*Pause.*) I thought he was joking. Then he said: I suppose Mickey – that's his accountant – said we ought to change it. And that was that.

> KELVIN *raises his wine glass and sips the wine.*

KELVIN. Do you know how I got the idea for Buster Crook?

> *There is immediate, deferential silence.*

I had a cousin called Charlie. His father was a miner, lost a leg in the war. Charlie was a plump, sensitive lad. At sixteen, he already looked like a middle-aged queen. From his father's point of view, Charlie was provocative. I mean, Charlie hated their poverty . . . their vulgarity . . . and cultivated a passion for art nouveau and various other cultural quirks. You couldn't exactly say Charlie fitted in with the life around . . . one downstairs room, oilcloth on the table, a black horsehair sofa, a china bird of some improbable species on the sideboard . . . mother cleaned three banks for a few shillings . . . dad on the booze most of the time. (*Pause.*) Charlie's bent for beautiful and delicate things must have been pretty staunch, to survive the environment. Who knows how it started. The grammar school? Some sinister friend, some ageing Nottingham pouff picked up in an art gallery? For the time and place, young Charlie was a sociological absurdity. What extraordinary genetic mutation had taken place in Charlie's mother's womb? (*Pause.*) However, one Sunday there was a terrible row between father and son. Charlie'd stuck a rose in a glass of water and started painting it in water-colours. His father burnt the rose, smashed the glass, and poured gravy over the drawing. (*Pause.*) After that they had their Sunday dinner. Charlie's little sister went to Sunday school. His mother went upstairs to bed. His father took off his wooden leg and got down on the horsehair sofa for a nap. (*Pause.*) Charlie packed a few things, put his dad's wooden leg on the fire – left. Never seen again.

25. *Interior. Room.*

KELVIN *now huddles in a corner, in a mass of filthy straw.*

VOICE. Do you intend to do to me what you did to Sladek? (*Pause.*) I loved Sladek. (*Pause.*) Broken ribs, teeth kicked out . . . executed when and where? Certainly for no crime, except that of being a fine poet . . . an intellectual . . . a witty parodist of all your stupidities, your brutalities, your lies in the name of this that and the other revolutionary ideal. (*Pause.*) When I get back to England, make no mistake – I shall have plenty to say about the fate of Sladek and all the others. (*Pause.*) No, Comrade! One day it will all come out, even here. (*Pause.*) And then what will you say? Will you say we stamped on Sladek's balls for the revolution? For party discipline? For the treasonable action of telling the truth out loud?

26. *Interior. Dining room.*

HOLLAND. Put his father's wooden leg on the fire?

KELVIN. Burnt it to a cinder. I've often wished I could have been there when he woke up.

BARBARA. So what became of Charlie?

KELVIN. He was last seen disappearing into the men's lavatory at St. Pancras Station. (*Pause.*) Nineteen nineteen. (*Pause.*) Last seen, that is, by his loving family.

BARBARA. And by you, Robert?

KELVIN. Just after the last war. (*Pause.*) He'd become to all intents and purposes French. Beautiful flat near the Boulevard St. Germain . . . a wild collection of erotic drawings and books . . . Arab boy friend . . . false papers . . . having quite a vogue as a minor, off-beat art critic . . . and dying of some obscure disease which he referred to as 'my obscene condition'.

HOLLAND. Doesn't sound much like *The Last Days of Buster Crook*!

KELVIN. No, it doesn't – does it?

BARBARA. One of your fantasies, Robert?

KELVIN. By no means. Can I have some brandy or something?

EMMA. *I* can see the connection –

KELVIN. Can you? Can you, darling? (*Pause.*) There's no doubt, the most microscopic connection between any two things . . . ideas . . . memories . . . couldn't escape old Emma. (*Pause.*) Emma makes impertinence seem like a caress!

EMMA. I'm sorry, Robert –

KELVIN. Why be sorry? Why apologize for the terrible natural logic of your own priggishness. One might as well apologize for breathing.

27. *Interior. Room.*

The room now contains a desk and two chairs. At one-side of the desk, KELVIN *dressed in shirt and trousers. At the other, a man in some anonymous uniform.*

MAN. Name?

KELVIN. Robert Kelvin.

MAN. Age?

KELVIN. Forty-two.

MAN. How long in the party?

KELVIN. Never in the party.

MAN. *Never in the party?*

KELVIN. Not amenable to discipline, that's the sad fact of it. Never could tolerate. Never could face inane directives from people I despised. Independence. Balance. Some idea of objectivity. Always tended to be more of a spectator. (*Pause.*) No. Not good party material.

MAN. Cigarette?

KELVIN. Thank you.

MAN. All we want . . . is the truth . . . in your own words, d'you see . . . about this woman.

KELVIN. About Emma.

MAN. That's right.

28. Interior. Dining room.

KELVIN *sits smoking, his eyes closed, his fingers round a glass turning it gently.*

KELVIN (*murmuring*). I have to put it on record that one couldn't even *fart* without being reported to Ruth's analyst. (*Pause.*) Was it my aggression? My anal fixation? Was it a regressive trick, reminding Ruth of her maternal obligations to me? (*Pause.*) All I can say is it's bloody weird living with someone who's being psychoanalysed. Everything one does has a ghostly meaning, everything one says is fraught with complex implications. (*Pause.*) You can't imagine . . . suppose, for example, you inadvertently pour tomato sauce over your wife during dinner . . . that humble accident . . . positively opens up whole worlds you never suspected. Dimensions. Areas of significance. You are beaten, battered, brought to your knees with the obscure content of what you had taken to be a humdrum moment of clumsiness. (*Pause.*) Your illusions about free will are scorned . . . your choices become symptoms . . . your whole life is nothing but the outward performance of some inward drama . . . of *which*, mark you, you yourself are totally unaware. (*Pause.*) Now: if I poured tomato sauce over you, Holland, what would you make of it?

> *Close-up* HOLLAND'S *face : he is laughing and talking, but we hear nothing.*

29. Interior. Room.

As in Scene 27. The MAN *holds out a paper to* KELVIN.

MAN. Would you just care to read it over?

KELVIN. Well. Let's see.

KELVIN *reads. The* MAN *begins to pace up and down the room occasionally stopping to look over* KELVIN'S *shoulder.*

VOICE. Height: five foot five inches. Eyes: blue. Hair: fair to brown. Figure: slender. Breasts: quite large, and that believe me is a piece of luck I had not reckoned on in my declining years. (*Pause.*) Education: grammar school and Cambridge. Father: insurance executive. Politics: agreement with my politics. One should enlarge on this last statement; what I mean is, should I throw out some observation, prejudice, dialectical prognosis . . . Emma will struggle to adjust her universe accordingly. Believing nothing, she is quite bemused by the ideological rubble and ruins through which I still pick my lonely way. Emma can see what should have been done, hates what *was* done, and is alternately frightened and exhilarated by what *might* be done. (*Pause.*) But the breasts really are quite large, of an astonishing beauty . . . and by no means pendulous. (*Pause.*) Age: young. *Young young young.* (*Pause.*) Intelligence: well, what does the word mean?

30. Interior. Dining room.

A WAITER *is serving strawberries. We follow him from one guest to the next. Silence.* KELVIN *is upright, but rather slumped in his chair. As the* WAITER *serves him he straightens up.*

KELVIN. Trotsky said that barricades are not some kind of fortress, or military position . . . but rather the point of physical and moral confrontation with the forces of repression. (*Pause.*) That's what Trotters said. (*Pause.*) I take it you've read your Trotsky, Holland. If not I shall fine you one bottle of V.S.O.P.

HOLLAND. Have some strawberries.

KELVIN. Emma, have some strawberries.

EMMA. I am doing.

KELVIN. Are they delicious?

EMMA. Lovely.

KELVIN. And the wine the right temperature?

EMMA. I wouldn't know about that.

BARBARA. Do you remember, Robert – we had strawberries in Karlsbad in . . . that summer . . . nineteen forty-seven, wasn't it? You, and Ruth, and me . . . and John.

KELVIN. Karlsbad?

BARBARA. Karlovy Vary.

KELVIN. Ah! Karlovy Vary!

HOLLAND *is fairly drunk, now he fixes on* KELVIN.

HOLLAND. I honestly do think . . . I'm beginning to think . . . you're beginning to bore me, Robert.

KELVIN. Right at this minute?

HOLLAND. Right at this very minute.

KELVIN. I daren't contemplate the mentality of someone who refers to Karlovy Vary as Karlsbad.

BARBARA. Never mind, love. Ruth was pregnant – wasn't she?

HOLLAND. I've always had a sneaking suspicion that . . . politically . . . you've been a phoney, Robert.

Pause.

KELVIN. The breasts really are quite large. (*Pause.*) You might not think so. You might refuse to believe it. But there it is. And I can assure you, it's a fact. (*Pause.*) Ruth was *not* voluptuous in that respect. When Gerald was born, they vanished altogether. I was writing *The Quiet Frontier* at the time, and I began to wonder whether we should ever see Ruth's mammary equipment again. (Pause.) And *she* used to talk about aggression. That's why the boy became an actor. After all, what's an audience to an actor if not a large tit? (*Pause.*) As for politics, Ralph, you'd have done better if you'd gone in for a policy of enlightened self-loathing.

HOLLAND. Say what you like – Ruth's a sweet woman.

KELVIN. I must say, they were quite decent to us in Karlsbady Vary. But never take the waters there. They give you the squits for days.

HOLLAND. I think *The Last Days of Buster Crook* is a damn' fine book, Robert. What's more – I propose a toast to that effect.

HOLLAND *raises his glass and drinks. The others follow suit, except for* KELVIN.

31. Interior. Kelvin's study.

As from the end of scene 13. KELVIN *still lies with the blanket over him, glaring in the direction of* EMMA'S *exit*

KELVIN. And she flung a half-eaten peach into the water. (*Pause.*) I have white hairs growing out of my ears. (*Pause.*) Should I clip them? (*Pause. Shouting.*) *Emma?*

EMMA *enters from the bedroom, in a dressing gown.*

EMMA. Did you call me?

KELVIN. I did.

EMMA. What's the matter, Robert?

KELVIN. I want to know if I should clip these hairs.

EMMA. What hairs?

KELVIN. These ones sticking out of my ears. Don't say you haven't noticed them. There must have been times, during the still small hours of the night when you've said to yourself: he has hairs growing out of his ears. D'you deny it?

EMMA. Don't be absurd, Robert!

KELVIN. What's absurd about it? I'm beginning to sprout in the most unlikely places. (*Pause.*) I want to know *your* line on my new crop of hairs. Should I be resigned? Should I attack them, at great danger to my person, with a pair of sharp surgical scissors? Should I ignore them? (*Pause.*) If *I* worry about them, why the hell can't you?

EMMA. *Please*, love – I'm tired out.

KELVIN. You shave under your arms. That seems to imply you have a point of view about hair. And I think they're coming on in my nose, too.

EMMA. I don't see why you have to turn something perfectly commonplace into an obsession!

KELVIN. Do you find them *aesthetic*, Emma?

EMMA. Robert – I'm going to bed.

KELVIN. Supposing *you* started getting furry in a non-regulation area?

EMMA. I won't have you drive me into a quarrel about your *age*!

KELVIN. My back feels as if somebody rammed a spear into it.

> EMMA *kneels beside him, concerned.*

EMMA. Darling –

KELVIN. Leave me here. I shall sleep here.

EMMA. Let me help you to bed –

KELVIN. *No!*

> There is a long pause. She is holding his hand. She lets go, and goes into the bedroom.
>
> He lights a cigarette. After a moment he dials a number.

KELVIN. Jane? (*Pause.*) Yes I know it's late. What? Yes I know I might have woken . . . I know . . . I know . . . yes. (*Pause.*) My God, if a dying man can't take a few liberties . . . what? I rang you because I thought of you. How the hell can *I* predict when I'm going to think about you. Yes. That's right. And if I didn't ring you straight away I'd soon forget I'd thought about you. Then there'd be no bloody communication between us at all, would there? (*Pause.*) You don't think I'm dying? (*Pause.*) You rang my doctor? (*Pause.*) I should think he was trying to spare your feelings. (*Pause.*) Yes I know it's late. But listen. Listen. Jane. I've got long white hairs growing out of my ears, and –

> There is a click, and the phone is dead. KELVIN *replaces the receiver.*
>
> Pulling the blanket round him, he goes into the bedroom and stands looking down at EMMA, who lies in bed with her eyes closed. A pause. She opens her eyes.

EMMA. You look like a red Indian.

> KELVIN *kneels beside her.*

KELVIN. I'm pretty drunk.

EMMA. I know.

KELVIN. I want a piss. I daren't go down. Might fall. Might snap one of these brittle bones. Might crack the skull in on the stairs. (*Pause.*) I rang Jane. (*Pause.*) I shall burst. (*Pause.*) I rang Jane. (*Pause.*) I don't want to go to this bloody celebration dinner. (*Pause.*) Jane rang off. She's never forgiven me that abortion. (*Pause.*) Has anyone ever forgiven me anything?

EMMA. I've nothing to forgive you, Robert. You've never hurt me.

KELVIN. I've done my bloody best. Sometimes I think you're plain *thick!*

EMMA. I expect I am.

32. Interior. Dining room.

Close-up HOLLAND.

HOLLAND. I always liked Jane. Always liked Ja –

KELVIN. Shut up, Ralph.

HOLLAND. Then she had that long illness . . . and Robert can't bear people to be ill. Can you Robert?
     Again the sound cuts out. We track round the table, with Holland silently mouthing. Close-up KELVIN.

KELVIN. Where's the lavatory?

EMMA. Down the corridor. Second right.
     KELVIN *rises and goes to the door.*

33. Interior. Corridor.

We follow him to the lavatory.

34. Interior. Lavatory.

He is running water into the basin. He rinses his face. Dries himself slowly.

VOICE. Emma, I feel . . . murderous. I actually . . . I'm serious . . . have looked at you, and known the temptation to kill. (*Pause.*) Then I review my list of charges against you. (*Pause.*) I will say, I've never seen a meaner . . . more petty . . . spiteful . . . trivial . . . never seen a more puerile list of reasons for becoming so resentful of somebody. (*Pause.*) All my life, I've really had nothing to complain of. Money, success . . . what those numbrains call a firm and established place in the English Novel. Capital E capital N. (*Pause.*) Forty years or so of being a marxist without the unbearable problem of having to live in a so-called socialist society. (*Pause.*) What's been my ironic fate? To step off the plane in East Berlin, Prague, Warsaw, Budapest . . . and be whisked away to a large comfortable hotel . . . receptions . . . conferences. (*Pause.*) Not even guilt. (*Pause.*) All in all, a career to turn the stomach of a genuinely honest man. (*Pause.*) Someone like Sladek, for example.

He goes out of the lavatory.

35. *Interior. Corridor.*

Making his way back slowly and unsteadily to the dining room.

VOICE. In the circumstances . . . to feel the squirming desire for all this breast-beating . . . this . . . despicable . . . self-indulgent . . . whining (*Pause.*) Sladek would have smiled.

36. *Interior. Dining room.*

The door from the corridor opens. The dining room is dark – everyone is sitting motionless. KELVIN *gropes his way to his chair. Sitting down, he knocks over a glass of wine. As he sits, in a panic, the room is suddenly light again.*

Everyone is preparing to go. Laughing and talking, one by one they come and shake KELVIN'S *hand. We hear nothing. Finally, there are left:* BARBARA, HOLLAND, EMMA, KELVIN.

BARBARA. Can you manage him, Emma?

HOLLAND. Oh, Robert's all right! Aren't you, Robert?

KELVIN. Fine. Absolutely fine.

EMMA. We'll be all right.

BARBARA. It's been quite an evening. I can't see straight.

 BARBARA, HOLLAND, EMMA *go on chatting for a few moments. Silence.*

VOICE. You would have liked Charlie, Emma. He looked like . . . like a bald mole. (*Pause.*) I saw him in a café. Followed him to his flat in the rue de Seine. Knocked on the door. It's our Charlie, I said. It's our Robert, he said. (*Pause.*) The Arab boy made a pot of some sort of scented tea, and Charlie told me exactly what would happen in France during the next ten years. Most of it did happen. (*Pause.*) Why did you burn your father's leg, Charlie, I asked him? (*Pause.*) It was badly designed, he said. The ugliest wooden leg I've ever seen. (*Pause.*) Then he showed me his Fuseli drawings, and a little Miro he'd stolen from a queer in Zurich in nineteen twenty-eight. I have to be careful these days, Robert, he said. I have to be careful, because of my obscene condition.

   Close-up KELVIN.

37. *Stock film: repeat of Scene 14.*

The street of a northern or midlands mining village in the thirties. Unemployed miners lounge at doors, squat with their backs against walls.

38. *Interior. Dining room.*

BARBARA. Well, Robert – it's been super. And thank you. And I hope the book's a tremendous success –
   She shakes hands with KELVIN *and leaves.*

HOLLAND. Come on, old sport –

EMMA. Ralph – will you just leave us here?

HOLLAND. What? Oh – yes. I see. Yes. They'll call you a taxi. Yes. Well. Goodnight, my dear –

HOLLAND. 'Night, Robert. Bear up, eh? Ring you tomorrow –
   He goes out. KELVIN *doesn't move.* EMMA *begins a slow circling of the table, looking at him from time to time.*

EMMA. When you're ready –

KELVIN. Do you know what Charlie's 'obscene condition' was?

EMMA. What?

KELVIN. A side opening.

EMMA. *What?*

KELVIN. A side opening. Into the bowel.

EMMA. Oh.

KELVIN. Oh.

EMMA. I thought it was just a story.

KELVIN. Well – it was. In a way.

EMMA. How in a way?

KELVIN. It was the first part of the first draft of *Buster*.

EMMA. You mean Charlie never existed?

KELVIN. Charlie existed all right.

    Pause.

EMMA. I wish you'd come home, Robert –

    Pause.

KELVIN. I was very fond of Charlie.

    Pause.

EMMA. I'm going to have them call a taxi, Robert.

    She goes out. As she closes the door behind her, the room darkens.
    Faintly, the sound of 'The Internationale'.

39. Interior. Train

As before – but KELVIN *is wrapping a travelling rug round* JANE.
He makes her comfortable, and resumes his own seat.

KELVIN. That better?

JANE. Yes thanks.

KELVIN. The pain better?

JANE. It comes and goes. I'm O.K. just now.

KELVIN. I preserve you all intact, inside my head.

JANE. Preserve who?

KELVIN. You. Ruth. The children. Emma. (*Pause.*) I suppose you
    had the worst time of all.

JANE. Because I had this done?

KELVIN. Of course, I get confused now and then. My memory
    infuriates me . . . it slips and slides . . . I get the children mixed
    up . . . the holidays. (*Pause.*) I never wanted you to have this
    done.

JANE. I know. You think so. But you did. The most serious choices
    in your life have always been made by other people. (*She looks*
    at him.) You've never decided anything, have you? You've

always been overtaken by the consequences of leaving it to others –

KELVIN. I've been writing a journal for Emma. A journal . . . a letter . . . something of the kind.

JANE. To vindicate yourself?

Pause.

KELVIN. After that evening in Cambridge . . . I brought her back to London with me. And she simply – stayed. (*Pause.*) I love her. (*Pause.*) I need her. (*Pause.*) Yet I can't stand the sight of her. (*Pause.*) She stayed with me as if it were the most simple and obvious . . . and . . . *good* thing to do.

JANE. For you or her?

Pause.

KELVIN. I'm a bit . . . dazzled by that kind of simplicity. I couldn't possibly have sent her away . . . or provoked a break.

JANE *starts laughing.* KELVIN *stares at her – she goes on laughing.*

40. *Interior. Dining room.*

The door opens – EMMA *enters. The light fades up.*

EMMA. Will you come, Robert?

She waits at the door. He gets up and they go out together.

41. *Interior. Taxi.*

KELVIN'S *head is slumped forward on his chest.* EMMA *sits looking in front of her – she is holding his hand.*

Close-up KELVIN.

VOICE. What haunts me, Emma, is nothing more than . . . just the sheer . . . amount . . . of time. All that *time.* Years and years and years and years. (*Pause.*) I'm tired. (*Pause.*) Where am I going? (*Pause.*) Where?

42. *Stock film: repeat of Scene 14.*

The street of a northern or midlands mining village in the thirties. Unemployed miners lounge at doors, squat with their backs against walls.

43. *Interior. Taxi.*

KELVIN. I'm afraid, Emma. (*Pause.*) All I ever wanted you to understand . . . was . . . this . . . fear.
  Close-up EMMA. *Close-up* KELVIN.
VOICE. Sladek . . . disappeared, you know. He – disappeared. (*Pause.*) No one mentioned it.
KELVIN. In a truck . . . going up into the Sierra Maestra . . . the dusty road, winding round the mountain . . . an eagle . . . was it an eagle? Was it, Emma?
EMMA. I think it was an eagle. Yes.
  KELVIN *seems to go to sleep.*

44. *Interior. Room.*

The bare room with the straw – KELVIN *huddled in a corner with a blanket round him. His eyes are closed.*
KELVIN. Charlie was extravagant . . . preposterous . . . absurd . . . and yet . . . formidable. Go on, Charlie, burn that damned wooden leg. Burn it, burn it, burn it.

45. *Interior. Cheap photographer's studio : repeat of part of Scene 4.*

FATHER. What do we want to be doing this for? Bloody nonsense.
MOTHER. Nay, we want some pictures –

46. *Interior. Taxi.*
Close-up EMMA. *Close-up* KELVIN.

47. *Interior. Bedroom.*

KELVIN *is lying in bed,* EMMA *holding his hand. He has just died.* EMMA *puts his hands by his sides. There is a knock at the door.*

EMMA. Come in –

    HOLLAND *enters.*

HOLLAND. Emma.

    Pause.

EMMA. He died a moment ago.

    HOLLAND *crosses to the bed and looks down at* KELVIN. *He hands a book to Emma.*

HOLLAND. I brought an advance copy of his new book. (*Pause.*) I thought ?

EMMA. I wish he'd seen it.

    She turns the book over and over in her hands. The title: 'The Last Days of Buster Crook.'

HOLLAND. It was sudden, wasn't it?

EMMA. Yes.

HOLLAND. I'm sorry, Emma –

EMMA. I knew he was often in pain, but I could never quite accept that he was really ill.

HOLLAND. You know –

EMMA. What?

    Pause.

HOLLAND. I'd planned a bit of a celebration dinner. For the book. Next Wednesday evening. (*Pause.*) It's a pity.

EMMA. He would have hated it.

HOLLAND. Oh, I know. Yes. But he would have come. (*Pause.*) He'd have come . . . and bitched . . . and got drunk . . . but he could never resist a good dinner and the chance to show off a bit.

EMMA. Show off?

HOLLAND. You know what I mean. Play the irritable, exhausted old man. He liked people to indulge him in that one. (*Pause.*) He knew about the dinner. (*Pause.*) We always gave him a dinner on the eve of publication –

    Pause.

EMMA. He never mentioned it to me.

    She goes out. HOLLAND *follows her. Close-up* KELVIN.

The Cellar and the Almond Tree

The Cellar and the Almond Tree was first broadcast by BBC Television on 4 March 1970 with the following cast:

VOLUBIN	*Peter Vaughan*
COUNTESS ISABEL VON REGER	*Celia Johnson*
MARENKA	*Patsy Byrne*
BLAUSTEIN	*Sydney Tafler*
BERNARD	*Peter Jesson*
GESTAPO AGENT	*Jon Rollason*
PAVEL	*Leonard Cracknell*
ROBERT KELVIN	*Bernard Kay*
LITTLE GIRL	*Lysandre de-la-Hay*
MAN	*Gerald Case*
LITTLE BOY	*Richard Beaumont*
INTERROGATOR	*Godfrey James*

Directed by Alan Bridges

1. Exterior. The square of an old town in central Europe.

It is bordered by former eighteenth-century palaces – a vast cobbled expanse with modern asphalt roads crossing it.

A hazy distance of spires, cupolas: we might feel the square is on high ground, like the Hradčany in Prague. A detachment of motorized troops is grinding slowly through the square – light carriers, trucks, etc. The noise is deafening.

One side of the square is open, with a stone rampart overlooking the town. Here, we see a MAN (VOLUBIN) with a briefcase. He is leaning on the wall and looking out over the town, smoking. VOLUBIN is in his early fifties – a rather heavy, stern-looking man in a neat dark suit.

From VOLUBIN'S point of view the camera finds the tower of an ugly building – a prison or a barracks. Camera holds on the tower.

2. Interior. A cellar.

VOLUBIN is being coldly and systematically beaten by two men. The sound of trucks and carriers heard in Scene 1, is muted almost to silence, and we hear the loud crack of the MEN'S fists on VOLUBIN'S body. There are silences, heavy breathing. Finally VOLUBIN is swaying on his feet, and collapses.

3. Exterior. Square.

VOLUBIN throws away his cigarette, picks up his briefcase and crosses the square. On the far side, an archway leads into the courtyard of one of the palaces. Here there is a sentry. VOLUBIN shows a pass to the sentry and goes into the courtyard.

VOLUBIN stops a moment, looking round. He might be in the eighteenth century. Baroque façades, doorways, statues. Some of the statues have heads, arms, legs broken off. From one wall hangs a torn and filthy poster in some indecipherable language.

It is hot and sunny. Quiet. VOLUBIN looks up at the sky.

4. Interior. Corridor.

The beaten VOLUBIN, *half conscious and bloody, is being dragged along with his feet trailing by the two* MEN *from Scene 2.*

5. Exterior. Palace.

VOLUBIN *crosses the courtyard and enters a spacious doorway. On the threshold he hesitates and looks out and upwards again, up the façade across the square. We see the rows of windows on each floor of the palace.* VOLUBIN *goes in.*

6. Exterior. Window.

COUNTESS VON REGER'S *face. An old woman in her seventies: the face lined, gentle, vague – yet still handsome and strong, with a latent astuteness, a surviving 'hauteur'.*

7. Interior. Palace: an apartment.

COUNTESS VON REGER'S *drawing room is a timeless salon. Curtains, pictures, furniture, are eighteenth-century – tasteful, elegant, exquisite details. The stillness in the room, the figure of the* COUNTESS *at the window – all seem frozen, bound in a sombre desuetude. From the* COUNTESS'S *point of view – an almond tree in full blossom, a lovely tracery of branches and flowers. She raises her lorgnette: Beneath the tree we see* VOLUBIN *standing motionless, with his briefcase. She turns, as her servant,* MARENKA, *comes into the room.* MARENKA *is about thirty – a stocky, bustling, sensible woman. She sets down a tray with coffee.*

COUNTESS. Thank you, Marenka. (*Coming away from the window.*) The almond tree is lovely this year.

MARENKA. I'm busy.

COUNTESS. What a sullen child you are!

MARENKA. If you're not satisfied –

COUNTESS. Let's not bicker. Shall we?

MARENKA. That's hard work with you. Not bickering.

COUNTESS. *Do* look at the tree.

Pause.

MARENKA. What's the point of looking at what isn't there? I'd say that's definitely impossible. We've had it all out before. You look out the window you see God knows what. *I* look out the window I know what's there and I see what's there. Cobblestones. (*Pause.*) You want almond trees, you put my wages up. (*Pause.*) I was in the middle of skinning a rabbit when you asked for that coffee.

The COUNTESS *pours her coffee.*

COUNTESS. There was a man standing under the tree. A man with a briefcase.

MARENKA. Almond trees, briefcases . . . !

COUNTESS. I love the spring.

MARENKA. It's summer.

COUNTESS. I didn't recognize his face. I've never seen him before.

MARENKA. I'd call it lucky if you never saw him again. Or the bloody tree either.

8. Interior. Palace: wide, ornate staircase.

VOLUBIN *is mounting slowly to the first floor. On the landing, he stops. Two high, open doors are apart, giving on to a large gallery. VOLUBIN goes into the gallery, a long bare room with polished parquet floors and paintings lining the walls. He begins to wander round, looking at the paintings.*

9. Interior. Palace: apartment.

The COUNTESS *is drinking coffee and laying out a game of patience. She takes a Russian cigarette from a box and lights it.*

10. Exterior. A country avenue.

A dusty road, lined by trees. An open carriage, with COUNTESS VON

REGER *and a* LITTLE BOY. *She has a parasol open against the sun – she is smiling.*

A MAN *on horseback rides up beside the carriage. He is early middle aged, attractive, laughing. He leans from his horse.*

MAN. Isabel –

COUNTESS. Bernard –

MAN (*laughing*). Martin said a funny thing last night.

COUNTESS. How unlikely.

MAN. Now now. We were playing cards, you know. And he suddenly said – apropos the *defeat*. (*Pause.*) He said: the Von Regers have one root in Germany and one in Poland. But their bloody leaves wave about in the most extraordinary places!

COUNTESS. Leaves?

MAN. Yes, Isabel. Family trees. Leaves. Isabel *do* give me a little smile!

COUNTESS (*humourlessly*). Martin has never understood the difference between wit and mere facetiousness.

> *With a grimace, the* MAN *kicks his horse's flanks and gallops away.*

BOY. What defeat did he mean, mother?

> *Pause.*

COUNTESS. It's not important, my dear. It's something called the Treaty of Versailles. Would you like some turkish delight?

> *From the back, the carriage is now a diminishing, swaying shape going down the avenue.*

11. *Exterior. Palace : staircase.*

VOLUBIN *is mounting to the second floor. He is asthmatic and stops a moment, to lean against the wall. His breathing is hoarse and strained. The briefcase drops at his feet.*

12. *Interior. A cellar.*

VOLUBIN *lies battered and exhausted on a straw pallet. A* GESTAPO AGENT *in civilian clothes is let in by a* WARDER. VOLUBIN *eyes him. Says nothing. The* AGENT *goes to the barred window and looks out.*

AGENT. Well. Sladek?

VOLUBIN. Volubin.

> *Pause.*

AGENT. Whichever you prefer.

> *Pause.*

VOLUBIN. When's the murder? I mean, of course, the execution.

> *Pause.*

AGENT. There isn't going to be one. We're letting you out, Sladek.

VOLUBIN. I see. The Gestapo, in its boundless clemency. Etcetera etcetera.

AGENT. We shall all remember you for your delightful sarcasm, Sladek. (*Pause.*) Naturally, we'll kill you if you *insist.*

> *Close-up the* AGENT *smiling.*

13. Interior. Palace : staircase.

VOLUBIN *retrieves his briefcase and goes up the last few steps to the second landing.*

Here, large double doors are open wide on to a large room.

Inside, there is a U-shaped grouping of tables draped with white cloths. Two WAITERS *and a* WAITRESS *are desultorily moving about with plates, glasses etc.*

On the far wall, a huge banner from one side to the other with portraits of Marx, Lenin and Stalin.

There is a serving room off this main room, and the WAITERS *come and go. The* WAITRESS *begins to arrange flowers at intervals along the tables. The room has large high windows. By one of them stands a harassed-looking man dressed similarly to* VOLUBIN. *This is* BLAUSTEIN. VOLUBIN *enters and* BLAUSTEIN *turns to him in exasperation.*

BLAUSTEIN. Volubin! Where the hell have you been?

VOLUBIN. I'm sorry. My asthma –

> BLAUSTEIN *is not unsympathetic, but gestures rather wildly round the room.*

BLAUSTEIN. You have asthma. What have I got?

VOLUBIN. What *have* you got? .

> BLAUSTEIN *points to one of the chairs at the end of the U-shape.* VOLUBIN *gratefully sits down.* BLAUSTEIN *looks at him desperately.*

BLAUSTEIN. What haven't I got! If not having is trouble. Which it is. (*Pause.*) I don't know where to begin. (*Points up at the ceiling.*) I mean: shall we start with the trivial? Let's not strain the tendons of the mind. I mean: how does one refer to *her*? Tell me that.

VOLUBIN. The old lady?

BLAUSTEIN. Old lady! My friend, that is not exactly a form of address. *Old lady*? The phrase rests on its laurels as an inadequate description. Squeeze *your* imagination and what does it bring forth? A tame, limping *fact*!

VOLUBIN. I'm sorry, Tonda –

BLAUSTEIN. *Sorry* he is!

> Pause.

VOLUBIN. I'm sorry I'm sorry.

BLAUSTEIN. We should descend to bad jokes at this point?

> VOLUBIN *rests his arms on the table for a moment. Takes out a handkerchief and wipes his face.*

BLAUSTEIN. Look. Is it bad?

VOLUBIN. I'm all right.

> BLAUSTEIN *is really agitated and begins to walk up and down.*

BLAUSTEIN. Betrayal. Occupation. War. Resistance. Social democracy. *Revolution.* And where is Blaustein now? He is focusing his entire mental capacity on the following problem: how to refer to some doddering old aristocrat who's out of her wits! We sweep away titles? Fine. We give her a nice little apartment in the family palace? Fine. (*He jabs his finger upwards again.*) And *she*? Her desiccated brain is jammed around nineteen forty-three. Not so good. What is the Revolution? *Formalin?* (*Pause.*) I'm just a poor German Jew. A communist thirty years. I can wrap my tongue round the expression

'Comrade Countess' for example? We have logic for this kind
of outrage to semantics? (*Pause.*) Klement, I need a beer.

    He waves to one of the WAITERS *and asks for a beer.*

VOLUBIN. What about 'Madam'?

BLAUSTEIN. Klement, in this case *I'm* sorry. To you the problem
is delegated. As of now, comrade, *you* are liaison man between
us and her. (*A* WAITER *hands him a cold beer, which he puts to his
lips.*) She's probably anti-semitic anyway. (*Drinks.*) Did I tell
you *why*? No I didn't. It's the wine cellar.

VOLUBIN. She's anti-semitic because of the wine cellar?

    There is a long pause. BLAUSTEIN *looks at* VOLUBIN *despair-
ingly.*

BLAUSTEIN. I never liked your sense of humour.

VOLUBIN (*a little too quickly*). Neither did the Gestapo.

    BLAUSTEIN *turns away, drinking.*

BLAUSTEIN. Of course, in this country we never did have what
you might call an indigenous title system. But these Junkers!
(*Pause.*) Were the Von Regers Junkers? The word is too
emotive for a man like me. (*Rounding on* VOLUBIN.) La – shall
we use 'La'? La von Reger has the keys of the wine cellar.
Rationality being what it is, the wine is *in* the wine cellar. Ergo:
the City Committee, on the historic occasion of tonight's
dinner – wants its wine. We may not have nationalized the
Countess, but her property is – you will no doubt take the
dialectical point – her *booze*, is the property of the State. And
yum yum say I for one!

VOLUBIN. Tonda –

    BLAUSTEIN *turns back to him.*

BLAUSTEIN. I know I know. *I* don't like your sense of humour.
You don't like my tone. Huh?

VOLUBIN. Well I –

BLAUSTEIN. Frivolous. Isn't that it?

VOLUBIN (*sharply*). Yes.

    Pause.

BLAUSTEIN. Have a beer.

    Pause.

VOLUBIN. I think I will.

  BLAUSTEIN *waves at the same* WAITER.

BLAUSTEIN. I'm a caterer. Not a diplomat. (*Points out of the window.*) So you were out there in the woods bombing trains when I was in England baking good bread for the Anglo-Saxon war effort! *So?* These tragi-comedies, I know what it is. They've *corrupted* me. Huh? I'm a man of suspicious levity. (*The* WAITER *gives* VOLUBIN *a beer.*) All I can say is: food we have. Vodka we have. Flowers we have. (*Points.*) A nice red banner we have. (*Shouting.*) *And the wine is in the cellar and we haven't got the fucking keys!* (*Quiet and resigned.*) All this in the middle of a revolution. (*Pause.*) Lenin would have split a gut – why shouldn't I?

VOLUBIN. And did you split a gut those four years in the concentration camp before you came here? Before you went and baked all that English bread?

  VOLUBIN *sips his beer. The two men look at each other warily. A pause.*

BLAUSTEIN. Two Zen priests are going through a muddy village in pouring rain. A woman wishes to cross the street. One Zen priest picks her up and takes her over. He and his friend plod on through the rain. Two kilometres outside the village, the priest who carried the woman says: I put her down. Why are you still carrying her? (*Long pause.*) The Countess never goes out. She lives up there with a maid. I suggest you pay her a call.

  VOLUBIN *gets up, takes his briefcase and makes for the door.*
  BLAUSTEIN *calls out:*

BLAUSTEIN. Klement –

  VOLUBIN *turns.*

BLAUSTEIN. Watch out for the maid. She's a plain woman with a tongue like a rhino's horn.

  Pause.

VOLUBIN. And the Countess's tongue?

BLAUSTEIN. I should know about aristocrats?

  VOLUBIN *continues on through the doors and up the third staircase.*

14. Exterior. Almond tree.

The image of the almond tree dissolves into:

15. Interior. Palace: apartment.

The face of the COUNTESS, *still playing patience. She pulls negligently at a bell-rope beside her.* MARENKA *appears at the door.*

MARENKA. What now?

COUNTESS. Did I hear you say 'rabbit'?

    MARENKA *suddenly brings out one hand from behind her back: she is holding a skinned rabbit.*

MARENKA. That's it. Name of Anton. Could be a cat, though.

COUNTESS. And might one ask what poor dead Anton is *for*?

MARENKA. Supper.

    Pause.

COUNTESS. My brother-in-law. I refer to George von Reger. Manages to live very well in Berlin. War or no war.

    Pause.

MARENKA. It's peacetime.

COUNTESS (*vaguely*). George has, to my mind, an impeccable attitude towards the Nazis. He despises them without provoking them.

    Pause.

MARENKA. Your brother-in-law was killed in an air raid on Berlin.

COUNTESS. Whatever else may be the case, he is certainly not eating rabbit.

MARENKA. No, madam. He's *being* eaten. By the worms. And if that's all for the moment –

    Pause.

COUNTESS. I think I shall have an omelette. And a green salade. And perhaps – half a bottle of champagne.

MARENKA. No eggs.

COUNTESS. I suppose the English and the Americans have been bombing the chickens too.

MARENKA. There's just no eggs. Not today.

COUNTESS. For such an unsubtle person, Marenka, you have a remarkable facility for being enigmatic.

MARENKA. I don't *have* to go on working here, you know. This is a democratic people's republic. I could work in a factory. On the trams. You'd better watch out. I mean the trouble I went for to get skinny old Anton here. D'you realize that rabbit was hopping around my nephew's little hutch yesterday. (*Pause.*) Tears, tantrums, the lot we had. Unsubtle I may be, madam, but rabbit's in – eggs are out. Madam should remember we've expropriated the exploiting classes. What's more *I* think it's about time.

COUNTESS. What a lot of rubbish you do talk!

MARENKA. Thirty years off your back and you never know. Might be in a factory or hoeing turnips yourself. Want to be thankful they couldn't even get you down the bleeding stairs. (*As she exits.*) Wouldn't mind seeing *you* bent over a lathe! *Madam!*

16. *Interior. Palace : apartment.*

The door closes behind MARENKA. *The countess sits quietly, her hands folded in her lap.*

17. *Exterior. Country avenue.*

Repeat the shot from Scene 10, where BERNARD *gallops away from the carriage.*

18. *Interior. Palace : banqueting room.*

The room is where we saw VOLUBIN *and* BLAUSTEIN – *but it is empty. The tables are gone. Only a few dust-sheeted chairs remain. We close up on a big, glittering chandelier.*
Beneath it, the COUNTESS *is dancing with a young man :* PAVEL. *It is early summer and the large room is filled with light.*
The music they dance to is in the 1920's idiom.

After a moment they stop. The COUNTESS *leads* PAVEL *to the window.*

The almond tree.

COUNTESS. I planted that tree when I was four, Pavel.

PAVEL. When are you going to marry me, Isabel?

COUNTESS. Shush!

A long pause. PAVEL *is at the window looking at the tree.*

PAVEL. I think your son likes me.

COUNTESS. *I* don't like the set you're mixed up with. Bernard. Martin. Your gambling and all the rest of it.

PAVEL. Where *is* your son?

COUNTESS. He's at Laugstein, with George von Reger's boy. And George is another, by the way. What's the matter with you all? Ludendorff called the British soldiers 'lions led by donkeys'. I sometimes think you and your friends are fools led by hedonists. What if the communists win in Germany?

PAVEL (*wryly*). I never imagined you were so 'political', Isabel!

COUNTESS. I don't pretend to be. But my husband died fighting for the Austro-Hungarian Empire. One wonders what you and your friends will *live* fighting for.

PAVEL (*smiling*). My dear. We are now an independent social democracy. Let the lawyers and shopkeepers get on with the squalid business. One lives to amuse oneself, thank God.

Pause.

COUNTESS. I shall not marry you. And you know it.

Pause.

PAVEL (*looking round*). I like big houses in the summer. When everyone is away in the country. (*He laughs.*) I *like* the dust-sheets.

Laughing, PAVEL *takes her by the waist and dances her round the room in a circle. They stop by the window overlooking the almond tree.*

PAVEL (*looking out*). Now *why* should you plant a tree in the Von Regers' courtyard when you were such a little girl.

The COUNTESS *smiles, but to herself. She turns away. We close up to her face.*

COUNTESS. Perhaps I was already in love with Gunther von Reger when I was four –

Close-up a horned phonograph in a corner of the room: the 1920's music continues to blare out.

19. Interior. Palace: apartment.

The COUNTESS *is calling out:*
COUNTESS. Marenka –

20. Interior. Palace: staircase.

VOLUBIN *stands at the door to the* COUNTESS'S *apartment. He stops, turns away from the door and leans over the banister lighting a cigarette.*
A high shot from VOLUBIN'S *point of view to the bottom of the staircase.*

21. Interior. Cellar.

VOLUBIN, *now marked only by a strip of sticking plaster across his forehead, stands dressed in his own clothes ready to leave prison. A* WARDER *holds the cell door open.*
The 'Agent' from Scene 12 sits smoking on the bed.
AGENT. Dear me. You seem to have lost a little weight since we took your own clothes from you.
Pause.
VOLUBIN. Yes. I've been doing exercises.
Pause.
AGENT. Sladek –
VOLUBIN. Yes?
Pause.
AGENT. We expect one of two things. (*Pause.*) Either you will cease to be an active communist – and after all who cares what you are inside your head? (*Pause.*) Or you will . . . lead us somewhere. (*Pause.*) The first is unlikely. The second . . . well we nearly killed you and you told us nothing. Perhaps your

special combination of fanaticism and arrogance will result in a tiny slip one of these days. (*Pause: smiling.*) It's all just a nasty game. Isn't it? (*Pause.*) You're a professional. So am I. (*Pause.*) So they are in Moscow, I understand!

Without answering, VOLUBIN *leaves the cellar.*

22. *Interior. Palace: staircase.*

VOLUBIN *turns from the banister, to the apartment door. It is in a dim corridor. Beside the door there is a framed photograph.* VOLUBIN *looks at it: a family group of Czar Nicholas II, wife and children.* VOLUBIN *sniffs. He rings the door.* MARENKA *opens it. She stares at him: says nothing.*

VOLUBIN. I'd like to see Countess von Reger.

MARENKA. And who might you be?

    Pause.

VOLUBIN. Volubin. Secretariat. City Committee.

MARENKA. She's listening to her gramophone.

VOLUBIN. Er – I'm sorry?

MARENKA. I usually have to play her a record, about this time of the afternoon. Always the same one. But then it would be, wouldn't it?

    Pause.

VOLUBIN. Why would it?

MARENKA. I thought you'd know all about it. (*Sarcastically.*) Being one of *them*.

    She is holding the door only slightly ajar. VOLUBIN *examines his shoes.*

VOLUBIN. Do you think I might be allowed inside?

    She opens the door wider and gestures him into a large, gloomy hall. Points to a faded period straight-backed chair.

MARENKA. Nothing to stop you sitting there.

    VOLUBIN *sits, his briefcase on his knees.* MARENKA *looks down at him impassively.*

VOLUBIN. Can you tell me? I mean: *what* should I know all about?

MARENKA. Her. (*Thumbs at a door.*)
>   *Pause.*

VOLUBIN. Comrade – I know nothing about the Countess.
>   *Pause.*

MARENKA. If it's anything I can deal with. You'd better let me.

VOLUBIN. Why?

MARENKA. Well I'm no spiritualist. But she's you might say not of this world. And don't give *me* any funny looks, either! *My* father was killed before the Red Army got here. (*Pause.*) He was a garage mechanic. And he blew himself up trying to blow a German tank up. (*Pause.*) *There's* a heroic death for a man known to be good with his hands!

VOLUBIN. I'm sorry.

MARENKA. Everything has its comic side. (*She cocks her head, listening.*) Can you hear it? That's her record playing now –
>   VOLUBIN *listens. We hear a cracked old recording, the music from Scene 17.*

MARENKA. She's a bit gone in the head, see? Haven't you talked to Blaustein?

VOLUBIN. Well I did. Yes.
>   *Pause.*

MARENKA. Stuck at nineteen forty-three, she is. (*Pause.*) Or forty-four. (*Pause.*) Rich memories, some people have. Me, I was scrubbing floors and making soup in nineteen forty-three. What am I doing now? Scrubbing floors and making soup. (*Pause.*) Being a party man, you'll gather I've got my class-conscious side accordingly. (*Pause.*) I actually *voted* communist. *Before* you and your friends decided to pull a fast one on the government. (*Exiting.*) Put *that* in your *Pravda* and smoke it.
>   MARENKA *disappears into the gloom and through a far door.*
>   VOLUBIN *is left self-consciously perched on his chair.*
>   *The music continues, but finally grinds to a halt.*
>   MARENKA *reappears, on her way to the salon.*

MARENKA. If I get you in – you're on your own.
>   *She goes into the salon and reappears a moment later.*

MARENKA. Come on, then –

VOLUBIN *gets up and makes for the salon door. As he is about to go through:*

MARENKA. Well as Marx said: history is conflict. I expect that's why you're down there with the Wiener schnitzel and vodka, and we're up here with the jugged rabbit. I suppose you're after the wine cellar keys?

VOLUBIN. I am, as a matter of fact.

MARENKA (*grinning maliciously*). You're not the first, either.

23. Interior. Palace: apartment.

MARENKA *precedes a bewildered and unsettled* VOLUBIN *into the* COUNTESS'S *salon.*

MARENKA. Comrade Volubin, Madam –

    And she exits rapidly.

    The COUNTESS *is standing by the old gramophone we saw in Scene 17.*

    She turns to VOLUBIN, *smiling graciously.*

COUNTESS. My dear Volubin! Safe and sound. Back from the front. The Ukraine, was it?

    Pause.

VOLUBIN. Countess, there seems to be a mis –

COUNTESS. Has Marenka given you something to eat? A glass of vodka?

VOLUBIN. Er –

COUNTESS. You can't imagine what it is like managing without a butler. But these are confusing times. One loathes the Nazis, at the same time one loathes the Bolsheviks even more. As a patriot, I doubt your poor mind knows *where* to put itself. I imagine technically you are a collaborator. As far as I'm concerned, you are our dear Volubin – and the finest butler this house has known since nineteen twenty-six. Mind you, your predecessor was excellent too. But then he was English. (*Pause.*) I hope you are being careful, dear man?

VOLUBIN. Careful?

COUNTESS. Do sit down. Do, please. In wartime, one tries to be flexible. You are puffing and wheezing. Have you been ill? Or is it the stairs? *I* never go out any more.

> *Rather overcome,* VOLUBIN *sits down almost involuntarily.*

COUNTESS. Marenka shall bring you some tea. (*She pulls the bell rope.*) She's getting quite insolent. As soon as the war is over, she'll have to go.

VOLUBIN. I –

COUNTESS. Why, for instance, did she refer to you as 'comrade'? Isn't that somewhat quaint? (*Pause.*) Or is it sinister?

VOLUBIN. I –

COUNTESS. Do you see what I mean? Half the time when I ring the bell she doesn't answer. (*Going to the door.*) The surly chit.

> *The door closes behind her.* VOLUBIN *gets up, looking round the room. He goes to the window and stands looking out.*

24. Interior. Cellar.

The cellar exactly as vacated by VOLUBIN *in Scene 20. The* GESTAPO AGENT *sits on* VOLUBIN'S *bed smoking. The cellar door is open.*

25. Interior. Palace : apartment.

Close-up VOLUBIN'S *face as he looks out. The* COUNTESS *enters, surprisingly agile for her age. She smiles to see him at the window.*

COUNTESS. Nature refreshes at all times, does it not, Volubin?

VOLUBIN. Nature?

COUNTESS. I planted that tree myself, you know. Well of course you know. Marenka plays a nasty little game with me. She pretends it isn't there.

> VOLUBIN *stands looking into the old woman's serene face.*

VOLUBIN. It's . . . beautiful.

COUNTESS. As I remember, you were brought up in the country yourself. Now. You shall have your tea. And you shall tell me *everything.*

> *Pause.*

VOLUBIN. I'm authorized by the City Committee to –

MARENKA *comes sullenly in with tea. This preoccupies the* COUNTESS *at once. She waves* MARENKA *out of the room and busies herself with the tea things.*

COUNTESS. What Committee?

VOLUBIN. I am not your butler, Countess von Reger.

COUNTESS. You see? Marenka actually procured me a lemon this morning. (*Waves the lemon.*) Wasn't that a triumph?

VOLUBIN. I saw some in the market. I nearly bought one. (*Pause.*) I live alone. (*Pause.*) I like to slice the lemon very thin. Then hold it down in the glass with a spoon. And watch the colour of the tea change. (*Pause.*) That clear honey colour you get. Round the piece of lemon.

The COUNTESS *has listened distractedly. Now she snorts.*

COUNTESS. Yes. And since Marenka has not deigned to slice this one, I shall do so myself.

VOLUBIN *watches her take a thin sharp silver knife from a saucer on the tray, and begin to slice the lemon.*

26. *Interior. A café.*

A hand is pushing a spoon down on to a slice of lemon in a glass of tea. We see VOLUBIN *sitting alone at the table.*

Close-up the tea glass.

A copy of 'The Times' drops on to the table beside the glass. We hear a voice (an English writer: ROBERT KELVIN*) say:*

KELVIN. Sladek!

VOLUBIN *looks up startled. Then he smiles. He springs to his feet and the two men put their arms round each other, touching cheeks.*

VOLUBIN. Robert Kelvin –

They both sit down.

KELVIN. There was one of those bloody silly conferences in Moscow. I thought: stop off and see Sladek on the way home. (*Pause.*) I arrived yesterday evening and I've rung you about a dozen times.

There is a long silence. VOLUBIN *is looking towards the café door. Two* WEHRMACHT OFFICERS *come in and go to a table.*

VOLUBIN (*quietly*). I haven't been at home.

KELVIN *sits looking at the two* GERMANS *for a moment.*

KELVIN (*quietly*). Well. For you the war's started –

VOLUBIN. Yes. (*Pause.*) Next, they'll go into Poland. Then maybe you and the French will wake up. (*Pause.*) And whilst you are all rubbing your eyes, Comrade Stalin will do a deal with these bastards.

KELVIN *knows this is unanswerable. He fiddles with the newspaper.*

KELVIN. Where've you been?

VOLUBIN. The Gestapo treated me to a little holiday. (*Pause.*) It was painful for two or three days. Then they stopped.

KELVIN. I couldn't stand torture. I'd tell them any bloody thing they wanted to know as soon as they breathed on me.

Pause.

VOLUBIN. You know what's really going on in Moscow?

Pause.

KELVIN. Yes.

Pause.

VOLUBIN. I was going to offer you some tea. But you generally . . . stick to alcohol. Don't you?

KELVIN. I'll have a slivovitz.

VOLUBIN *beckons a* WAITER *and orders. Their voices are a murmur – we are close up on* KELVIN'S *face.*

VOLUBIN. Well. Did they put the red carpet down for you in Moscow?

KELVIN. More or less.

VOLUBIN (*drily*). That's the only red thing left in the Soviet Union: the carpet they roll under the feet of their guests from abroad.

KELVIN. I can see torture must make people self-righteous, if nothing else! (*Pause:* VOLUBIN *is looking at him stonily.*) I'm sorry.

VOLUBIN. But you are right!

KELVIN. I'm *bored* with feeling guilty.

VOLUBIN. Blaustein's family got him released from the concentration camp. I should think he's on his way to London.

KELVIN. What are you going to do?

27. *Interior. Palace : apartment.*

Close-up on VOLUBIN *sipping his lemon tea. The* COUNTESS *watches him smiling.* MARENKA *stands over them.*

COUNTESS. This is the man I told you I saw under the tree, Marenka. So there. What about that?

MARENKA. Only one thing wrong with that.

COUNTESS. What?

MARENKA. You said you didn't recognize the man under the tree. Now you say *he* (*Points at* VOLUBIN) used to be your butler.
    Pause.

COUNTESS. At my age, one's eyesight –
    MARENKA *rounds on* VOLUBIN.

MARENKA. You see our pretty almond tree when you came through the courtyard?
    Close-up the COUNTESS'S *hands : she has them both clasped round her tea glass. She is trembling.*

28. *Exterior. A large formal garden.*

A SMALL GIRL *of four stands holding a gardening trowel. She has dug a hole and is looking up at a* MAN *who is holding a small sapling. He is dressed expensively in the fashionable style of the late nineteenth century, and is smiling at her.*

GIRL. Will it grow high?

MAN. Very high.

GIRL (*pointing into the distance*). Higher than Laugstein?

MAN (*laughing*). Maybe not quite so high.

GIRL. And it'll never die?
    Pause.

MAN. Never.

Laughing, she takes the sapling from him, puts it in the hole and begins to pack the earth back round it.

29. *Interior. Palace : apartment.*

MARENKA *has gone. The* COUNTESS *is still holding her glass in both hands.*

COUNTESS. Volubin. Will you play my record again? Please?
> VOLUBIN *hesitates. Then he goes to the gramophone and winds it up. Sets the needle on the record. He stands beside the gramophone as it plays.*

30. *Interior. Palace : banqueting room.*

The tables are laid for the dinner. The WAITERS *and* WAITRESS *stand in a row.*
BLAUSTEIN *moves round the tables, adjusting a plate here, a bowl of flowers there.*
The WAITERS *watch him in silence. Finally he goes to them and inspects them, walking slowly down the little row of people.*
BLAUSTEIN. Could be worse. Could be better. Hands, please?
> *They put out their hands for inspection.*
> *Satisfied,* BLAUSTEIN *looks benignly from one end of the row to the other.*

BLAUSTEIN. In the army. I speak of bourgeois times, let it be said. Men have been known to spit under an officer's fried egg. Before placing it under the Imperial nose. (*Pause.*) Now I – a graduate Doctor of Law at Cracow University – I have often meditated upon such things. (*Pause.*) How does a Doctor of Law become a catering functionary? You might well ask. The road is long and difficult. (*Pause.*) I wish to make the point that there is no task so humble that the Revolution does not bestow on it its true social worth. (*Pause.*) Tonight we celebrate our liberation by the Red Army. (*Pause.*) If I omit to say: the 'glorious' Red Army this is not because I am lacking in zeal. It merely expresses a wholly personal distaste for the overworked adjective. (*Pause.*) That is what is known as subjectivism. (*Pause.*) Subjectivism is, ideologically speaking, a kind of sin. (*Pause : shouts.*) SINFUL BLAUSTEIN EXPECTS PERFECT SERVICE FROM EACH AND EVERY ONE OF YOU TONIGHT! (*Pause : quietly.*) Right. Blaustein does not wish to depart this world via a coronary thrombosis brought on by the ineptitude of a Comrade Waiter. You catch my drift?

WAITERS (*together*). Yes, Comrade.

    Pause.

BLAUSTEIN. In the immortal words of those who served under General Eisenhower: O.K. you guys.

    The WAITERS *trail off to the serving room.* BLAUSTEIN *lights a cigar and stands surveying the tables.*

BLAUSTEIN (*meditatively*). Avant la purge – c'est moi!

    He turns to the red banner, and gently puffs smoke rings in the direction of Marx, Lenin and Stalin.

31. Exterior. A wire fence.

Beyond the fence stands BLAUSTEIN, *dressed in the pyjama-like striped uniform of a prisoner. He stares bleakly into the camera.*

32. Interior. Palace : apartment.

VOLUBIN *is once more by the window. The* COUNTESS *sips her tea. The music plays. Close-up* VOLUBIN.

33. Interior. Café

As in Scene 25. KELVIN *is drinking his slivovitz.*

VOLUBIN. I'm not getting out. If that's what you mean –

    Pause.

KELVIN. I shouldn't think you're very popular in the party. (*Pause.*) They must think it's a pity the fascists didn't get you in Spain. That would have been convenient.

VOLUBIN. Yes. Also, much more romantic to go like some of yours! Like –

KELVIN (*cutting in*). John Cornford. Julian Bell –
> *Pause.*

VOLUBIN. Yes. Like them.
> *Pause.*

VOLUBIN. I don't write poetry any more. (*Pause.*) I wonder if I shall again? If I survive what's coming. (*Pause.*) I'm sorry, but it makes me angry to sit here talking to you.

> *There is a long silence. We cut backwards and forwards between* VOLUBIN'S *and* KELVIN'S *faces.*

34. Interior. Palace: apartment.

The gramophone is grinding at the end of the record. VOLUBIN *lifts it off.*

COUNTESS. Will you come back to us after the war?

35. Interior. Café.

The scene is where we left it in 32. But VOLUBIN'S *eyes are on the* GERMANS' *jackboots under the table where they are sitting. Pan up from the boots to one chair where there is a Wehrmacht officer's hat. Another chair at the same table: another hat.*

We follow the two OFFICERS *eating, from* VOLUBIN'S *point of view. Whilst this is going on we hear the* COUNTESS'S *voice over.*

COUNTESS. The Germans have been very polite. I've dined several high-ranking officers here from Berlin. (*Pause.*) I was only nineteen when the first war broke out. (*Pause.*) We all thought George von Reger was so brave and outrageous . . . we thought he wouldn't live through it. (*Pause.*) But it was George who lived. And my poor Gunther who got killed. (*Pause.*) Since the Russians took Poland this time, I haven't heard from my own family. (*Pause.*) Family connections do cut across the intricacies of wartime alliances, don't they? (*Pause.*) The English must feel the same way

about their monarchy. (*Pause.*)
It can't be true . . . what they
say about the Nazis . . . and
these camps. Can it? (*Pause.*) I
once met Scott Fitzgerald.
(*Pause.*) I suppose you wouldn't
know about him. He drank too
much – and he was a wonderful
man. (*Pause.*) Those summers
in the south of France –

36. Interior. Palace : apartment.

Close up VOLUBIN'S *face. The* COUNTESS *is smiling to herself abstractedly.*

VOLUBIN. It's two years since the Revolution. This palace was
requisitioned. You are fortunate – you were allowed to keep this
apartment. (*Pause.*) I am, as I said, from the Secretariat. I am
empowered to demand the keys to the cellars.

COUNTESS. My dear Volubin –
    Pause.

VOLUBIN. I appreciate . . . I think I understand what you . . . I
understand your confusion. (*Pause.*) But I must have those
keys.

COUNTESS. Of course, it wasn't easy bringing up my son without
his father. (*Pause.*) I was so young when he was born.
    Pause.

VOLUBIN. I have no children –

COUNTESS. I was grief-stricken. Anxious. I didn't trust the
nurses, the tutors. And I didn't trust myself either. (*Pause.*)
My son was . . . it turned out . . . delicate.
    Pause.

VOLUBIN. Going back to what you said about the Russians
taking Poland. 'This time', you said. And I suppose you mean
nineteen thirty-nine.
    Pause.

COUNTESS. Delicate! Surrounded by men coming and going who knew nothing but what was *physical*. (*Pause.*) Fencing. Hunting. (*Pause.*) Always shooting things. (*Pause.*) I remember the heaps. The piles. Of bloodstained animals and birds. (*Pause.*) Their glazed eyes. And mauled feathers.
    Pause.

VOLUBIN. The Soviet Union did not exactly 'take' Poland. (*Pause.*) History is a butcher. But who ever carved up more nations than families like yours?
    Pause.

COUNTESS. I think he was always frightened –
    Pause.

VOLUBIN. Your son –

COUNTESS. Not like George von Reger's boy. (*Pause.*) I think his way was to *imitate* his father.
    VOLUBIN *crosses to the table and lifts his tea glass. Close-up his face.*

37. *Interior. Café.*

As in Scene 34. KELVIN *looks hurt.*

KELVIN. Angry? I make you angry?
    Pause.

VOLUBIN. It's not you, Robert. No. (*Pause.*) The trouble is, I'm tired. (*Pause.*) All the worst is still to come. And I'm tired *now*.
    VOLUBIN *looks across at the* GERMAN OFFICERS.
Look at them. (*Pause : he smiles.*) Can you imagine them in a London pub? (*Pause.*) Isn't it . . . inconceivable.
    Pause.

KELVIN. Yes.
    Pause.

VOLUBIN. But all the same you know it's possible. And you know when they move the next time – they'll take Europe. (*Pause.*) They'll occupy the French coastline. And there'll only be that absurd ditch between you and them, Robert.
    Pause.

KELVIN. Stalin has virtually destroyed the Revolution. But he might save the Soviet Union.

VOLUBIN. If the Americans come out of their kennel! (*Pause.*) I'm sorry. I really can't talk about anything just now. (*Pause.*) Sitting here talking to you . . . What do you want? To talk about the Moscow Trials? Trotsky? (*Pause.*) I'm one of your favourite luxuries, Robert. (*Laughs.*) You have a peculiarly false admiration for me. I think I must reassure you. (*Pause.*) You assume another war . . . the Germans will lose . . . and there will be more revolution. Either because we take the people with us, or the Red Army puts a line as far West as Stalin can reach. (*Pause.*) And when one or the other happens, you'll feel better for knowing that there will be a few thousand like me. (*Pause.*) On the other hand, you know what will probably happen to us too – eventually. (*Pause.*) Never mind. You'll still be on the other side of the ditch! (*Pause.*) Over there, where no one will ever make a distinction between what you are talking about and what *happened* in the Soviet Union. Mon pauvre Robert! I should think none the less you're in for a great big fat literary honour one day. (*Pause.*) Anyway, your writing deserves it. (*Pause.*) If there must be prizes –

KELVIN. I can't stomach those silly euphemisms you go in for! The Gestapo 'treated you to a little holiday'! And: 'It was painful for two or three days'! You deprecate something vile so as to invite pity. That's what you do *really* –
    Pause.

VOLUBIN. It was only a feeble joke. I was trying to parody the 'English style'. And I thought you might find that amusing.
    Pause.

KELVIN. I was going to ask you about Katie –
    Pause.

VOLUBIN. She is dead. (*Pause.*) That was my last poem: after Katie.
    Pause.

KELVIN. Here?
    Pause.

VOLUBIN. No. (*Pause.*) In Moscow. (*Pause.*) Or wherever they took her. (*Pause.*) I wrote a poem about her and me here. On one of the river steamers. (*Pause.*) She wore a green and white striped dress. And she leaned against the rail of the boat. (*Pause.*) People were laughing and drinking. (*Pause.*) She took my face between her hands and kissed me. And smiled. And said with that sweet irony of hers: I think you're turning into a Trotskyite fascist. (*Pause.*) And kissed me again. (*Pause.*) We'd been eating sausages with mustard. And I tasted the mustard on her mouth. (*Pause.*) We both laughed. (*Pause.*) She went to the Soviet Union. I assume she must have done or said *something* over-impetuous. (*Pause.*) All the same. I don't envy her interrogator whoever he was. (*Pause.*) She was fiendishly clever. And funny. (*Pause.*) And before she went too far with him, I'll bet the bastard took a few permanent psychic wounds!

    Pause.

KELVIN (*softly*). Katie!

VOLUBIN. I miss her so much that I think my very capacity for love is rotting.

KELVIN. Can I see the poem?

VOLUBIN. Oh, I did one of those stupid things. Like an adolescent. I wrote it. Then I walked out one night. On to one of the bridges over the river. (*Pause.*) And crumpled the sheet of paper. (*Pause.*) And threw it into the river. (*He laughs.*) I wonder what Mayakovsky would have done?

    Pause.

KELVIN. Poor Katie –

38. Exterior. The almond tree.

VOLUBIN *stands beneath it with his briefcase.*

39. Interior. Palace : apartment.

Close-up the COUNTESS'S *face. Close-up* VOLUBIN'S *face. He looks towards the window.*

40. Interior. Cellar.

As before, but it is now empty. Camera explores it a little.
We hear brass band music, Czech style. Glasses are clinking. Voices and laughter. These sounds fade. KATIE'S *voice is heard over.*

KATIE'S VOICE. I think you're turning into a Trotskyite fascist! (*She laughs, then we hear* VOLUBIN'S *laugh.*) I can taste mustard on your mouth. (*Pause.*) Nice. (*Pause.*) My love –
    The brass band music and other sounds fade up again.

41. Interior. Palace: apartment.

VOLUBIN *is looking closely at the* COUNTESS. *She is not looking at him. There is a long silence.*

VOLUBIN. You shelter. (*Pause.*) You hide. (*Pause.*) Because your thoughts are the only privileges left to you. (*Pause.*) Old people should have some privileges. (*Pause.*) So you wander. (*Pause.*) But. (*Pause.*) You might be playing with me. You might.

COUNTESS. When will it all be over? When will you come back? (*Pause.*) Or shall I die first? (*Pause.*) I would like everything . . . to be . . . as it was. (*Pause.*) Before this terrible war.

VOLUBIN. Go outside. Look. (*Pause.*) Listen. (*Pause.*) Let the truth into your mind. (*Pause.*) I've no wish to probe. To hurt.
    Pause.

COUNTESS. Do you remember when we used to pack up every summer? Everything. (*Pause.*) Dust sheets on the furniture. (*Pause.*) Everything. (*Pause.*) And we went . . . servants and all . . . to Krejczyn. Or to Laugstein. (*Pause.*) So much fuss. And noise. And packing. And girls giggling.
    Pause.

VOLUBIN. The keys –
    Pause.

COUNTESS. Did you like Krejczyn best? Or Laugstein. (*Pause.*) George's poor wife! That poor woman! She busied herself with such *small* things. (*Pause.*) My boy refused to try to ride when

George von Reger was there. You see George laughed at him. (*Pause.*) It wounded my son. (*Pause.*) It hurt me. (*Pause.*) And he always made the children drink champagne. He put the glasses in their little hands. He stood there smoking those long thin cigars of his. 'Let the bubbles go up your noses,' he used to shout. 'Go on! Go on!' (*Pause.*) Then he'd vanish to Berlin. Sometimes in the middle of the night. (*Pause.*) I wonder what it was the children adored about George? (*Pause.*) These *physical* men. These arrogant men. (*Pause.*) These men who behave exactly as they wish, and indeed thrive on scandal. As he did. (*Pause.*) What? How? How is it that . . . such men . . . can ignore the pain around them. (*Pause.*) In their women. (*Pause.*) Whilst my Gunther. Who was so gentle. So charmingly correct. So touchingly formal. (*Pause.*) Seemed dull, to others. (*Pause.*) Why are the qualities of restraint and responsibility something to be sneered at by men like George?

> *Pause.* VOLUBIN *is suddenly almost convulsed. He shouts:*

VOLUBIN. We have put an end to all their nonsense. All of it!

> *Long pause. The* COUNTESS *seems not to have heard.*

I am *not* your servant!

> *Close-up the* COUNTESS *watching him serenely.*

42. *Exterior. A large open window : country house.*

The window is open. Within, gauze curtains billow and sway – we see only the curtains.
Inside the room, someone is playing a piano softly.

43. *Exterior. A paddock.*

The music from Scene 42 is heard throughout this scene.
Countess von Reger's SON *is timidly astride a horse. The* COUNTESS *holds a training rein : the horse moves slowly in a circle round her. She is in a summer dress, smiling. The* BOY'S *face is clenched: he is making a big effort to control his fear of being on the horse.*
(Music : Schumann or Des Abends.)

44. Interior. Palace: apartment.

VOLUBIN, *self-conscious about his outburst, stands breathing heavily. Close-up his face.*

45. Interior. Cellar.

As in Scene 2, except that we cut in the COUNTESS'S *face and the music from Scene 42 several times.*

46. Interior. Palace: apartment.

VOLUBIN *is calm now. The* COUNTESS *goes to the window.*
COUNTESS. The tree was planted. Of that I am certain. (*Pause.*) But then how –? (*Pause.*) Did we bring it here? From Laugstein? Or could it have been Krejczyn? (*Pause.*) Somebody's whim. Indulging me. (*Pause.*) It must have been from Laugstein. Because I remember George's father standing over me as I put it into the ground. (*Pause.*) He was wearing city clothes. (*Pause.*) He had just arrived from Berlin. (*Pause.*) That's right. I remember. The carriage brought him from the station. There were servants. (*Pause.*) I was standing in front of the house in white stockings and a little blue dress. (*Pause.*) He got down from the carriage. He had a kind of parcel. He came up to me smiling and said: Isabel! You are here for the summer again? And I was tongue-tied. And he led me into the house and showed me what was in the parcel. (*Pause.*) A little tree!

47. Exterior. Large formal garden.

Repeat Scene 28. A small GIRL *of four stands holding a gardening trowel. She has dug a hole and is looking at a* MAN *who is holding a small sapling. He is dressed expensively in the fashionable style of the late nineteenth century and is smiling at her.*

48. Interior. Palace: apartment.

VOLUBIN *sits slumped in a chair. The* COUNTESS *is still at the window with her back to him.*

49. Interior. Corridor.

Repeat Scene 4: The beaten VOLUBIN, *half conscious and bloody, is being dragged along with his feet trailing by the two* MEN. *Over, we hear* KATIE'S *voice repeated from Scene 40.*

KATIE'S VOICE. I can taste mustard on your mouth. (*Pause.*) Nice. (*Pause.*) My love –

50. Interior. Palace: apartment.

VOLUBIN. Has nothing touched you? Nothing but your own life? Those houses in Poland and Germany. (*Pause.*) Laugstein. (*Pause.*) Krejcyn. (*Pause.*) And of course . . . *this* house! (*Pause.*) I wonder what kind of a resistance fighter a butler would have made? (*Pause.*) As good, or bad, or mediocre as . . . any other man.

There is a long silence. Now VOLUBIN *too goes into a reverie.* I have a room in the house of a film director. We knew each other before. (*Pause.*) He was in our air force in England during the war. (*Pause.*) I haven't much. (*Pause.*) Haven't much by way of things, I mean. (*Pause.*) A few books. (*Pause.*) We all have to work so hard. And there's such a . . . such a muddle. (*Pause.*) That's why, I think, I mentioned the market. Because I like to walk through it on my way here. When I get off the tram. (*Pause.*) Because when they've come in from the country with something . . . a few apples . . . carrots . . . I don't know what. (*Pause.*) I like to walk through it. And today, as I said. (*Pause.*) It was lemons. (*Pause.*) Lemons where from? (*Pause.*) A miracle! (*Pause.*) From Georgia maybe? A few got here by mistake? (*Pause.*) Miraculous lemons. (*Pause.*) Poets have often written about fruit. (*Pause.*) Neruda. (*Pause.*) You won't have read Neruda. (*Pause.*) No. (*Pause.*) I wish the young could grow up very quickly – and throw us out! (*Pause.*) But who wants to wish anyone's youth away? (*Pause.*) And if they did . . . some of us . . . would crush them like insects. (*Pause.*) Do you hear me, Countess? (*Pause.*) I know I am a bitter man. (*Pause.*) It shows through.

COUNTESS (*turning*). *I* remember when you broke something. What was it? Something quite valuable. (*Pause.*) Those ivory statues of my husbands. (*Pause.*) Chinese? (*Pause.*) Japanese? (*Pause.*) I never cared for ivory. But I rebuked you. (*Pause.*) I distinctly remember that. (*Pause.*) And I felt guilty afterwards. I'm sure it wasn't your fault. (*Pause.*) I rebuked you unjustly, and I am sorry. (*Pause: she comes and sits near him.*) But why was I unjust? What was it about? (*Pause.*) One so often takes one's feelings out on servants. (*Pause.*) And they are defenceless. (*Pause.*) And it is dishonourable for a master or mistress to do such things. (*Pause.*) Although we are human. We are human too. Isn't it funny? Because servants nearly always throw *that* in one's face! I'm only human, they say. (*Pause: she smiles.*) Master and servant: perpetually asserting how human they are. (*Pause.*) A glass. A dish. Something spilt. Something forgotten. (*Pause.*) A guest neglected over some small touch of attentiveness. (*Pause.*) The brutalities of domestic relationships mirror, perhaps, our larger feelings. (*Pause.*) But how often do we notice that? Think of it?

Long pause.

VOLUBIN. How can I break into your mind? (*Pause.*) Not break in. No. I didn't mean that. Not *break.* (*Pause.*) But how can I . . . since I am not whoever he was. How can I . . . where do we . . . what do we? How *begin?* (*Pause.*) Or else I shall pick up the phone. The police will arrive. (*Pause.*) You will be ignored. (*Pause.*) I wish you weren't as you are. I think you'd be amused. (*Pause.*) Then *I* could be amused.

He crosses to the window as the COUNTESS sits down.

51. *Interior. Cellar.*

As in Scene 12, VOLUBIN lies battered and bruised in the cell. But the GESTAPO AGENT *has not come in –* VOLUBIN *is alone.*

52. *Interior. Palace : apartment.*

Close-up VOLUBIN'S *face.*

53. Interior. Café.

Following on from Scene 37.

Repeat KELVIN'S *last line of dialogue:*

KELVIN. Poor Katie –

> *The* WEHRMACHT OFFICERS *get up and leave. There is a silence between* KELVIN *and* VOLUBIN.

KELVIN. The capacity for love? Rotting? Now who's the romantic?

> *Pause.*

VOLUBIN. *You* go through women like a terrier hunting rats in a barn. You sink your teeth into their necks. Toss them in the air. And then you're barking and pawing about in the next heap of straw!

> *Pause.*

KELVIN. I do?

> *Pause.*

VOLUBIN. A well-known novelist. Something of a public fellow-traveller. (*Pause.*) A drinker. (*Pause.*) A great bull for causes. (*Pause.*) The image is so potently stereotyped that I should think many women find it irresistible. (*Pause.*) Spine-snapping and all.

> *Pause.*

KELVIN. When they *possess* spines!

> *Pause.*

VOLUBIN. I'm very fond of you, Robert.

KELVIN. And I you.

> *Pause.*

VOLUBIN. Do you pick on spineless women? Whatever you mean by the word.

> KELVIN *sips his slivovitz. He is both tender and irritated.*

KELVIN. The aforementioned stereotype has a distinguished ancestry.

> *Pause.*

VOLUBIN (*tiredly*). Don't *bother* to talk to me like that, Robert.

(*Pause.*) Not when I've known several of your women. (*Pause.*)
Wives. Mistresses. (*Pause.*) I'm afraid I must leave in a moment. (*Pause.*) There's never any point is there? In saying to
someone: don't drink so much. Is there?

KELVIN. My dear Klement Sladek – *no*!

> Pause.

VOLUBIN (*smiling*). I have two names now. Sladek – my very own.
And Volubin. (*Pause.*) For reasons you will understand. (*Pause.*)
And the Gestapo knows my – what do you call it? – my double
barrel.

KELVIN. Third name lucky. I hope.

> Pause.

VOLUBIN. I hope (*Pause.*) And I apologize for the . . . euphemisms
about the Gestapo. (*Pause.*) I've little tolerance for pain. And it
was very bad. (*Pause.*) I simply didn't know the things they
wanted to know. (*Pause.*) They realized that. Which is why I am
free. (*Pause.*) Free. (*He laughs.*)

54. Interior. Palace: apartment.

Close-up on the COUNTESS'S *face, again through the image of the
almond tree.*

COUNTESS. Amused? (*Pause.*) I am *bemused*!

> VOLUBIN *takes a step back from the window, still looking out.*

VOLUBIN. Out there. Our country is . . . can one reasonably
speak of *your* country? (*Pause.*) The country is in the hands of
the Communist Party. (*Pause.*) In effect. (*Pause.*) There is a
revolution, Madam. (*Pause.*) Can you imagine the turmoil?
(*Pause.*) Whilst you continue to live. Up here. At the top of your
palace. (*Pause.*) Because some very decent man or other per-
suaded some overworked committee to deal with the tiny problem of *you* . . . in a humane fashion. (*Pause.*) You look strong.
(*Pause.*) I should think you might still be alive up here turning
over your memories when good, innocent communists . . . are
beginning to be arrested. (*Pause.*) Because so far, that is the
logic of revolutions.

Close-up the COUNTESS'S *face.* MARENKA *enters. Somewhat gloatingly she says:*

MARENKA. Blaustein is in the hall, comrade. He looks as if he's either had an enema, or needs one.

VOLUBIN *exits at once through the door to the hall.*

55. *Interior. Palace: apartment – hall.*

BLAUSTEIN *is moodily but gently kicking at* VOLUBIN'S *briefcase. He looks up as* VOLUBIN *enters the hall from the salon, closing the door gently behind him. They face each other in silence a moment.* BLAUSTEIN *is hot, and sweating heavily. He takes out a large handkerchief and mops his face.*

BLAUSTEIN. Well?

Pause.

VOLUBIN. She thinks I'm her butler.

Pause.

BLAUSTEIN. Downstairs. You should see downstairs. A Jewish wedding it could be ready for. If we took down the banner. (*Pause.*) All we *need* is a butler!

Pause.

VOLUBIN. The Countess and I – stalemate.

Pause.

BLAUSTEIN. A butler she thinks you are! Then *be* a butler –

VOLUBIN. Tonda –

BLAUSTEIN. Please be a butler! Be anything. For a goy, you bring out my soft side. Have pity! Where's *your* soft side? You played cowboys and Indians with the Germans. You can be a butler!

Pause.

VOLUBIN. She's impossible. She's resolutely in the past –

BLAUSTEIN. And so are some other people.

VOLUBIN. What the bloody hell do you mean by that?

Pause.

BLAUSTEIN. Outside is twenty-nine degrees of heat. Of good old sun. (*Pause.*) What do you see before you? Blaustein is a ball of fat. Melting. It is a melting effigy of Blaustein bouncing off your retina. (*Pause.*) You want to kill me? You want me to suffer the trauma of dissecting your negative tendencies under your *nose*? Don't do this! Klement, every man's feet sweat. But even my toe *nails* are sweating. The spine – a river. The navel – a lake. The crutch – a swamp. I am a physiological miracle. I distil at a rate of litres per second. *Klement!*

VOLUBIN. Why don't you sit down?

BLAUSTEIN. Even my piles are sweating –
    Pause.

VOLUBIN. Sit down, Tonda.
    BLAUSTEIN *sits – on the chair occupied by* VOLUBIN *when* MARENKA *first let him into the hall.*

VOLUBIN. We break into the wine cellar.
    Pause.

BLAUSTEIN. We can break through a mediaeval door? It must be a foot thick.
    Pause.

VOLUBIN. I'm not (*pointing*) going back in there.
    Pause.

BLAUSTEIN. No breaking down of doors. (*Pause.*) It is a question of respect. (*Pause.*) And self-respect. (*Pause.*) We kicked those social democrats up the arse. That's one thing. This is. (*Pause.*) This is an old lady. A *michugene*! (*Pause.*) Dotty she is? She's lucky. (*He points at the salon door.*) Back to the front line, Klement.
    Pause.

VOLUBIN. The whole thing's ridiculous.

BLAUSTEIN. The celebration?

VOLUBIN. Yes.

BLAUSTEIN. Sacrilege!

VOLUBIN. Maybe.
    Pause.

BLAUSTEIN. See you in jail one of these days!
    Pause.

VOLUBIN. One of these days . . . we'll be in jail for nothing at all. Not even sacrilege.

BLAUSTEIN. I need this further information *now*? (*Pause.*) Why do I still love you? Huh? Even when I have to hear you saying what I *think*?

> BLAUSTEIN *smiles. He stands,* VOLUBIN *grins back at him. The two men put their arms round each other and touch cheeks.* BLAUSTEIN *steps back a pace.*

BLAUSTEIN (*mopping his cheek*). You see? (*With the handkerchief wrapped round his finger, he prods his cheek.*) Never mind. Sweatbruderschaft!

VOLUBIN. Go away! Go away and have a bath or something.

BLAUSTEIN. Do I smell? I knew it –

VOLUBIN. You smell of American deodorant, you dripping bastard. Which you got *where*?

> *Pause.*

BLAUSTEIN. There is a lady. At the embassy. Who types all day beneath their fucking great eagle. (*Pause.*) She has deodorant. (*Pause.*) Blaustein dear, she says: When communism puts this in the shops I'll marry you. (*Pause.*) A nice lady. From Detroit. You want communists and bourgeois democrats should smell the same, I ask? (*He hesitates.*)

VOLUBIN. Well? And what did *she* say?

BLAUSTEIN. She said it'd be a start, the silly bitch. *But.* Deodorized I walk the streets of our city. In the trams – Blaustein is a scented oasis. A flower's armpit.

> *He goes to the main door, turning.*

I don't want to have to climb those stairs again this afternoon. Each one a cliff. An escarpment. (*Pause.*) Tonight we'll get drunk.

VOLUBIN. *You* will.

BLAUSTEIN. Shalom!

> *He goes out.* MARENKA *comes out of the salon door into the hall.*

MARENKA. Comrade Volubin –

VOLUBIN. Yes?

MARENKA. It doesn't make sense.

VOLUBIN. I quite agree.

Pause.

MARENKA. That Blaustein!

VOLUBIN. He's a dear old friend of mine.

MARENKA. Is he now? (*Pause.*) You know what you've gone and done? She thinks she's giving a dinner tonight. All because of you two and those bloody keys!

Pause.

VOLUBIN. Why do you stay with her?

MARENKA. What should I be doing? Hodding bricks? Digging holes?

VOLUBIN. I didn't mean to –

MARENKA (*tiredly*). I know what you didn't mean to.

Long pause.

MARENKA (*tartly*). *I* know what's going on. *I* go to evening classes. And not for Karl Marx – for a man! (*Pause.*) Do I get one? (*Pause.*) Look at me –

Pause.

VOLUBIN. You stay with her because she's dependent on you. Don't you?

MARENKA (*quickly*). Not for the power of it!

Pause.

VOLUBIN. Yes. I think I believe that.

Pause.

MARENKA. Well, are you going back in? Or aren't you?

VOLUBIN. I am.

MARENKA. I don't envy you. She's expecting a lot of people for dinner.

MARENKA *vanishes into the far gloom of the hall.*

After a moment, VOLUBIN *goes to the salon door – opens it, goes in.*

56. *Interior. Palace : Apartment.*

VOLUBIN *enters. There is a barely definable change in the* COUN-

TESS – *a lightness, a more noticeable agility. She is between the window and the table.*

VOLUBIN *faces her, saying nothing.*

COUNTESS. Volubin, my dear man. What I hadn't realized. Is that you must be very busy. (*Pause.*) There you were asking for the cellar keys. And there was I rambling on and rambling on! (*She laughs – but to herself.*)

VOLUBIN. It's true. I *am* busy.

COUNTESS. Nothing must go wrong! Every detail must be . . . exquisite.

   Pause.

VOLUBIN. Your son –

   Pause.

COUNTESS. What?

VOLUBIN. You didn't say. You didn't *mention*. Exactly what became of him.

   Long pause.

COUNTESS. But – (*Pause.*) I don't understand. He died in your very own arms. (*Pause.*) How *can* you!

   Long pause.

VOLUBIN. I am sorry. I meant: did he . . . was he taken to Laugstein? Or to Krejczyn.

   A long pause. The COUNTESS'S *eyes are glazed, she struggles with her shifting memories. She looks at him pleadingly.*

VOLUBIN. I was . . . forcibly conscripted. I mean, what the Germans called 'volunteered'. The morning after. After he died.

COUNTESS. Yes. Now I do remember. (*Long pause.*) We took him to Laugstein. (*Pause.*) George said. (*Petulantly.*) He was very astute I must admit. George *said* the Russians would take Poland to the west of Krejczyn. (*Pause.*) And they did. Didn't they?

   Pause.

VOLUBIN. Yes, Madam.

   She is laughing again.

COUNTESS. As soon as Marenka said you need the wine for dinner, *I* understood – you see.

   VOLUBIN *crosses to the window.*

57. Interior. Café.

As at the end of Scene 53.

KELVIN. Why the hell did Katie *go* to the Soviet Union? Why?
    Pause.

VOLUBIN. Katie was never . . . very . . . rational. About her
    politics. (*Pause.*) They needed all kinds of people. Scientists.
    Technicians. (*Pause.*) She was a very good biochemist. And she
    went. To help install a new laboratory. (*Pause.*) It was to be for a
    year. (*Pause.*) Only a year.
    Pause.

KELVIN. I'm surprised you've never been thrown out of the party.

VOLUBIN. So am I.
    Pause.

KELVIN. Why do you think?
    Long pause. VOLUBIN *rises. He puts out his hand.*

VOLUBIN. I've always come to heel in the end. In my discomfit-
    ing fashion – I'm a good party man. (*Pause.*) Split right down
    the middle.
        KELVIN *has taken his hand. Their hands grip tightly for a
        moment.*
    Goodbye, Robert –
    Pause.

KELVIN. I shall see you again!

VOLUBIN *smiles. He turns and walks away. Close-up on* KELVIN'S
    face.

58. Interior. Palace : apartment.

VOLUBIN *turns from the window to look at the* COUNTESS. *She is
walking backwards and forwards. She stops.*

COUNTESS. You'll take the greatest care. Won't you?

VOLUBIN. I will.

59. Interior. Cellar.

Repeat Scene 2 without the sound. VOLUBIN *is being coldly and systematically beaten by two* MEN. *Finally he is swaying on his feet and collapses.*

Over, we hear KATIE'S *voice:*

KATIE'S VOICE (*softly*). I can taste mustard on your mouth. (*Pause.*) Nice. (*Pause.*) My love –

> *This is repeated until the end of the scene, ending itself, abruptly when the scene ends.*

60. Interior. Palace : apartment.

VOLUBIN *moves away from the window a little. The* COUNTESS *goes to it.*

COUNTESS. I shall dress. How I shall dress!

> *She looks outside. We see the almond tree. Cut to: Close-up* COUNTESS'S *face.*

COUNTESS. Marenka shall do my hair –

> *Close-up* VOLUBIN'S *face and cut to: the empty cellar as in Scene 39*
>
> *Cut to: Close-up* COUNTESS'S *face. She looks out of the window.* VOLUBIN *looks out of the window.*
>
> *We see the cellar, and gradually superimposed on it the image of the tree. Tree and cellar are held for a few seconds.*
>
> *Cut to:* COUNTESS'S *face.*

COUNTESS. You will wear your best livery, Volubin –

> *Pause.*

VOLUBIN. I shall wear my best livery.

COUNTESS. The red velvet.

> *Pause.*

VOLUBIN. The red velvet.

> *She crosses to a cabinet and takes from it a ring with a bunch of large keys on it.*

COUNTESS. And now I shall give you the keys.

> *She hands him the keys.*

That will be all, Volubin –

VOLUBIN. Thank you, Madam.

He stands looking at her a moment – her face is alive, happy. He goes out.

61. *Interior. Palace : staircase.*

We follow VOLUBIN *down the staircase, keys in one hand, briefcase in the other. He is smiling to himself. For* VOLUBIN, *his movements are almost jaunty.*

Outside the banqueting room hovers BLAUSTEIN, *looking worried. Behind him are two inconspicuous* MEN. VOLUBIN *goes up to* BLAUSTEIN, *jangling the keys under his nose. He is taken aback when* BLAUSTEIN *reaches for the keys automatically, and with no sign of his usual manner.*

VOLUBIN. What's the matter with you? You've got them. You can all drink yourselves silly –

BLAUSTEIN *says nothing, but looks behind him to the two* MEN. *One of them comes forward. He looks at* VOLUBIN *and nods towards the stairs.* VOLUBIN *looks at* BLAUSTEIN *questioningly.*

BLAUSTEIN. Klement, I'm sorry. It's nothing to do with me. Well you know that. They've been waiting for you the last ten minutes.

VOLUBIN *says nothing. The two* MEN *move up beside him.* BLAUSTEIN *touches his arm gently.*

VOLUBIN *and the two* MEN *continue on down the stairs.*

62. *Interior. Palace : apartment.*

The COUNTESS *sits in a long petticoat, with a soft linen towel round her shoulders.* MARENKA *is doing her hair. We close-up* MARENKA'S *fingers. Close-up the* COUNTESS.

63. *Interior. A bare room.*

There is only a plain deal table. The two MEN *from scene 61 stand at one side –* VOLUBIN *at the other. One of the men holds a canvas bag. The other is writing a list, as* VOLUBIN *empties his pockets. Each item is listed: Keys, handkerchief, wallet, small change, spectacles case, wrist-watch – then put into the canvas bag.*

64. *Interior. Palace : apartment.*

MARENKA *is holding up a dress for the Countess to see – a beautiful ball gown in the style of the late thirties.*

65. *Interior. Corridor.*

The same corridor as in Scene 4. VOLUBIN *is walking down it between the two* MEN.

66. *Interior. Cellar.*

The same cellar as in Scene 12. Empty. The door is opened, and VOLUBIN *led in by the same* WARDER *as in Scene 12. The* WARDER *goes out. The door clangs behind him.* VOLUBIN *stands looking round this familiar space.*

67. *Interior. Palace : staircase.*

From the back we see MARENKA *helping the* COUNTESS, *looking majestic in her piled hair and ball dress, down the stairs.*

65. *Interior. Corridor.*

The same corridor as in Scene 4. VOLUBIN *is being led back to the bare room of Scene 63 by his* WARDER.

66. *Interior. Bare room.*

The room of Scene 63. Now, an INTERROGATOR *in civilian clothes sits at one side of the table smoking, with a file in front of him.*

The door opens. The WARDER *ushers* VOLUBIN *into the room, and leaves. The* INTERROGATOR *points to the other side of the table. There is no chair.* VOLUBIN *goes and stands in the indicated position.*

INTERROGATOR (*looking at the file*). Now then. Comrade Volubin. (*Pause.*) Ex-Krauner. (*Pause.*) Ex-Sladek. (*Pause: musingly.*) I wonder why you never took your own name back?
    Pause.

VOLUBIN. Sladek was a poet. Krauner was a partisan. Volubin was somewhere in the middle. (*Pause.*) It's up to you to decide whether there's any significance in that.
    Pause.

INTERROGATOR. There are certain State charges against you –
    VOLUBIN *is hardly listening. He seems neither frightened nor particularly interested.*

VOLUBIN. The last time I was in this room, it was a Gestapo pig sitting where you are.
    Pause.

INTERROGATOR. One might paraphrase Voltaire, and say: If history made us in its image, we have certainly returned the compliment!

VOLUBIN. One might also paraphrase the Communist Manifesto and say: there is a spectre haunting communism. (*Pause.*) Is it people like you? Or people like me?
    The INTERROGATOR *launches into a long speech, but we do not hear him. Close-up* VOLUBIN'S *face. We hear* VOLUBIN'S *voice.*

VOLUBIN'S VOICE. My dear Robert –

67. Exterior. An Austrian-style letter box.

We hold the letter box in close-up. A hand appears, drops a long envelope into the slot.

68. Interior. Bare room.

The INTERROGATOR *is still speaking. We cannot hear him. We close-up* VOLUBIN'S *face and hear his voice.*

VOLUBIN'S VOICE. My dear Robert. A friend is holding this letter for me in Vienna. (*Pause.*) Should it reach you, you will know that I am in prison – and they are probably embarked on a further series of Show Trials. (*Pause.*) You did get the big literary prize, I saw it in a newspaper. I congratulate you. (*Pause.*) I know, if you get this, you will not fail to undertand what is happening –

The INTERROGATOR *jumps to his feet, shouting:*

INTERROGATOR. Will you pay attention!

69. *Interior. Palace : staircase.*

Outside the banqueting room stands BLAUSTEIN. *The big doors are open –* BLAUSTEIN *to one side, a* SECURITY MAN *to the other.*
Beyond, in the banqueting room, we see that the tables are filled : a MAN *stands beneath the red banner making a speech, but we only hear a muffled sound.*
Down the stairs comes the COUNTESS – *resplendent.* BLAUSTEIN *sees her and jumps. Smiling, she slowly comes towards him. Standing in front of him she stands offering her arm.*

COUNTESS. Gunther darling . . . will you take me in then?

BLAUSTEIN hesitates, but only a few seconds. He gives her his arm, and she rests her hand on it. BLAUSTEIN *prepares to lead her in. The* SECURITY MAN *steps forward anxiously. He is frozen by a savage look from* BLAUSTEIN.

70. *Interior. Palace : banqueting room.*

The speech-making MAN *is raising his glass.*

MAN. Comrades : the Soviet Union!

From the assembly a loud : 'The Soviet Union!' They drink and put their glasses down. They remain standing and we hear 'The Internationale' played very loudly. As this begins : BLAUSTEIN *enters through the big doors with the Countess on his arm.*

To the sound of 'The Internationale' they slowly walk down between the U-shape of the tables.
We track them the whole distance, cutting in the consternated faces all around them.
Now BLAUSTEIN *and the* COUNTESS *are facing the* SPEAKER *– and the red banner behind him. Cut to:*

71. *Interior. Bare room.*

The INTERROGATOR *has resumed his seat before the open file. He unscrews a fountain pen – looks up at* VOLUBIN.
INTERROGATOR. Shall we begin?
    Close-up VOLUBIN'S *face.*

Emma's Time

Emma's Time was first broadcast by BBC Television on 13 May 1990 with the following cast:

EMMA	*Michele Dotrice*
KELVIN	*Andrew Keir*
MICHAEL	*John Quentin*
ARNOLD CRAIL	*Norman Scace*
JANE WOOLLER	*Pauline Yates*
EMMA'S MOTHER	*Elizabeth Kentish*
EMMA'S FATHER	*Jack May*
MARK LANG	*Ian Holm*
KELVIN'S MOTHER	*Mary Merrall*
RUTH	*Kay Newman*
SLADEK	*Peter Vaughan*
CHARLIE	*John Sharpe*
ROBERTO	*Mike Briton*

Directed by Alan Bridges

1. Interior. Robert Kelvin's house: study.

The study as seen in 'On the Eve of Publication'.
From a high shot, three people: EMMA (*Kelvin's mistress when he died*), *an accountant,* MICHAEL, *and a lawyer –* ARNOLD CRAIL.
CRAIL *is speaking.*
MICHAEL *fiddles with a pencil – they are both sitting at Robert Kelvin's desk.*
EMMA *sits staring at a wall covered with framed photographs of writers.*
Close-up EMMA. *Close-up* CRAIL.

CRAIL. Well there it is, Emma. Robert's affairs were very complicated but we seem to have it all straightened out.

> EMMA *seems not to be listening.*
> *From her point of view we have close shots of three photographs: Sartre, Camus, Ehrenburg. She sits very composed, her hands in her lap.*

Emma –

EMMA. Yes?

> *Pause.*

CRAIL. I was wondering if . . . if you were listening . . .

EMMA (*turning*). I was listening.

CRAIL. I mean. I realize none of this is very pleasant for you. But as Robert's lawyer –

EMMA (*cutting in*). It's neither pleasant or unpleasant.

> *The two men are discomfited.*
> EMMA *looks down at her hands.*

CRAIL. The point is that Robert left ample provision for his ex-wives and children. All the same, he's left *you* quite a rich woman –

> EMMA *gets up and faces them both, her face neutral.*

EMMA. So I'm sort of well-heeled, am I?

> *Pause.*

CRAIL (*a little distastefully*). If you choose to put it that way.

(*Pause.*) And if in any way I can continue to help you, I shall be more than willing. (*Looking at* MICHAEL.) I'm sure the same goes for Michael. After all he was Robert's accountant for many years –

Pause.

EMMA. I wonder how many novelists made such a lot of money –

CRAIL. Well . . . of course there were huge sales on some of his books. And then film rights. (*Pause.*) And after he won the Nobel Prize –

EMMA (*cutting in*). After that he was worth even more, was he?

CRAIL *looks down, straightening some papers. He thinks she is hard, and he is beginning to get annoyed.*

CRAIL. That's nothing to do with me. I'm just giving you the facts.

EMMA *crosses to the photographs. There is one of Robert Kelvin sitting at a café table with Ernest Hemingway.* EMMA *looks hard at it and we close-up the photograph.*

EMMA. He never liked Hemingway. (*Pause.*) I wonder what they were saying that day. At that café table.

Pause.

MICHAEL. Have you any idea what you want to do, Emma?

She goes back to her chair and resumes her original posture.

EMMA. No idea. None at all.

2. *Exterior. Cambridge backs. Night.*

There is a thunderstorm. ROBERT KELVIN *is kneeling by the river being sick.*

EMMA *stands over him. He retches for a moment, then stands wiping his mouth with a handkerchief.*

KELVIN. Ever tasted anybody else's vomit? *Kissed* a mouth fresh, as you might say, from a recent puke?

Pause.

EMMA. No I haven't, Mr Kelvin –

KELVIN (*irritated.*) *Mister* bloody Kelvin! And who the bloody hell are you, anyway?

Pause.

EMMA. Emma. (*Pause.*) When you left the party you asked me to follow you. (*She smiles.*) You were being very rude to me and then you wanted to be sick.

> *There are loud claps of thunder and flashes of lightning, but the rain has passed.*
>
> *They stand peering at each other in the dimness.*
>
> KELVIN *sways, and puts his hand on her shoulder. She holds his wrist gently and he maintains balance.*

KELVIN. Emma. (*Pause.*) Emma.

EMMA. Yes. First you quoted Jane Austen to me –

KELVIN. Wha'?

EMMA (*quoting from 'Emma'*). One half of the world cannot understand the pleasures of the other –

> KELVIN *leans his head on her shoulder.*

KELVIN. Oh Christ!

EMMA. Yes. And then you said I looked as if I had the capacity for pleasure of a chloroformed virus.

KELVIN. Oh Jesus!

EMMA. And then you said I looked as if I might be nauseatingly intelligent.

KELVIN. Good.

EMMA. But '*pseudo*', you added.

> *Pause.*

KELVIN. Emma – can you get me somewhere quiet where I can go on getting even drunker.

EMMA. If that's what you want –

KELVIN. A peaceful vomitorium. Away from youth. And dons. And King's bloody College. And that *deafening* music –

> *Pause.*

EMMA. I'm young. Will you want me to leave you as well?

KELVIN. I'll make a bargain. Get me away with a minimum or indeed an absence, of scandal. And I'll take you on despite your age.

EMMA. What an ugly person you are, Mr Kelvin.

KELVIN. Inside, or out?

EMMA. Both.

KELVIN. Now you see why I dragged Jane Austen into the conversation you cheeky little bugger.

EMMA (*quietly*). There's a friend of mine has a flat. She's away for the weekend. (*Pause.*) But – what about the party?

KELVIN. The next time I throw up it won't be into this river, I can assure you. It'll be into the face of that newt-arsed little tutor of yours.

He totters a few steps back from her, his arms spread out and downwards. Declaims in a poor imitation of a posh voice.

I thought in your last novel, Mr Kelvin, you were trying to reconcile marxism with phenomenological psychiatry. Would you say there's something in that?

He falls down flat on his face. Glares up at her.

The globe, the very earth did tilt beneath my poor old feet. Can you see my face?

EMMA. Not very well –

KELVIN. It is signalling hatred in the direction of your crutch.

EMMA. Why my crutch?

KELVIN. For the simple reason I can't get my bloody head off the ground. What's up? Did they spread glue on the grass in deadly anticipation?

Pause.

EMMA. I don't think I can lift you –

KELVIN. Then you'll just have to bring your friend's bloody flat over here – won't you?

Pause.

EMMA *kneels beside him.*

EMMA. Come on then. I'll try.

KELVIN (*glumly munching*). Even the muck tastes rotten in Cambridge!

EMMA. Come on – (*Taking his arm.*)

KELVIN. I've got nothing *against* your crutch. Nothing at all. I want you to know that before I die. We don't like to think of you growing up neurotic, now, do we?

3. Interior. Robert Kelvin's house : study.

As in Scene 1, except that CRAIL *now stands in front of* EMMA *holding his briefcase.*

MICHAEL *is looking at the photographs.*

CRAIL. I'll be in touch with you again soon, Emma –

EMMA. Thank you.

> *Pause.*

CRAIL. Why don't you ask Robert's secretary to stay on in the house a while?

EMMA. I already have.

> *She looks up at him coolly.*

Only because she needs the job whilst she finds something else.

> *Pause.*

CRAIL. I'll let myself out –

> *He exits.*

> EMMA *watches him go.*

> MICHAEL *is lounging in front of the photos with his hands in his trouser pockets.*

MICHAEL. Sartre . . . Camus . . . Ehrenburg . . . Simone de Beauvoir . . . (*Pointing at one.*) Who's *that*?

EMMA. Aragon.

MICHAEL (*turning on her*). Why do you dislike Arnold? (*Pause.*) Letting him go out like that –

> *Pause.*

EMMA. I don't dislike him. It's his embarrassment about all this. It makes me feel aggressive. I've always had a bit of a problem with aggression. Instead of pulling fierce faces I go stony.

> *Pause.*

MICHAEL. Well, Robert never had much trouble being aggressive. Did he?

EMMA. No. (*Pause.*) I expect that must have attracted me from the very first. (*Grins at him.*) Don't tell me there's nothing original about *that*, or I shall go all stony on you as well!

MICHAEL. *I've* never minded your stony mug. Makes you look

like a china teapot. I often used to think Robert should've lifted
you up and poured the hostility out.

He scuffs the carpet with his foot.

Might have burnt the carpet, I suppose –

JANE WOOLLER – *Kelvin's secretary – knocks and enters.*

JANE. The ghoulish session is over, I take it? I saw Arnold Crail
scuttle across the hall with his tail in his briefcase –

MICHAEL. It's all over. And we're all ready for a large drink.

Pause.

Looks from EMMA to JANE.

Aren't we?

JANE. I've a suspicion you put away even more booze than Robert
did. Where do you keep it? I mean where do you keep the *effects*?

She goes to a drinks table and pours him a large scotch.

As she does so :

Don't your clients ever get nervous about it? Think you might
get their columns of figures crossed or something?

MICHAEL. Robert was a jag man. I'm just a quiet, harmless
soaker –

JANE. Emma?

EMMA. A vodka, please, Jane –

MICHAEL *takes his drink from* JANE.

JANE (*to* EMMA). A man from TV wants to do a sort of retrospective portrait of Robert. Whose jurisdiction does *that* come
under?

As she takes EMMA her drink, she says :

Does it even make *sense*?

MICHAEL (*deadpan*). *You* might make a few bob out of it. Great
man's secretary for seven years. Bound to be a *few* secrets up
your skirt, or down your –

EMMA (*cutting in*). Oh, shut up, Michael!

Pause.

MICHAEL. I'm sorry. I thought we all had a tacit understanding we
wouldn't get soft about Robert. (*Pause.*) Publicly. (*Pause.*) I
mean. They might even stick in a commercial about his
accountant. Eh?

Now JANE *has a drink poured for herself.*

JANE. That's right. We don't get soft about him. We just get edgier and edgier. (*Drinks.*) Up yours.

Pause.

EMMA. Michael, you're very tiresome when you're trying to be flip. What's more it tends to give *me* the impression you're just going to start crying.

Close-up of EMMA'S *face – very impassive.*
She raises her glass to her lips.

4. Interior. Cambridge flat. Bedroom. Early morning.

A shabby, messy room.
In the bed, ROBERT KELVIN *lies hunched and snoring with his back to* EMMA.
Close-up of EMMA. *She has tears rolling down her cheeks.*
KELVIN *stirs.*
At once, EMMA *takes the sheet and dries her tears. Closes her eyes.*
Close-up of KELVIN – *his ageing face is suddenly livened, as his eyes open. He is very hungover.*
His eyes take in as much as they can of the room without things getting too painful. They move to one side. He is aware of EMMA.
He puts a hand gently on her thigh over the bedclothes, but does not turn towards her.
She opens her eyes.
There is a long silence.
KELVIN *coughs, and moistens his lips.*
Slowly, EMMA *takes her arm from under the bedclothes and puts her hand on his.*
A long silence.
KELVIN. I feel like something that's been shitten through a coffee strainer.

Pause.

EMMA (*quietly*). So do my insides!

He painfully raises up on one elbow to look into her face.

KELVIN. Did I give you a hammering then?

Pause.

EMMA. A bulldozing.

    KELVIN *collapses on to his back, staring at the ceiling.*

KELVIN. I remember *bits* of it –

    Pause.

EMMA. That's very consoling.

KELVIN. For Christ's sake don't feel insulted!

EMMA. I don't.

    He hauls himself up on both elbows now.

KELVIN. Let me see you –

    We see her begin to pull the bedclothes aside from her body, and go into a close-up of her face.

    Close-up of KELVIN *looking.*

    Close-up of EMMA'S *face, immobile.*

No blood? No martyred virginity?

    He falls back on the pillow.

God. That sort of anxiety's a bit out of date. Isn't it?

EMMA. Years and years and years. (*Pause.*) Besides. We didn't want to grow up neurotic. Did we?

KELVIN. I bet that's something *I* said, you bitch!

    Pause.

EMMA. That's right. Lying flat on your face in the Backs.

    Pause.

KELVIN. Don't pinch my –

EMMA (*cutting in*). Robert. Do you want to just get up and go away or what?

    Pause.

KELVIN (*shiftily*). Where are we?

EMMA. In somebody's flat.

KELVIN. And where is *that*?

EMMA. Cambridge.

KELVIN. Just wondered. Matter of orientation. To know where one is is one thing. To know where that may be is another. And where's Billy?

EMMA. Who's Billy?

KELVIN. The bloke that drives my car, dammit.

EMMA. How should I know? Where's the car?

KELVIN (*tetchily*). How should *I* know? Billy usually dumps me down and goes off to play Black Jack in obscure places. But he has a tremendous knack of being able to find me. (*Pause.*) Usually. (*Pause.*) Has someone foiled my Billy boy? (*Pause.*). I'm a very frightened man, you know. Paranoid. Delusional. (*Pause.*) Christ. Am I going to have to *walk*?

EMMA. *I'd* like to look at *you* –
    She twitches the bedclothes off him and KELVIN *roars – but tails off into a humiliated silence as we close-up* EMMA *looking at him. Close-up* KELVIN. *Looks down his body.*

KELVIN. I should point out. In its feeble defence. That it has been *through* a lot –
    Pause.

EMMA. Mmmmm – m.

KELVIN. Don't be smug. How would yours look after more than six decades of strenuous degeneration?

EMMA. Funny. All the bits of it are the same shape. Just different sizes.

KELVIN (*yelping*). Same *shape*?

EMMA. Looks as if you were carved out of a large, rancid Hungarian sausage.

KELVIN (*thundering*). *Now just you* –
    She twitches the bedclothes back and this somehow shuts him up whilst she again cuts in, lying back on her pillow.

EMMA. *I* don't mind, Robert –
    Pause.

KELVIN (*suspiciously*). Eh?

EMMA. I said I don't mind.
    Pause.

KELVIN. I don't pretend that this near-cadaver is an exciting aesthetic experience. (*Pause.*) But . . . er . . . aren't you even a tiny bit revolted? (*Pause.*) Or are you overwhelmed by the spirituality of the inner contents?
    EMMA *turns away from him, on her side.*

EMMA. Oh – I just think it's irrelevant.

KELVIN. Now look here. I'm *all* relevant. *Totally* relevant. I'll not disown a single blemish. (*Pause.*) Look.

He jabs a finger at the side of his neck.

See that scar? That *scar* – was caused by a flower pot in Hungary. (*Pause.*) Which fell upon me. (*Pause.*) Who *says* there was no counter-revolution in nineteen fifty-six? Eh? White Hungarian old ladies hurling flower pots down upon strolling marxists!

EMMA. Strolling, were you?

Pause.

KELVIN. Strolling quickly.

EMMA. I see. Strolling quickly.

KELVIN (*shouting*). All right then! Bloody running!

EMMA turns on him quickly.

EMMA. What do you want? What are you going to do? When are you leaving? Maybe if you just whistle, your Billy'll come to you –

KELVIN huddles down in the bedclothes, his face sombre.

KELVIN. Are you going to come and live with me, Emma?

He lifts an arm high, pointing down towards his navel with a forefinger.

With this? Since it and I are clearly inseparable. Mutually parasitic.

Pause.

EMMA (*softly*). Yes, Robert.

Pause.

KELVIN. Soon?

Pause.

EMMA. In a few weeks. When I've taken my degree –

KELVIN (*wildly*). When you've taken your god-damned bloody blasted *degree*?

EMMA. Well. If you don't last long I might need it. Mightn't I?

But EMMA is laughing, and rolls over on top of him kissing him.

5. *Interior. Robert Kelvin's house : study.*

Close-up EMMA, taking the glass from her lips.

EMMA. What's the television man like, Jane? Does he wear tight pants and one of those flowered scarves tied round his neck?

JANE. From our brief telephone conversation I'd say – yes. Very likely. (*Pause.*) Robert used to bark at them. What are you going to do, love? Bite?

> EMMA *stands, placing her glass down firmly. She says to* JANE, *without visible feeling.*

EMMA. I haven't bitten *you* yet. Have I, Jane? Despite the fact that Robert was screwing you for five of those seven years Michael mentioned. (*Pause. Quietly.*) And despite the fact that you hung on here like a leech.

> *She goes to the door. Turning, she looks at them both.* JANE *is sipping her drink, her eyes dark and resentful over the glass.*

Will you arrange an appointment for the TV man to come here?

> *She goes out.* MICHAEL *raises his glass.*

MICHAEL. In the words of St Augustine: Rome has spoken. The case is concluded.

> *Pause.*

JANE. Robert adored her. *I* can't understand why he even liked her.

6. *Interior. Robert Kelvin's house : bedroom.*

The room is dark, except for lamplight from the street.
EMMA *lies, clothed on the bed, holding a glass of vodka.*
KELVIN'S VOICE. What are you like, Emma? (*Pause.*) What do you think? Believe? Need? Want? (*Pause.*) Where's your bloody rage?

7. *Exterior. Kelvin's house : street.*

A taxi stops. EMMA *gets out, pays the driver, and hauls a large suitcase off the platform beside him. She lugs it up the stairs to the front door and rings the bell. After a moment,* JANE *comes to the door. She holds it open, looking at* EMMA *without saying anything.*
EMMA. My name's Emma Foster. Robert Kelvin's expecting me.

(*There is a long silence,* JANE *staring.*) I've just come down from
Cambridge.

    Pause.

JANE. I've just come down from Robert. He had a three hour
lunch at the White Elephant and he's lying pissed in his bedroom—

    JANE *moves a little way back into the hall, waiting.* EMMA
    picks up her case and goes in. The door closes behind them.

8. *Interior. Robert Kelvin's house : bedroom.*

Mid-afternoon. KELVIN *lies sprawled across the large double bed,
parallel to the pillows. A bottle of whisky and glass are next to his
right hand, where it dangles on the floor. The door opens –* JANE
stands holding it open whilst EMMA *goes in with her suitcase, then
closes it.*

EMMA *puts the case down and goes to the foot of the bed.*

KELVIN'S *boozy, alert eyes fix on her.*

KELVIN. My publisher is a fatuous toad. But toads can write chits,
sign bills. (*Pause.*) And an *enormous* bill he signed at lunch.
(*Pause.*) Not without a frown. (*Pause.*) For the greater part of the
food and booze lay boiling in Kelvin's gut. (*Pause.*) I sent Billy
to meet you at the station.

    Pause.

EMMA. I didn't expect that. I took a taxi. (*Pause.*) You look bloody
awful, Robert –

KELVIN. According to Montaigne, a man who fears suffering is
already suffering from what he fears. (*Pause.*) I (*As he sits up.*)
believe I exemplify that condition. (*Pause.*) Did you encounter
the snotty Jane? Secretary, etcetera?

EMMA. At the door. (*Pause.*) *Very* cool.

KELVIN. Yes. Well you might carry out a bit of research there.
(*Pause.*) I couldn't say Jane *warmed* this bed before I met you.
(*Pause.*) But she – how shall we put it? – simulated ardour. By
tangling the sheets one or two nights a week. (*Pause.*) I can't
remember whether you're a sheet-tangler or not. (*Pause.*)
After all, one week-end in Southwold doesn't make a sexual
case history. Does it?

EMMA. It wasn't Southwold.

KELVIN. Eh?

EMMA. It was Aldeburgh.

KELVIN. I get vague, south of Nottingham.

> *His eyes close. He begins to snore. His hand twitches – knocks over the glass on the floor.* EMMA *goes to pick up the glass and the bottle. Looks round the room. Gets her case on the floor, and kneeling begins to unpack the things in it into piles on the floor.*

9. *Interior. Robert Kelvin's house : bedroom.*

As in Scene 6. EMMA *is drinking. She puts the glass down on the bedside table and lies supine, her arms by her sides. We hear her mother's voice :*

MOTHER'S VOICE. I thought you wanted to do a post-graduate degree. I thought you wanted a career. I thought you despised the idea of a man and woman living together. (*Pause.*) One expects anything these days – and God knows certainly not marriage. (*Pause.*) So what I'm criticizing, Emma, is this complete reversal of your own ideas. Not mine. Not your father's. *Yours.*

10. *Interior. The Fosters' house : bedroom.*

A large, comfortable room furnished as a room to live and work in. Its provincial suburban character is overlaid with EMMA'S *personal style – books everywhere; in one corner a music stand and violin case; a tailor's dummy draped and decorated grotesquely; a large still of Buster Keaton on one wall; a skull with tendrils of ivy threaded through it – the ivy growing out in a long slender branch from a large green bottle; a small desk with a typed manuscript.*

EMMA *is packing. Her* MOTHER *sits watching her. Her* FATHER *stands with his back to the open casement window. He is a thin, strained-looking man of fifty. His* WIFE *slightly plump, a little younger, dressed in a rather smart suit – but her hair style is vaguely out of date. As* EMMA *talks she is taking things from neat piles on the bed and putting them expertly in the case.*

EMMA. I don't mind contradicting myself.
> *Pause.*

FATHER. But if you could explain, Emma –

EMMA. I want to be with Robert Kelvin.

MOTHER. That's not an explanation –

EMMA. What is it then?

MOTHER. It doesn't *tell* us anything.

EMMA. It tells you everything.

MOTHER. Why haven't you brought him here?

EMMA. It never occurred to me.

MOTHER. We know nothing about him –

EMMA. Read his books. (*Pause.*) There are also two books about him. (*Pause.*) And if you can be bothered, there ought to be quite a collection of newspaper and magazine articles. (*Pause.*) Hire a detective agency. Do your thing.
> *Pause.*

FATHER. He must be over sixty –

EMMA. There you are. Dad's made a start. (*Pause.*) Sixty-two, to be exact.
> *Pause.*

MOTHER. I've seen him on television. (*Pause.*) He's a communist.

EMMA. Define 'communist'.
> *Pause.*
>
> Her MOTHER *stands slowly, looking at her.*

MOTHER. There's something so . . . *inaccessible* about you, Emma.
> *Pause.*

EMMA (*quietly*). I know. I'm sorry about that. (*Pause.*) *He* ignores it. (*Pause.*) That's an enormous relief to me. (*Pause.*) He's a very honest, brutal, desperate man – and he doesn't peck away at my 'inaccessibility'. He will eventually, of course, I hope I shall be ready for it by then.

MOTHER. You're emotionally deficient. (*Pause.*) You're brainy – and empty. Of anything normal.

EMMA. Define 'normal'.

FATHER. Is there something you resent *us* for?

EMMA. Nothing. (*Pause.*) That's probably abnormal as well.

(*Pause : to her* MOTHER.) What, in your opinion, would be the ideal *me* – mother?

Pause.

MOTHER (*quietly*). I don't sense any love in you.

She goes to the door. Turning :

When you were eleven, I took you to a psychiatrist. He said you were a very well adjusted child. (*Pause.*) I should have taken a second opinion.

And she goes out. EMMA'S FATHER, *during her speech, has turned to the window.*

FATHER (*quietly*). I had nothing to do with that.

Pause.

EMMA. *I* did.

Pause.

FATHER. You remember it?

Pause.

EMMA. I think I must have engineered it.

FATHER (*Slowly*). *Why*, Emma?

Pause.

EMMA (*wryly*). Because I strongly disapproved of seeming to have no feelings.

FATHER. At eleven?

Pause.

EMMA. Yes. (*Pause.*) *I* thought I was abnormal. (*Pause.*) Nowadays, I think *psychiatrists* are abnormal. (*Pause.*) But I can't explain a damn thing – to you or anyone else. (*Pause.*) Because I don't concede there's anything to explain –

She looks up at him. He leaves the room, passing her without looking at her.

11. Interior. Robert Kelvin's house : bedroom.

As in Scene 6 EMMA *lies on the bed. She gets up, goes to the window, stands with her back towards it looking at the bed.*
In glaring white light we see KELVIN'S *dead body – the sheet under his chin, his arms straight by his side.*

12. Interior. Robert Kelvin's house: study.

EMMA *sits in her characteristic pose – straight in her chair, hands folded in her lap. We open on a close-up of a* MAN *in his early thirties –* MARK LANG *– sitting opposite* EMMA *talking. As he talks,* JANE *brings in a tray with coffee, and goes out without speaking or looking.*

MARK. I thought of using a lot of the existing material on Robert Kelvin. You know. Telly interviews, newspaper stuff . . . quotes and readings from his books. (*Pause.*) Then I wanted to do quite a bit of filming myself. Places and people . . . some of the *locations* of his books. (*Pause.*) His mother's still alive. (*Pause.*) Did you meet her?

EMMA *is scrutinizing him carefully. He is not at all what she and* JANE *had predicted. He is small and dark, with a sharp, handsome face. Dressed in a black roll-top sweater, an old, loose sports jacket, levis, nondescript shoes. He is almost diffident, yet searching – a sympathetic presence.*

EMMA. I went up to Nottinghamshire once. With Robert. (*Pause.*) She's very old. Over eighty, anyway. (*Pause.*) She seemed a bit unsure who Robert was. And I'm sure she wouldn't remember me. (*Pause.*) Otherwise . . . Robert . . . quite unconsciously . . . at least I think so . . . tended to keep things separate. I mean his work, one or two friends. (*Half smiling.*) His limited contact with his last wife. (*Pause.*) His children.

Pause.

MARK. You.

Pause.

EMMA. Yes. Me too.

Pause.

MARK. Separate territories? (*Pause.*) Sort of zones? (*Pause, grinning.*) Attention! You are now leaving the *Mother Sector*!

Pause.

EMMA. Why are you so obsessed with Robert's life and work?

Pause.

MARK. I was born in Hungary. Came out with my parents in nineteen fifty-six. (*Pause.*) Kelvin lectured at my university in Budapest . . . just before the Russians came in. (*Pause.*) His work . . . he always seemed to me one of the few English novelists with a – what to call it? – a kind of European consciousness. (*Pause.*) What was it? A spin-off from his marxism?

    There is a long silence. EMMA *pours them both coffee.*

Do you want me to just go away? Does all this upset you? Bother you?

    Pause.

EMMA (*calmly*). No. You contrive to avoid that. (*Pause.*)

MARK. I once saw you with him. At the première of a film based on *The Quiet Frontier.* (*Pause.*) You looked beautiful, and self-confident and – isolated. (*Pause.*) Good book. Lousy film. (*Pause.*) He never wrote any of the filmscripts from his books, did he?

    Pause.

EMMA. Can't you just do the programme and leave me out of it all?

    Pause.

MARK. Yes. I've got the permission of his trustees. (*Pause.*) But obviously you're important.

EMMA. Am I?

MARK. The way I want to do it.

EMMA. And how is that, exactly?

    Pause.

MARK. Don't you think it would be interesting if *you* did the various interviews?

EMMA. Why? And what did you mean by "isolated"?

    Pause.

MARK. You looked as if . . . whatever existed between you and Robert Kelvin . . . had nothing to do with the world at large. (*Pause.*) Nothing whatsoever.

EMMA. Does it concern the world at large?

MARK (*carefully*). There's no point in my denying I'm curious about where Kelvin's death leaves *you* –

EMMA. Which has nothing to do with the programme.

Pause.

MARK. No.

Pause.

EMMA. I'd like to think about it.

MARK. Yes, of course – but how soon could you let me know?

Pause.

EMMA. Ring me in the morning.

MARK gets up, his coffee cup still in his hand. He seems suddenly very shy and uncertain. EMMA takes one cup from him. There is a silence, then he takes a briefcase from the floor beside his chair.

MARK. Thank you very much, Miss Foster –

EMMA goes to the door and opens it.

I'll let myself out –

EMMA. Robert was once in love with a woman in Budapest. (*Pause.*) Or he said he had been. (*Pause.*) It was always difficult to extricate his fantasies from what had actually happened. (*Pause.*) I seem to lack the fantasizing faculty. (*Pause.*) Call me, then –

Pause.

MARK. I will –

He goes out. She shuts the door behind him slowly and deliberately. Close-up EMMA.

13. Interior. Robert Kelvin's house : bedroom.

As in Scene 3, except that now the case is unpacked and EMMA sits on a chair near the bed. She is looking at KELVIN, who is snoring in a drunken stupor.

EMMA'S VOICE. Aldeburgh, not Southwold. (*Pause.*) Southwold has sand. Aldeburgh has pebbles. (*Pause.*) The Saturday night was brilliant moonlight. And about one in the morning we walked on the beach. (*Pause.*) You did an Edwardian song and dance act, and ended up in the sea declaiming that if everybody had their just desserts – you'd be Poseidon (*Pause.*) Then later in bed you talked about the Polish actor, Cybulski. (*Pause.*)

You loved him. (*Pause.*) He was a dear friend. (*Pause.*) You mourned him. (*Pause.*) I shall never get used to your knowing people who to me are names, legends, items in journals and magazines and newspapers. (*Pause.*) Everything still has its violent life in you. (*Pause.*) You forget nothing. No one. (*Pause.*) When you and Cybulski were boozing round Warsaw, I was just going into the sixth form –

> KELVIN *grunts and rolls over on the bed.* EMMA *goes to window, looks out.*

14. Clip from 'Ashes and Diamonds'.

The initial shooting scene. Bullets from CYBULSKI'S *gun rip into a man's body, a lacework of smoking holes in the fabric of his coat.*

15. Interior. Kelvin's mother's house. Nottinghamshire mining village.

A kitchen-living room in a back-to-back terrace. Kelvin's MOTHER, *an old, gnarled woman, sits facing* EMMA *at the table. There is a pot of tea and two cups. The light seems overbright and unreal.*

MRS. KELVIN (*bewilderedly*). I don't know what you all want, young lady. (*Pause.*) Or what it's all about. (*Pause.*) Yes, his dad was a local man. (*Pause.*) I was born in Northallerton. (*Pause.*) So you knew our Robert, eh? (*Pause.*) I couldn't get down there, you know. Not to London. (*Pause.*) For the funeral. (*Pause.*) It's me arthritis. I can't hardly move, some days. (*Pause.*) I can't tell nobody nothing. (*Pause.*) Famous, they say he was. Oh yes. I know. (*Pause.*) I'm very old and very tired. (*Pause.*) What do I know, but year after year of baking an' cooking? (*Pause.*) His father coming in in his pit muck. (*Pause.*) He was a man with a temper, that one. (*Pause.*) You'll never know what it's like down t'pit, he used to say. (*Pause.*) He'd knock you down as soon as be argued with. (*Pause.*) Children come, and *they* go down t'pit if they're lads. (*Pause.*) And if they're lasses, they marry pit lads. (*Pause.*) Hard work. And worry. How would you like it? (*Pointing.*) Every day your man went out yon door; and whether he'd come back from his shift you couldn't know. (*Pause*.) Course, the *men* made light on it. (*Pause*.) Daft, laughing devils a lot on them. Fine men, but daft as children. (*Pause*.) Then they'd get paid. And sup it. And put barely enough in your hand on Friday nights to keep body and soul together. (*Pause*.) Who could blame fellers in that sort of work, for their drinking? (*Pause*.) Our Robert got all them scholarships. And got out. And good luck to him. (*Pause*.) His youngest brother was killed in a fall. Many a year later.

>   *Pause*.

EMMA. What was it . . . do you think . . . that made Robert different?

>   *Pause*.

MRS KELVIN. If you knew him, young lady – you knew him.

>   *Pause*.

EMMA. What did you think about it?

>   *Pause*.

MRS KELVIN. Postcards from all over t'world, we had. (*Pause*.) They're all in a box in yon sideboard. (*Pause*.) His father'd try an' chuck 'em on t'fire. (*Pause*.) And I'd cry. (*Pause*.) So he chucked them at me instead. (*Pause*.) We didn't *want* nothing from Robert, if you understand me. (*Pause*.) What *could* I think about it? What *can* you think about summat you don't understand? (*Pause*.) Still, he was getting on – wasn't he? (*Pause*.) He was a lovely bairn. He was a kind boy. Shy. He wasn't strong. (*Pointing*.) Spent a year in that corner wi' a plaster cast round one leg, and up to his chin nearly. (*Pause*.) We had to bring his bed down. He couldn't hardly move. All he wanted was books an' books an' more books. (*Pause*.) I used to buy him them cowboy stories, for tuppence in t'market. (*Pause*.) I don't know what you *was* exactly to our Robert, Miss –

>   *Pause*.

EMMA. I lived with him two years until he died. (*Pause*.) We came to see you once –

>   *Pause*.

MRS KELVIN. I couldn't never keep track on his lady companions.

(*Pause.*) I'm none narrow-minded, for all I'm old. When he got divorced the second time, well, I thought to me sen. Pack it in for good, lad. Live in sin, if tha' must. With somebody can bide you. And be damned. (*Pause.*) For his wives couldn't bide him, you know. (*Pause.*) That much *was* clear. (*Pause.*) Four letters we had from Robert in God knows how many years. Two saying he was getting married; and two saying he was getting divorced. (*Pause.*) Mind, I used to read about him in the papers now and then. Folks'd send me cuttings. (*Pause.*) Busy-bodies half on them. You know. Trying to 'ave a sharp dig whenever there was a bit of scandal. (*Pause.*) You'll hardly need *me* to go on about his drinking. (*Pause.*) I thought his father could sup. But Robert could've supped his father, if he'd been a row of pints. (*Pause.*) Did you love our Robert?

    Pause.

EMMA. Yes.

    Pause.

MRS KELVIN. You're a bonny young woman. (*Pause.*) You'll be lonely.

EMMA. Yes.

MRS KELVIN. It's bad, to lose your man. (*Pause.*) But you're right at life's beginning. (*Pause.*) I can sense you're not one gets over things easily.

    Pause.

EMMA. Not Robert. No.

MRS KELVIN. Must have been over forty years between you. That *is* too much.

EMMA. *He* was obsessed with his age. To me, it never mattered.

    She stands suddenly, turning into the camera.

Mark – stop this. Please.

    Camera pulls back – there are sound and light technicians, a cameraman with a hand-held camera, and MARK.

MARK. *Cut!*

    EMMA *goes to him.*

EMMA. Will you all go away. Please?

    She is shaking, standing rigid with her fists clenched. Everyone

looks at her in consternation. MARK *nods at the cameraman.
The lights go out. They begin to pack up.*

MARK. (*Quietly*). I told you, Emma. Nothing will go in without your approval.

EMMA. I know you told me.

She sits down again. MRS KELVIN *looks vague and uncomprehending.*

MRS KELVIN. You're upset, bairn!

EMMA. Aren't you?

Pause.

MRS KELVIN. Nay girl, I'm past it. (*Pause.*) What do I grasp about television? (*Pause.*) Something to remember our Robert by, I thought it might be. (*Pause.*) I'm long past upsetting. (*Pause.*) If there's owt in life after death, our Robert'll be killing his sen looking down on this lot. (*Pause.*) He wasn't short on vanity! (*Pause.*) He had his vain side. (*Pause.*) And should a man deny having made summat on his life? When (*She gestures vaguely.*) he come out on *this*. (*Pause.*) It was hell on earth round here. But it's changed, I'll give them that. (*Pause.*) Do you know they go to t'pit in their cars nowadays? (*Pause.*) What about that? Colliers *driving* to t'pit. Like a gang o' nobs, and bosses.

Pause.

MARK. Emma –

EMMA. I'll see you back at the hotel in Nottingham.

MARK. *Emma* –

The TECHNICIANS *are getting their equipment out. Mrs Kelvin pours tea into* EMMA'S *cup – then she feels the pot.*

MRS KELVIN. It's as cold as t'devil's charity –

But EMMA *takes the cup and drinks. She looks straight into* MRS KELVIN'S *eyes.*

16. Clip from 'Ashes and Diamonds'.

The scene where CYBULSKI, *in the hotel, lights glasses of vodka in memory of his comrades killed fighting during the war.*

17. Interior. Hotel bedroom.

EMMA, *in a dressing gown, is pacing up and down. She has a bottle of champagne in one hand, a glass in the other. She sits on the bed, gripping the bottle and glass tightly.*

KELVIN'S VOICE. Cybulski had passion . . . and charm . . . and violence . . . and intelligence . . . and I had an uncanny certainty he wouldn't live much past forty. (*Pause.*) Really, he was a grieving romantic – as well as an obdurate communist, after his own idiosyncratic fashion. (*Pause.*) And Poland now. (*Pause.*) Well. Bugger you. D'you hear me? *Bugger* you! (*Pause.*) My absurd recollections! Memories! Always raking it over and raking it over. (*Pause.*) Like Sladek. (*Pause.*) When Sladek was young, he wasn't unlike Cybulski in some ways. (*Pause.*) Did I tell you Sladek isn't dead? (*Pause.*) I was sure he was dead. (*Pause.*) They got him just before the Slansky trials. (*Pause.*) They were preparing it all. (*Pause.*) Sladek . . . 'bulski . . . look, isn't there any more of this brandy? Lousy though it is. (*Pause.*) I told you. I'll have nothing but Hine in this bloody house, Emma –

There is a long silence. Then a knock at the door.

EMMA. Yes?

MARK'S VOICE. Mark –

EMMA. Come in.

He enters – stands looking at her.

KELVIN'S VOICE (*drunkenly*). I mean, I thought the Gestapo got Sladek. Well they did of course. No, I mean then the second bunch of rats. Yes. That's it. First the Gestapo rats. Then the Stalinist rats.

Pause.

EMMA. Have some champagne.

Pause.

MARK. Do you want to stop the whole thing?

Pause.

EMMA. Have some bloody *champagne*! And sit down, or something. Stand on your head.

She goes into the adjoining bathroom, comes out with a glass, and pours champagne.

MARK sits tensely in a comfortable chair by the wall facing the bed.

I hope you can salvage something out of it. I just can't go on myself. (*Pause.*) It was a ridiculous idea. I'm going away. (*Pause.*) Out of the country. (*Pause.*) Meanwhile I shall have Robert's house sold. And everything in it. And when I come back, I shall . . . I want to write something myself.

Pause.

MARK. Write . . . what?

EMMA. I don't know.

Pause.

MARK. I'm sorry, Emma –

EMMA. About what? Your programme? If you can do it at all, you can do it without me.

MARK. Yes. I can.

Pause.

EMMA. Well then?

She is drinking constantly, refilling her glass, walking up and down.

MARK. Are you drunk?

EMMA. A bit.

Pause.

MARK. Where will you go?

Pause.

EMMA. To Paris. Robert used to talk about a cousin of his there. (*Pause.*) He may or may not exist.

MARK. Charles Bourne?

EMMA. I might have known you'd have traced him if he *did* exist! *Pause.*

MARK. He's a decrepit old queen. He's very ill. (*Pause.*) I asked if we could interview him –

EMMA. Why didn't you tell me?

Pause.

MARK *sips his champagne, half smiling wanly.*

MARK. We received a very large very thick postcard, bordered in black. It said: Robert Kelvin was a self-lacerating fool. His sole redeeming quality was to be quite incapable of self-deception. He took to Karl Marx before he was properly equipped to think; and I have taken to the Holy Roman Church before I am properly equipped to die. I consider it vulgar to wait until the last moment. Accordingly I linger on, I seek grace, I read St Thomas Aquinas, and I will permit you to interview me for thirteen minutes. Serviam. Charles Bourne. (*Pause.*) It had an address in the rue de Seine, it arrived this morning, and my secretary phoned it through from my office ten minutes ago.

EMMA *pours the last of the champagne into her glass and lies on the bed.*

EMMA. Charlie Bourne burned his father's wooden leg. (*Pause.*) I thought he might turn out to be a complete invention of Robert's. (*Pause.*) Robert Kelvin was someone who can't be gradually eased out of one's mind, one's life. Not to be forgotten, ever. But might be exorcized if you see what I mean. (*Long pause.*) You want to sleep with me, don't you, Mark?

MARK. Yes.

EMMA. Correction. You want, to begin with, to know whether I'm available to be slept with.

Pause.

MARK. No. (*Pause.*) I want you, Emma.

Pause.

EMMA. Love me?

MARK. I believe I do.

Pause.

EMMA. You shouldn't feel under any obligation to supply an impeccable motive. (*She sits up, vehement.*) I intend to get to Charles Bourne before you do!

MARK. There's no reason why you shouldn't.

Pause.

EMMA. Come to bed, Mark –

Pause.

MARK. Emma . . . listen –

EMMA. I'd rather you didn't say one more word.

> *She puts her glass on the bedside table, switches out the light.*
> *Close-up* MARK.
> *From his point of view we see her dressing gown fly across the*
> *room into a corner. He begins to undress.*
> *Close-up* EMMA.

18. *Clip from 'Ashes and Diamonds'.*

The scene where CYBULSKI *is in bed with the* GIRL *from the Hotel bar.*

> CYBULSKI *in the ruined chapel with the inverted crucifix.*

19. *Interior. Hotel bedroom.*

The intertwined bodies of MARK *and* EMMA.

MARK and EMMA *move and writhe together in slow motion.*

We see their hands and arms, their faces kissing, their bodies rolling over, their fingers on each other's backs.

And in a counterpoint with this: KELVIN'S VOICE:

KELVIN (*voice*). I know I'm going to die soon, Emma. (*Pause.*) Burn me. Bury me. Put me into lunar orbit. Anything. Only find somebody else *quick*. Do you hear me? Get into bed with somebody and get it over with. Then give him the push or keep him or do what the bloody hell you like, but *do* it. Will you, Emma?

EMMA (*voice*). I will if *I* want to. (*Pause.*) I've no intention of carrying out your instructions post mortem. (*Pause.*) What if I did it now? Why should I wait for you to die?

KELVIN (*voice*). Do it *now* then! Got anybody in mind?

> *Pause.*

EMMA (*voice*). No love. No. (*Pause.*) No.

20. Clip from 'Ashes and Diamonds'.

CYBULSKI *shoots the communist party official in the rainy street.*

21. Interior. Hotel bedroom.

MARK *and* EMMA *lie motionless side by side.*
Close-up EMMA.

22. Clip from 'Ashes and Diamonds'.

The macabre drunken dance scene in the hotel.

23. Interior. Hotel bedroom.

MARK. Well. That was a loathsome coupling for you! Wasn't it?
Pause.
EMMA. I'm sorry.
MARK. And I'm – humiliated.
Pause.
EMMA. I'm terrified. (*Pause.*) Numb. (*Pause.*) Nothing I want.
No one I need (*Pause.*) My mind's a blank. I don't even experience a flicker of lust! (*Pause.*) I don't masturbate. (*Pause.*) I'm
absolutely still. Quiet. (*Pause.*) I've no ambitions. No convic-
tions. Everything that moved Robert so hungrily seems now to
have belonged utterly to him. (*Pause.*) It isn't that I had a
pseudo-existence by just relating to Robert – and nothing else.
(*Pause.*) Though *he* often accused me of that. (*Pause.*) A lot of
people tried to put me down with that idea. (*Pause.*) And I
can't tell you what it's like now. (*Pause.*) At least I *am* angry! I'm
angry, and I've no volition. (*Pause.*) It's as if knowing Robert . . .
that huge, gifted, complex ruin of a man . . . as if *encompassing*
him . . . stripped life . . . for me . . . of its possibilities. (*Pause.*)
His despair. His disillusion. His sheer recollective insight
towards his whole life and experience . . . it you see, it really . . .

in the end . . . *exacted* nothing from me. (*Pause.*) He drank, and railed against me. But finally, as I understand it, he *demanded* nothing. He let me be. (*Pause.*) And in letting me be, he made it possible to live with my oldest suspicions. My coldness to life. My sort of . . . sensitive, erudite . . . inertia of self-pity . . . the refuge of feeling masochistic, of only being an object . . . and being incapable of *doing* anything, of taking any sort of *stand*. (*Pause.*) Then knowing all that and feeling nothing but contempt for it.

> *Long pause.*

MARK. Won't you – try? With me?

EMMA. What did I just do?

> MARK *slips out of the bed. He begins to dress.*
>
> EMMA *turns her face away, then suddenly shouts:*
>
> What did I just do?
>
> *Pause.*

MARK (*neutrally*). Nothing. I shouldn't think it even rated as a perverse act of self-sacrifice. (*Pause.*) All one learns through you is – Kelvin.

> *He goes out.*

24. Clip from 'Ashes and Diamonds'.

The scene where CYBULSKI, *in a chase, is trapped amongst pegged out sheets in an open space. He is behind one of the sheets.*
We see only the bulge of his shape, and a spreading stain from his wound.

25. Interior. Hotel bedroom.

EMMA *lies awake, staring at the ceiling.*

26. Interior. Robert Kelvin's house: study.

KELVIN *sits slumped in an armchair, clutching the inevitable glass.*
EMMA *sits opposite* KELVIN.

He is drunk, his head keeps dropping. He half mumbles :

KELVIN. When Cybulski stayed with me once . . . I watched him
go out on to the street . . . he was always convinced he'd lost
something . . . passport . . . an address . . . some vital piece of
paper with a name on it . . . his keys. (*Pause.*) He stood outside
my house turning his pockets out. He looked stricken . . .
turning round and round . . . fumbling with the things in his
pockets . . . I couldn't see his eyes . . . those tinted glasses . . .
and one time. In Warsaw. Pissed, we were. In his flat. Five in
the morning. The sun rising over the Vistula. I went into the
lavatory. Saw this battered tin, with his shaving soap and brush
in it. Took it back into the living room. (*Pause.*) What's this,
Zbyshek? (*Pause.*) It's an old mess tin, he said. A mess tin I
found. (*Long pause.*) Warsaw uprising. I don't know. *I* don't
know. *I* don't bloody well know. (*Pause.*) I was twenty odd
years older than him. (*Pause.*) Felt like a waxwork, suddenly.
(*Pause.*) We saw it, didn't we?
    Pause.

EMMA. Saw what, Robert?

KELVIN. I don't know. The mess tin. Didn't we see it? Don't you
remember?
    Pause.

EMMA. I haven't been to Warsaw, have I?

KELVIN. A mess tin. A leather jacket. (*Pause.*) Ashes and diamonds. Bloody legends. (*Pause.*) *He* didn't know where he was,
in . . . or out . . . or behind . . . legends. I'm going to . . .
going to . . . pass . . . pass right out, love . . . Emma –
    He slides out of the chair on to the floor.

27. *Interior. Hotel bedroom.*

As in Scene 25. EMMA *lies awake, staring at the ceiling.*

28. *Clip from 'Ashes and Diamonds'.*

CYBULSKI'S *death scene.*

29. Interior. Robert Kelvin's house : study.

EMMA *is standing over the prostrate* KELVIN.
*He manages to get to his knees. Starts singing drunkenly – a verse of
'Pirate Jenny'. Stops.*
KELVIN. *He* wouldn't speak German.

30. Interior. Hotel bedroom.

As in Scene 25. EMMA *lies awake, staring at the ceiling.*

31. Interior. Robert Kelvin's house : study.

KELVIN'S *body lies on the bed.
Two* MEN *lift and lower it into a coffin.*
EMMA *is watching at the door.*

32. Interior. Charles Bourne's flat, Paris.

*Charlie's living room/bedroom : shuttered, dimly lit, period furniture.
An enormous bed, where the mountainous* CHARLIE *reigns – a dying
heap of decrepit flesh. A queen who has seen and known it all for the
last half century – once a friend of Isherwood, Auden, the Bauhaus
Group.*
CHARLIE *is a kind of self-styled Oscar Wilde, with all the cultural
accretions of the twentieth century. The walls are covered with
Fuselis, Klees, pornographic drawings by Andrea Del Sarto, Dalis,
Bretons, reproductions of faded frescoes from Pompeii, tapestries.*
*He lies, Nero-like in the vast bed – which is littered with French and
Italian newspapers, magazines, intellectual journals in Russian and
German.*
CHARLIE *lies peering forwards into death – and presiding inwardly
and nastily over a past which lacked the violent and perverse poetry
of a Genet.*
His 'friend', ROBERTO, *is pouring champagne.* ROBERTO *wears a red*

shirt, tight blue denims, a flowered neckerchief, a plenitude of chains and bracelets.

ROBERTO: *Queer, loving, victimized, tender – a frail rowboat being towed beside* CHARLIE'S *overpowering body into the regions of death.*

CHARLIE *stares pettishly over his champagne glass at* EMMA, *who sits watching him, sipping champagne herself.*

CHARLIE. Wasn't Robert enough? Why search for him when he's dead? (*sipping.*) And don't tell me you're looking for *you*, dear! One's had quite enough of that sort of drivel in one's life from people. (*Pause.*) What's the *matter* with you all? Occupying your universities and squeaking your pathetic little slogans! (*Waves his hand.*) This place was full of tear gas in May 1968. I ask you! *Tear* gas! (*Pause.*) Roberto, *do* run away will you? And stop *crying!*

    ROBERTO *minces huffily out of the room.*

I will say. You're not garrulous. (*Pause: Tartly.*) I'm sure Robert appreciated that. D'you like the champagne? God knows where it goes in *my* viscera!

Whispers to one side of his hand.

Side opening. As if one didn't have *enough* holes in one of one sort or another –

EMMA. I don't talk much because I can't often think of anything to say.

CHARLIE. Well. It can't be stupidity. Robert never lived with stupid women. He only married them. He always began by thinking that practical. Then of course, he had to admit that it was merely tiresome. (*Pause.*) I hope *you* aren't political –

EMMA. No. I'm not.

CHARLIE. *That's* a relief, anyway. Does anyone think a bunch of dismal little bureaucrats can legislate for spirituality? (*Pause.*) I read Robert's last novel, you know. It was me to a *tee*. (*Pause.*) I really did begin life's great adventure in a lavatory on King's Cross station, you know. My only regret is that I am, you might say, a Genet without either his capacity for crime or his sublime talent. (*Pause.*) Imagine. *Tear* gas. And those abysmal CRS cracking the pates of students and innocent passers-by alike. (*Pause.*) Not that the CRS aren't quite sexy in their way. (*Pause.*) All that sinister *gear* –

　　Pause.

EMMA. I'm a bit desperate, Charlie –

CHARLIE. Did you expect to toddle from birth to death in a state of unadulterated bliss? (*Pause.*) I mean, you shouldn't have gone to live with Robert before you'd –

EMMA (*cutting in*). I've never liked young men. You may think that arrogant of me, but it's never been a question of my feeling superior. (*Pause.*) They bore me. (*Pause.*) It's curious how indifference attracts people. They want to smash through it. (*Pause.*) No one but Robert ever smashed through mine –

CHARLIE (*waspishly*). And what did he find on the *inside*, dear?

　　Pause.

EMMA. Nothing.

CHARLIE. That must have been very aggravating. Personally, I'm always delighted to find my worst suspicions confirmed. But Robert was *fanatical* at trying to drag out of people qualities they never had in the first place. People with genuine talents are often like that. They occupy a psychic jungle and it irks them to discover that most people subsist in a desert.

　　Pause.

EMMA (*smiling*). Desert?

　　Pause.

CHARLIE. There was a time when I could have turned a more subtle metaphor. (*Pause.*) You know. You cheer me up.

EMMA. *Do* I, Charlie?

CHARLIE. You do, you do! (*He wags a finger.*) Take no credit in the matter! It's just that here I am, learning day by day to turn my face towards death: and there *you* are! *Stuck*, dearie! *Stuck*. With decades and decades of the whole dreary trek in front of you. (*Pause.*) Why don't you commit suicide? It might give one one or two people a pang. They'll indulge themselves in thinking they are capable of mourning a life. Then that will be that. And *you* will have minutely diminished the sum total of pointless travail which passes for life on this planet. (*Pause.*) After all, you are not a Catholic. *I* must pursue the mighty legend of sin and redemption to its ridiculous conclusion. (*Pause.*) Can you conceive of anything more idiotic than passing through the hands of a priest before one snuffs it? (*Pause.*) Why can't they have little boy priests? Wouldn't mind passing through a pair of hands of *that* sort! (*Sighing.*) However, *lust* – apart from the problem of sin in that respect – has bid farewell to its monstrous host. Dammit, I'm even uglier than *Robert*! (*Pause.*) But you know, Emma, it's really only women and queers who can love without regard to the physical drawbacks of the desired body. (*Pause.*) How . . . (*Pause.*) how did a Nottinghamshire mining village produce a famous novelist and a cosmopolitan queen of such scabrous tastes as myself? (*Pause.*) Should they raise a monument of any sort to Robert in the vile place of our birth . . . I hope one night you will creep out there in the darkness . . . and underneath where it says: Robert Kelvin . . . take a hammer and cold chisel, dear . . . and underneath carve – in brackets of course – 'and Charlie'. (*Pause.*) Do you like that Klee over there? (*With pride.*) I stole it. From a Chilean millionaire who thought himself the bee's knees with a whip in bed. Whereas, darling, he wasn't even a gnat's knickers. (*Pause.*) A puny little fellow; but that may account for his delusions about his whipping. (*Long pause.*) Emma, you have no option – if you won't be reasonable and do away with yourself you have no option but to live stoically. (*Pause.*) *I* have never admired stoicism – but, as someone once said of the cavalry apropos warfare: it adds tone to what might otherwise have been simply a vulgar brawl.

Pause.

EMMA *speaks very softly and slowly, as if to herself.*

EMMA. Stoicism. (*Pause.*) Stoicism.

She goes to the bedside.

Why have you become a Catholic, Charlie?

CHARLIE *falls back among his pillows, his eyes closed, his mouth twisted.*

CHARLIE. Think of all the great schemes, the massive designs . . .

for justice, equality, the liberation of the human soul on earth. (*Pause.*) That was what crocked up poor old Robert. (*Pause.*) Tchah! Marxist! It neither illuminated his art nor uplifted his spirit. A self-disgusted spectator of other people's corrupted and abortive revolutions. (*He raises himself up.*) The Christians have done no better. And possibly worse. (*Pause.*) I decided, my dear ... to peg out in arbitrary allegiance to a great metaphor. (*Pause.*) Will that do? (*Pause.*) I mean, I decided ... that the Christ kick won on points aesthetically.

    EMMA *laughs.* CHARLIE *reaches out his glass. She fills his and hers.*

EMMA (*raising her glass*). *You* cheer *me* up, Charlie!

CHARLIE. Let us drink to that –

    They drink. EMMA *bends down and kisses his cheek.*

    Really! *That's* going a bit far, dear!

EMMA. No it isn't –

CHARLIE. You're a delightful child. I wonder why? You make no egoistic exertions ... and yet ... you emanate a curious peace.
    Pause.

EMMA. Then sleep now, Charlie. (*Pause.*) Would you like to sleep?

CHARLIE. I believe I would, you know –

    EMMA *takes his glass, moving away.*

EMMA. Shall I send Roberto in?

CHARLIE. I wish you would. (*Pause.*) He'll steal some trifle or other, but then I've never minded people stealing. (*Yawning.*) I've always thought it reveals a certain depth of character –

    His eyes close. EMMA *goes to the door.*

    As she opens it.

    Emma –

EMMA. Yes?

CHARLIE. You have genuine humility. I hope you will cherish that.
    Pause.

EMMA. Thank you, Charlie –
    Pause.

CHARLIE. Now send in that wicked boy. (*Pause.*) And tell him at least two of the Fuselis are fakes. *That'll* fox him.

    EMMA *laughs. She goes out.*

33. *Interior. Robert Kelvin's house : study.*

The furniture, including the bed, is shrouded. The door opens and one of Kelvin's ex-wives, RUTH, *enters.*

EMMA *is taking the framed photographs from the wall and stacking them on the bed. She looks up in surprise at* RUTH, *an attractive woman of fifty or so – poised, well-dressed, but a rather hard face.*

EMMA. Ruth!

    Pause.

RUTH. I've always kept my key to this house. When I divorced Robert I said you'd better change the lock because I'm hanging on to this key. (*Pause.*) I knew it would be very unlike Robert to have a *lock* changed.

    Pause.

EMMA. Why would it be?

    Pause.

RUTH. He simply wouldn't care whether I came or went. Made scenes or didn't. Dropped dead or stayed alive. (*Pause.*) I knew he'd just . . . forget all about it anyway.

    Pause.

EMMA. Did you come for any special reason?

RUTH. Yes. For those photos you are clearly about to run away with.

    Pause.

EMMA. Hardly 'running away with'!

RUTH. You think so?

    Pause.

EMMA. Robert left me the house, and the contents.

RUTH. I'm aware of that.

    Pause.

EMMA. Well then?

    RUTH *goes to the remaining pictures on the wall.*

RUTH. I knew most of these people. (*Turning to* EMMA.) I want
these pictures.

> *Pause.*

EMMA (*quietly*). They were all I was taking –

RUTH. You needn't lie. I naturally know the terms of the will.
(*Pause.*) You rapacious little bitch!

> *Pause.*

EMMA. Ruth. I've sold the house and the furniture . . . the paintings, the drawings. (*Pause.*) I gave the money and the capital
sum Robert left me to his Trustees. (*Pause.*) I didn't want it.
They can do what they feel is . . . proper . . . with it.

> RUTH *sits on the bed and lights a cigarette, eyeing* EMMA.

RUTH. I see. To prove what?

EMMA. To prove nothing.

> RUTH *rifles among the photos on the bed. Under one, she finds a
> small gramophone record.*

RUTH. And this?

> *Pause.*

EMMA. It's 'Guantanamera'. Robert bought it for me when we
were in Cuba.

RUTH. Sentimental value?

> *Pause.*

EMMA. I like it.

> *Pause.*

RUTH. How I detest you young cows! Maxi-coats and mini-skirts
and *minute* brains!

> *Pause.*

EMMA. Anyone would think Robert had left you for me. (*Pause.*)
Do you think I could have made him when I was ten years old?

> *Pause.*

RUTH. But you certainly *made* him. Didn't you?

EMMA. We chose to live together.

RUTH. *Chose!*

> *Pause.*

EMMA. Why are you so angry with *me*, Ruth?

RUTH. Don't be so arrogant. To me you aren't even a person.

You merely typify your generation. My daughter is like you and I loathe her too. You pretend to care about so much and value so little.

 Pause.

EMMA. You don't know me, Ruth.

RUTH (*rising*). One doesn't need to. That is precisely my point. (*Pause.*) They pulled something like you from between my legs twenty years ago – and she's taught me everything about all of you. (*Pause.*) Robert, needless to say, adored her. (*She smiles faintly.*) You might even usefully reflect upon that! (*Pause.*) He often used to say that as he grew older and older his women were younger and younger. (*Pause.*) He used to wax quite obscene on the problems of ending up with a six-month old.

 EMMA *takes her coat from the bed and puts it on. She picks up the record of 'Guantanamera'.*

EMMA. You can have the photos –

 And she exits.

34. *Interior. Large white room.*

Camera pans round the room, which is devoid of furniture except for a bed, a chair, and a record-player on the floor beside the bed. It is night, and the room is lit only by a small fat, nursery candle. We have the impression only of a bleak whitish space in the sporadic flickering of the candle.

EMMA *sits naked on the bed, staring down at the record-player. 'Guantanamera' is on the turntable, but not playing.*

KELVIN'S VOICE. I have this dream, Emma, that I'm being interrogated in a white cellar. (*Pause.*) A place of torture. (*Pause.*) A bit like an operating theatre, but I always know it is a cellar. (*Pause.*) Do you know that Sladek was tortured in the same prison after the revolution . . . the same place where the Gestapo tortured him. (*Pause.*) I know. I'm always telling you. (*Long pause.*) The point is. In the dream. I'm interrogating myself. Go on. Let's have one of your icy analyses of what the bloody post-Freudians would make of that. Go on . . . go on . . . go on . . . (*His voice fades.*)

> EMMA *bends down and turns on the record-player.* 'Guantana-mera' *fills the room very loudly.*
>
> *It plays right through, and* EMMA *sits on whilst the record turns noiselessly on the turntable.*

35. Interior. Robert Kelvin's study.

As it was when KELVIN *was dying. He lies on the bed, staring at the ceiling.* EMMA *comes into shot, kneels beside the bed.*

KELVIN. I'm going, Emma –
> *Pause.*

EMMA. I know, Robert.
> *Pause.*

KELVIN. Will you – will you go to see Charlie?
> *Pause.*

EMMA. Yes, Robert. Yes, I will.
> *Pause.*

KELVIN. And – my mother?
> *Pause.*

EMMA. Yes, Robert.

KELVIN. Charlie *did* burn his father's wooden leg, you know –
> *Pause.*
>
> Have I been worth the trouble? (*Pause.*) All the bloody drunken violent, abusive, maudlin trouble? (*Pause.*) The scenes. The vomiting. The aggression. The –

EMMA. Hush, Robert –
> *Pause.*

KELVIN. A Scotch, Emma. And a bloody great big one.
> *She gets him the drink. He takes a gulp.*

KELVIN. The last poem of Mayakovsky's –
> *Pause.*

EMMA. For God's sake, Robert –

KELVIN (*trying to shout*). Now!
> *She goes to the bookshelves. Takes a book and sits on the bed.*
> *As* ROBERT *drinks, she reads out the poem Mayakovsky wrote before he committed suicide.*

EMMA (*very quietly*).

Past one o'clock. You must have gone to bed.
The Milky Way streams silver through the night.
I'm in no hurry; with lightning telegrams,
I have no cause to wake or trouble you.
And, as they say, the incident is closed,
Love's boat has smashed against the daily grind.
Now you and I are quits. Why bother then,
To balance mutual sorrows, pains and hurts,
Behold what quiet settles on the world,
Night wraps the sky in tribute from the stars.
In hours like these, one rises to address
The ages, history, and all creation.
    Long pause.

KELVIN. Now piss off and come back when I'm dead.
    He goes on drinking.
    EMMA *closes the book, leaves it on the bed, goes to the door.*
    She stops and turns to look at him, then goes out.

36. Interior. Large white room.

As in Scene 34 – but Emma lies, still naked, face down on the bed. Her body is shaken with sobbing.

37. Interior. Large white room. Morning.
Close-up the door. We hear a bell ring outside. Pan to the window.
EMMA *sits by the window in her dressing-gown. The room is filled with bright sunshine. She goes to the door and opens it.*
An OLD MAN *stands there – he is over seventy and looks older, his hair very white, his face lined, his eyes dimmed by very thick glasses. He is dressed in an overcoat of central European cut, he carries a hat, and leans on a stick. It is Kelvin's old friend* SLADEK.

EMMA. Yes?
SLADEK. Miss Foster?
EMMA. Yes.
    Pause.
SLADEK. My name is Sladek. Do you know the name? Or perhaps you might know me as Volubin?

He smiles slightly, waiting. EMMA *is stunned. There is a long silence.*

EMMA. Robert's friend –
Pause.

SLADEK. Yes.
Pause.

EMMA. Will you come in?
She steps back into the room. He slowly follows her. They both stand looking round the room.

SLADEK. I had some trouble finding you –
Pause.

EMMA. How did you?

SLADEK. First Robert's publisher. Then his lawyer. (*Pause.*) You left Robert's house, then? (*Looking around.*) Your . . . your room . . . surprises me, somehow.
EMMA goes to the only chair.

EMMA. I've only got one chair –
Pause.

SLADEK. Could we go by the window?

EMMA. The window?
Pause.

SLADEK. I'm very nearly blind, you see.
Pause.

EMMA. But – you could see my room!
Pause.

SLADEK. I have . . . an impression of your room. (*Pause.*) Strangely familiar.
Pause.

EMMA *takes the chair to the window. She then goes to* SLADEK *and takes his arm, leads him to the chair. He sits down.*

SLADEK. Forgive me if I intrude –

EMMA. You don't. No. (*Pause.*) I can make some coffee –?
Pause.

SLADEK. My dear. How did Robert die?
Pause.

EMMA. Drinking.

Pause.

SLADEK (*smiling wryly*). That seems ... appropriate! (*Long pause.*)
He must have spoken of me then?

EMMA. Very often. (*Pause.*) I –

SLADEK. And now. How do you live?

Pause.

EMMA. I don't know. Not yet.

Pause.

SLADEK (*slowly*). I left Czechoslovakia. (*Pause.*) I went to Vienna.
Then Paris. (*Pause.*) I read of Robert's death. (*Pause.*) It had
the inexplicable effect of making me wish to come to London.
(*Pause.*) Your authorities are kinder to Czechs these days than
to ... some other would-be immigrants!

EMMA. That's what Robert said after the Russians went in to
Czechoslovakia. (*Pause.*) The Pakistanis had better start apply-
ing for Czech nationality, he said. Then they'll get into England.

Pause.

SLADEK. Robert could be a very ... *caustic* man.

Pause.

EMMA. I loved Robert.

Pause.

SLADEK. A long time ago – Robert and I loved each other.

Pause.

EMMA. He sometimes seemed ... obsessed by you.

Pause.

SLADEK. It may seem absurd at my age, but *I* would like to write
again.

Pause.

EMMA. To write – what?

Pause.

SLADEK. I have spent so much of my life in prisons. (*Pause.*)
Could we walk out? Could we take a walk?

Pause.

EMMA. I'll get dressed –

EMMA *goes out of shot.* SLADEK *takes off his glasses and rubs his
eyes. Sits with his face turned to the sun, his eyes closed.*

SLADEK (*in a whisper*). Forgive me, Miss Foster. (*Pause.*) Pardon this intrusion –
> *Close-up* SLADEK'S *face.*

38. *Exterior. Holland Park Gardens.*

In long shot, EMMA *and* SLADEK *are walking through the park. We move in on them as they come to a bench and sit down. There is a long silence, and he gently rests his hand on her arm.*

SLADEK. You are very sad –
> *Pause.*

EMMA. I'm – blank. If you understand me.
> *Pause.*

SLADEK. If I told you a very long, very complicated story – would you be interested?
> *Pause.*

EMMA. What is it?

SLADEK. It is my unwritten journal. (*He smiles to himself.*) I call it: A true history of the Czech Communist Party. (*Pause.*) I ask this of you – because of Robert. And my eyes, you understand . . . it is difficult to write. (*Pause.*) Let us write this together, and – dedicate it to Robert. (*Pause.*) Would you like that?
> *Pause.*

EMMA. Yes. I would. I'd like to do that.
> *She now takes his hand between hers. He is looking into the distance beyond her.*

SLADEK. For me, it really begins at Lenin's funeral. Can you imagine? (*Pause.*) I was at Lenin's funeral. (*Pause.*) A young man –
> *Close-up* EMMA'S *face.*

39. *Repeat clip from 'Ashes and Diamonds'.*

CYBULSKI'S *death scene.*

40. *Exterior. Holland Park Gardens.*

Close-up SLADEK'S *face.*
Close-up EMMA'S *face.*

SLADEK. It was a moving occasion. A most moving event. (*Pause.*)
And if you understand how Russia *was* at that time . . .
Fade out SLADEK'S *voice.*

41. Stock film: Lenin's funeral.

*We see several seconds of the funeral and hear 'The Internationale'.
'The Internationale' fades and becomes the Czech national anthem as
the credits come up over the funeral scene.
Fade out.*

After Haggerty

After Haggerty was presented at the Aldwych Theatre on 26 February 1970 by the Royal Shakespeare Company with the following cast:

BERNARD LINK	*Frank Finlay*
CLAIRE	*Billie Dixon*
CHRIS	*John White*
ROGER	*David Wood*
MR LINK	*Leslie Sands*
INTERPRETERS	*Margo Jenkins*
	Frederick Arle
	Helen Francois
ACTORS	*Tim Curry*
	Helen Francois
	Margo Jenkins
	Malcolm Kaye
UNDERTAKERS	*Lewis Wilson*
	Frederick Arle

Directed by David Jones
Designed by Alan Tagg

ACT ONE

Scene One

A big room with high windows, containing only a few sheeted chairs, a sheeted desk, two stepladders, pots of paint, etc. We hear a woman's voice, American, after a loud beating on the door. This is CLAIRE, *a bonily attractive woman in her late twenties.*

CLAIRE (*off*). Haggerty. You there? You *in* there? (*Pause.*) You *are* in there, you bastard. (*Pause.*) I can shout louder than this. As you know. (*Pause.*) Haggerty?

    The banging on the door starts again, louder. A tall, fattish Englishman of forty-five enters from another door. This is BERNARD. *The banging stops.*

CLAIRE. Haggerty, if you don't open up I shall push your goddam baby through the keyhole. I've got it here. In one of those kiddy chairs. (*Pause.*) Haggerty? Your child is shitting. (*Pause.*) Listen. I'm going to cram kid and shit right through your keyhole. Do you hear me, crabhead?

    BERNARD *is very upset by all this. Slowly, he goes to the door – and cautiously opens it.* CLAIRE *blasts into the room, but is naturally, since expecting* HAGGERTY, *somewhat taken aback at the sight of* BERNARD.

BERNARD. I'm not Haggerty.

CLAIRE. Prove it.

BERNARD. Well, I –

CLAIRE. Look. Let's get this straight. It's obvious at once your mind is kind of sluggish. And mine is *fast*. My mental processes go *whoosh*. Therefore, I know you are not Haggerty, but you're already under sentence. *You're* going to catch a big hunk of the aggression I've been working up from New York to that goddam door. And I'll tell you this. This is a fact. That was *Haggerty's* door. Once. (*Pause.*) And mine.

CLAIRE *stands looking round.* BERNARD *is somewhat traumatized and sinks on to one of the dust-sheeted chairs.*

Having the place done up?

BERNARD. Yes, I –

CLAIRE. Yeah. I saw, out in the square. The district sure is *going up.* (*Pause.*) Don't tell me. I'm cunning. I know. Haggerty leased you the apartment. Huh?

BERNARD. Yes. (*Pause.*) I've only been here a week.

CLAIRE. So you *know* Haggerty. I mean, I just want to know *how much* I'm confusing you.

BERNARD. No. His lawyer –

CLAIRE. Haggerty has lawyers now? Jesus. That's ironic. My lawyers have never managed to have *Haggerty.* If you knew him that would not surprise you.

BERNARD. I'm just a –

CLAIRE. Just a what? And just a who? But let me inform you before you go on to the defensive that you are the kind of Englishman I really hate. London is full of you. If human society was logical, you wouldn't have a name you'd have a number.

BERNARD. My name's Link. Bernard.

CLAIRE. I know why you're looking at me like that. You're wondering: is there anything human in that woman? Anything warm? Gentle? Kind? Reasonable? Anything *not* aggressive?

BERNARD. I –

CLAIRE. I can reliably inform you it's all there. But you have to work for it. Do you like that kind of work?

BERNARD (*pointing doorwards*). The baby?

CLAIRE. *Be* clever! *Strike* at the maternal areas! And you'll bust your chubby knuckles.

She goes to the window and looks out.

This used to be a real crummy square. Now look at it! Plum

doors. White façades. (*Pause.*) Do I see a coach lantern over there on the other side? (*Pause.*) Do I see a fairy peeping out from behind one of those polystyrene sculptures?

BERNARD. There are still a lot of poor families.

CLAIRE. Are there? Are there really? So I suppose you can still feel pretty good. Feel like you haven't *gone up too far.* (*Pause.*) I can see you have a real tender conscience throbbing somewhere inside that large bag of fat!

   Pause.

BERNARD. The baby –

CLAIRE. Leave the baby to me, Bernard. Bernard Link. Christ! Link! Did the other kids at school call you Missing? Don't answer. I realize you're bound to've heard it before.

BERNARD. You said the baby was –

CLAIRE. Shitting?

   Pause.

BERNARD. Yes.

CLAIRE. Do you wish to intervene? Have you got some ingenious scheme to prevent his rotten little bowels doing what physiology makes inevitable?

   Pause.

BERNARD. He's very quiet.

CLAIRE. I'll say for Haggerty's kid, he shits quietly. He gets contemplative. If he could think, he would be thinking: wait till she gets a whiff of *this* one!

BERNARD. When I came in this morning. With my groceries. There were three small children standing there staring at me. Quite unnerving. (*Pause.*) Well, I smiled. As one does. A friendly little smile for the small people. Who stare at you. (*Pause.*) And the girl – she couldn't have been more than six – said: Hello, fat man.

   CLAIRE *crosses to him.*

CLAIRE. Are you a defeated person?

   Pause.

BERNARD. No.

CLAIRE. So why didn't you kick her in the pussy?

Pause.

BERNARD. That would have been . . . disproportionate to the offence.

CLAIRE. You figured that out so quick with *your* mind? With the urge to kick out still embryonic?

Pause.

BERNARD. I think you've jumped to hasty conclusions about my mind. (*Pause.*) I resent that.

There is a loud yell from the baby outside. CLAIRE *goes out.* BERNARD *sits wondering things to himself. The baby's cries get louder, and go on for about half a minute.* CLAIRE *returns with a large bundle of Kleenex in one fist. The baby stops crying.*

CLAIRE. There it is.

BERNARD. I wish you wouldn't –

CLAIRE. You don't wish to know about Rass's crap? After what he's put into it, I mean? (*Pause.*) All that effort. All those thousands of articulated functions functioning? (*Pause.*) You're going to reject him?

BERNARD. Well. He hasn't met me. Has he?

CLAIRE. He and I don't like being in the same room as each other. Young as he is, we have arrived through God knows what primitive means of communication at this pact: we try to avoid each other. Since the child can't walk, on me falls the responsibility of respecting our wishes.

Pause.

BERNARD. What a curious name. Rass.

CLAIRE. His name, given its full credit of syllables, is Raskolnikov.

BERNARD. My God.

CLAIRE. Yes. It's worse than you being called Link. It knocks Link into a cocked hat. It makes Link sound unimaginative, and safe, and –

BERNARD. Children tend not to be familiar with questions of human evolution. It's only adults who've always said, I mean some of them: ha ha! I expect you were called Missing at school.

CLAIRE. So I'm glad you never suffered in that respect. May I now flush Rass's de-nurtured chicken purée down the john?

BERNARD. Yes. I wish you would.

CLAIRE. If you'd flown from New York to London at six months to find no father and a stranger in your apartment – *your* little turds would reach a new high in whatever goes for decibels in smell.

BERNARD. He doesn't know there's a stranger in the, the flat.

CLAIRE. I think I overwhelm you, Bernard.

She exits through the other door with the mass of tissue.
BERNARD *muses.*

BERNARD. Raskolnikov. Raskolnikov Haggerty.

He goes through the door to the hall. The child starts crying.
Fade out and fade in to

Scene Two

The stage is dark. An illuminated sign is lowered saying: BUDAPEST. *A single spot picks out* BERNARD *standing downstage centre. Another spot picks out an* INTERPRETER *standing just behind him, left.*

BERNARD *holds in one hand a small card of notes. He seems shy and humble, but speaks firmly. There are very faint and far sporadic bursts of submachine gun fire.*

BERNARD. This lecture was of course organized at a moment when the recent developments in your country had not reached the brink of outward, historical expression. (*Pause.*) I am amazed and confused to be here at such a critical time. (*Pause.*) And needless to say, I am grateful – and indeed humble – to find so many of you present this evening.

The INTERPRETER *comes forward and repeats what he has said in Hungarian. She then resumes her former position.*

To confront you as a drama critic from England is one thing. To confront you as a Marxist as well, may be to invite your justifiable derision. (*Pause.*) Returning to the question of the work of Christopher Fry and John Whiting –

There is a sudden and tremendous burst of machine gun fire off. The BUDAPEST *sign is raised, as the spots on* BERNARD *and the* INTERPRETER *fade.*

Darkness whilst BERNARD *removes his jacket and tie, and unbuttons his shirt cuffs.*

Fade up BERNARD *pulling forward a chair. He sits down, fastening his shirt cuffs. Spot on* BERNARD.

What about that, then, dad? Yes. Bloody well nearly killed, I was. (*Long pause.*) No. *Hungary*, dad. (*Pause.*) No, dad. Tito – he's Jugoslavia. (*Pause.*) Looking at your face I'd say you're entirely unmoved by the information I might have been killed. (*Pause.*) *What's* that? We'd never have got me Auntie Bertha over there for the funeral? (*Pause.*) Yes, I know I'm alive and well and you're entitled to your little joke. Ha Ha. (*Points.*) See that raincoat? There's a *bullet* hole in the sleeve of that raincoat. (*Pause.*) No. *Nobody* was shooting at me. I just got in the bloody way. And should you recount the horrendous tale to Auntie Bertha, you might as well add they don't go in for funeral ham teas in Hungary either. (*Pause.*) I was just having my little joke, dad. (*Pause.*) She's what? Having a varicose vein removed? (*Pause.*) Listen. (*Shouts.*) I nearly had my bloody life removed. Yes. My *existence*. Wiped out. (*Pause.*) You know. You have this habit. And it irritates me. Every time I tell you something that happens to *me* – you slap your thigh and say: eh, bloody hell, what'll happen next!

BERNARD *stands and takes his tie from his pocket, begins to put it on.*

I'll send you a map, dad. With a thick red ring drawn round Hungary. You might spend a minute or two with it between work and your allotment. (*Pause.*) If I don't get off now I'll never catch that train at Leeds. (*Pause.*) Yes, I know you never see me more than one day a century. Yes, I know. (*Pause.*) Well, I'm just going upstairs to pack.

Fade out and fade in to

Scene Three

BERNARD *sits at the desk, now cleared of its dust-sheet, and loaded with books, papers and a typewriter. He is typing.*

At the window, two young men, CHRIS *and* ROGER, *are painting the window frame.* ROGER *stops, with his brush poised.*

ROGER. By the way, Bernard. I can't make it here tomorrow.

BERNARD. Oh? Why?

ROGER. I've got an audition.

BERNARD. Where?

ROGER. Watford. Isn't it beastly.

BERNARD. The part, or the act of desertion?

ROGER. I'll die if I don't get something.

Pause.

BERNARD. There are bound to be hazards if one goes to a firm that employs out-of-work actors.

ROGER. Can't think why you did, love.

CHRIS *stops painting and goes to* BERNARD.

CHRIS. I'm not an actor. Nor a pouf neither.

ROGER. Chrissy – stop it! And be careful, you're getting wiggly paint marks all down the back of your hand. *You're* not a professional. Selling cars *he* was last week. Shouldn't be surprised they were you-know-what cars, either.

CHRIS (*to* BERNARD). I'm just telling you. That's all.

CHRIS *goes back to the window.* BERNARD *wearily turns for the inevitable chat.*

BERNARD. My last flat, it was anarchists.

ROGER. Smelly old lot!

BERNARD. They weren't as bad as actors. (*Pause.*) They were a bit of a trial though. (*Pause.*) They painted half the place, then disappeared. For ever.

ROGER. And of course – you'd paid them, dear, hadn't you? Silly old you.

BERNARD. I'd paid them half. (*Pause.*) Wherever they are, I suppose they can at least feel they kept their integrity. Half for half. (*Pause.*) I liked them, actually. I mean, for one thing they were terribly tidy and clean. (*Pause.*) One of them was sort of mad. (*Pause.*) They were very kind to him. And did most of his share. (*Pause.*) One day he forgot to wash his hands and just wiped the paint off on the towels in the bathroom. (*Pause.*) Two of them led him off somewhere and talked to him quietly. The other chap washed the dirty towels. (*Pause.*) He didn't actually get all the paint out. But I was touched by the gesture. (*Pause.*) They were all convinced mad people shouldn't be put in mental hospitals, and they looked after William like a baby. (*Pause.*) What's more, their William had a First in mathematics at Cambridge.

ROGER. Drive anybody mad, wouldn't it? All those sums! (*Pause.*) And talking of babies –

BERNARD. Look, I've got work to do.

ROGER. Yes, I know you have, love. I read that piece of yours about Brecht in Berlin and I thought it was fabulous. *But.*

CHRIS. He had a row with your friend upstairs this morning.

ROGER. I wouldn't exactly call it a row. It was the baby, Bernard. What I mean, I went into the loo for a pee. And I had this bottle of turps in my hand. Ever so absent-minded. Well, I put it on the ledge whilst I made my little contribution to the London sewage authority; and well, of course I nip away forgetting all about me turps, don't I? Well, with my luck *she* goes in there with what's-his-name. I forgot to tell you I hadn't put the screw on the bottle in the first place. And well, dearie – it's turps all over the little daemon's head, isn't it? The clumsy bitch knocked it over, and –

CHRIS. I wish you'd belt up.

ROGER. Chrissy, I shall sulk. Shan't I, Bernard?

CHRIS. You do lay it on a bit thick, you know.

ROGER. When you're as sensitive as I am, cherub, there's no point laying it on thin. Every nasty crude remark from people like you becomes a positive *spear*. As for Madam Haggerty, a spot of turps, I said, won't do it any harm. You can tell she loathes it, so why go all primaternal-donna over a drop of white spirit?

BERNARD. I'm paying you to paint a few bloody walls, Roger. That's all. I don't even ask for colours, which God knows you'd argue about till doomsday. Just a few walls. Whilst I get on with my trashy occupation of writing endless rubbish about the endless rubbish people like you want to act in. (*Pause.*) *Act!*

ROGER. Did I *ask* to be burdened with the absurd lust for it? Did I? (*Pause.*) I mean, I have to tell you, Bernard, and I'm not one for evasion – that is not a baby up there. It is a surviving miscarriage. You can put me through the door, dear, if you like. *But.* Christ. Raskolnikov! I'm not one to pass up a giggle in *any* circumstances. *But.* I expect when Madame first saw it, it was all blood and mucous and all that ghastly stuff that comes out *with* these things. And she thought it was normal. Then they wash the poor little mite and she takes one look and what comes into her mind, I ask you: Dostoevsky!

BERNARD. It's a perfectly normal baby. So get going with your brush and shut up.

ROGER. In all honesty, Bernard. Could you say it's a perfectly normal *mother*? Showers the object with turpentine, then blames me! I mean I've heard some pretty vivid language in my time. Frankly I turned red. Me!

CHRIS. Why don't you mind your own business? Eh? I've never known such a gush of gab. Not even from the scores of queers I've known besides you. 'Course, what they do at the office, they make sure you get put on a job with some poor sod like me. All tongue-tied and hard-working. They know somebody's got to do the graft, don't they?

He goes to ROGER *and waves the paint-brush in his face.*

You're *old-fashioned, Rodge*. Did you know that? Imagine.

Old-fashioned at twenty-six. And do you know what's aged you, sport? Your clacking tongue.

Taps ROGER'S *head.*

What you got in there? A bloody pianola?

Pause.

ROGER. *Chrissy!*

ROGER *begins to dab furiously if ineffectually at the window frame.* CHRIS *appeals to* BERNARD.

CHRIS. His sort – you can't deal with them. Know what I mean? He makes me wish I was prejudiced. If I let him yap he bores the arse off me. And if I spell out the odd home truth, then what? He's *hurt!* Look at him. You can see the blood pourin' out of his spiritual wounds. (*Pause.*) For god's sake I'm harmless enough. Ignorant. Uneducated. (*Pause.*) But at least I can take anything, can't I? Fairies, blacks, dykes, students –

ROGER *turns to him waspishly.*

ROGER. Place a tick against which noun is out of place in the above four!

CHRIS *goes over to* BERNARD.

CHRIS. I knew Haggerty, you know.

Pause.

BERNARD. I think I'll move into a hotel.

Pause.

CHRIS. He was great.

Pause.

BERNARD. How?

Pause.

CHRIS. You know what I mean? A great bloke.

ROGER. Listen to that! There's insight for you! *There's* a fully-rounded psychological portrait of Madam's lover boy! If that one had passed the eleven-plus, we'd have a psychiatrist on our hands now. Wouldn't we? Sock us the rest of it, Freud. Will you?

CHRIS. I'll duff him yet, Bernard. I'll have to.

ROGER. I take it all back, Chrissy. I'm still upset, that's all. I just can't cope with women. I adore them, but I can't cope. And when they're toting round their grisly wee progeny, they make me scream. One daren't *think* of that child's future. Start off with the name Rasputin and where on *earth* does one end up?

BERNARD. Ras – kolnikov.

ROGER. Kolnikov, then. Is she mad? Was Haggerty mad? The naughty mystery man. Where is Haggerty?

BERNARD. He's in Paris. I had a telegram from him after I signed the lease. It said: For interior decoration, go to 'Rely-On'. So I came to 'Rely-On' – did I not? Without even knowing me, Haggerty understood that I have a weakness for the unconventional. I'm not the sort of person who has his plumbing done by plumbers, building by builders, painting by painters. Oh no. Not me. I have to give work to the underdog – yes? Layabout actors. Anarchists. Earnest sixth-formers financing relief for the latest area of global devastation. What is the consequence? Every time I'm foolish enough to change flats, I live for weeks in some of the most dangerous environments in the world, short of actual warfare. (*Pause.*) I suspect Haggerty is some kind of genius. What else explains his knowing that I am a monument of vulnerability through his *lawyers*? The telegram was a masterpiece. It combined perceptiveness with sheer malice to a degree I have rarely experienced. (*Pause.*) I am labouring to explain, Roger, that without Haggerty you and I would actually have never shared the rich experiences we've had this last week. I hope the thought chills you – dear.

> Pause.

ROGER. I didn't come here to be rebuked, Bernard. It's time for our nice cups of nescaff, I think. Bags me the Gnome.

CHRIS. The bleeding *Gnome*?

ROGER. Bernard knows what I mean. That gorgeous big lumpy mug with the green spots. I call it The Gnome.

CHRIS. Oh, Jesus!

ROGER. *You* are getting the black chipped one with the wonky handle and I hope it draws blood.

Exit ROGER.

BERNARD *and* CHRIS *exchange a long, sympathetic glance.*

CHRIS. There's no holding some of them any more. Is there?

CLAIRE *strides in, holding an empty turps bottle.*

CLAIRE. Where is he?

BERNARD. Who?

CLAIRE. Ginger nuts.

BERNARD. *Please*, Claire –

CLAIRE. If he was any other sex, I'd ram it up his ass.

BERNARD. Wouldn't you like some nescaff?

CLAIRE. Bernard, the epoch of sociology may have brought them into their own – but Roger is a goddam maniac! Turpentine and babies' hair do not mix, Bernard. Like it kind of seeps down into their goddam *eyes*, if you get me.

BERNARD. I've had children. In my time.

CLAIRE. You did? And you bathed them in petroleum by-products?

BERNARD. For God's sake, one always has accidents with children around.

CLAIRE. Listen. I want Rass to live. That kid's gonna grow up and take his fair share of the crap that's flying if it's the last thing I ever do. With Haggerty's genes and my post-natal care he's going to be evil down to the toenails. (*Pause.*) What I have in mind is something like a Hitler. Or a Borgia. And don't think if you hang round my neck looking pained I'm going to crack. I cracked when I met Haggerty. And as far as I'm concerned the rest of life with him has become a treasured wound. (*Pause.*) Do you understand psychology, Bernard?

BERNARD. Well, I think over the years I've acquired –

CLAIRE. Yes. So dig this, man. Psychology is what I'm allergic to. Don't try to encircle me with comprehension, Bernard, or I'll go for your ego's jugular. I hope I inspire fear. If I don't, it means you're a loser in the natural selection stakes. It took millions of years to make American women out of dinosaurs, and I for one have no intention of throwing that achievement in the face of the Almighty. (*She pauses to enjoy* BERNARD'S *evident paralysis.*)

BERNARD (*almost yelping*). Claire – this is *my flat*!

CLAIRE. You mean you're kinky about *property*? Or is it just the problem of tenure? I thought Europe still had a few *genuine* socialists left! I mean, you don't even need *blacks* to get your kids on the barricades! (*Pause.*) Are you in touch, Bernard?

    Pause.

BERNARD. How long were you thinking of staying?

    CLAIRE *surveys* CHRIS, *who has been standing transfixed.*

CLAIRE. Why doesn't he get on with his painting?

    Now both BERNARD *and* CLAIRE *are looking at* CHRIS. *After a moment he goes to the window and resumes painting.*

You can move into my place on Long Island any time you like, Bernard. D'you know Amagansett? You'd like it. Those Atlantic breakers, they'd flip you over and shake you up and you'd feel as good as new.

BERNARD. But –

CLAIRE. And weekends, the psychiatrists settle in like locusts. You can't *move* for the amount of Nobel Prize material there is lying about on that sand.

BERNARD. What I'm trying to say –

CLAIRE. I'm not a colonizer. I'm an ejector. (*Pause.*) I thought bangle-bollocks was making coffee.

    Pause.

BERNARD. I thought I lived in London, if you'll pardon me.

CLAIRE. You don't seem to catch on. If there were such a thing as the supernatural and he were dead – I'd be Haggerty's ghost. Man, I'm haunting the fink already. Just calm down, will you? I saw the look in your eyes yesterday. I saw the crawling thought behind those moist peepers of yours. That I might turn out to be a *lay*. (*Pause.*) Bernard, I'm positive you don't wish to be thought unsubtle?

    ROGER *comes in with three cups of coffee on a tray. Ignoring*

CLAIRE *he gives one each to* BERNARD *and* CHRIS, *takes one himself. He holds the tray for a moment, then holds it out to* CLAIRE.

ROGER. I can't count.

CLAIRE *takes his nose between her thumb and forefinger. Squawking,* ROGER *drops his coffee.* CLAIRE *takes the tray from his other hand and holds it out to him. He takes it, and flounces out.* CLAIRE *looks at* BERNARD. *She reaches out and he automatically gives her his coffee.*

CLAIRE. Cheers.

Fade out as she drinks and in to

Scene Four

The stage is dark. An illuminated sign is lowered saying: MOSCOW. *A single spot picks out* BERNARD *standing downstage centre. Another spot picks out an* INTERPRETER *standing just behind him, left.*

BERNARD. The crucial development in our theatre in nineteen fifty-six was, as has been repeated and analysed ad nauseam: Osborne's LOOK BACK IN ANGER. (*Refers to notes card in his hand.*) At the Royal Court Theatre in London an entire generation seemed to have found its own vehement, articulate expression in the character of Jimmy Porter.

The INTERPRETER *comes one step forward and repeats what he has said in Russian. She resumes her former position.*

The spots on BERNARD *and the* INTERPRETER *begin to fade during his following speech, and his voice also dies away.*

Whether the artist consciously wishes it or not, his work often reflects the movements and currents of historical change. Of dialectical change –

Fade out spots on BERNARD *and* INTERPRETER, *as the* MOSCOW *sign is raised.*

Darkness whilst BERNARD *puts on a raincoat.*

Fade up BERNARD *pulling forward a chair and sitting down facing the audience.*

Yes, I know you gave me a key but I lost it. (*Looks at his watch.*) Made it up the M1 in just over three and a half hours this time. (*Pause.*) Well. When you weren't in, I drove round a bit. (*Pause.*) Drove down to the old house. By the canal. (*Pause.*) Doesn't look much different. A bloody dog rushed out and sank its teeth into me trouser leg. (*Pause.*) What? Oh, yes. Better than bullet holes. Aye. (*Pause.*) You're looking pretty fit. (*Long pause.*) That's not sciatica. It's all that bloody gardening. Your spine must be like a DNA molecule. (*Pause.*) Of *course* I don't expect you to know what I'm talking about. It's just a weak form of aggression, dad. Me displaying my cultural superiority. Or something. (*Long pause.*) She what? Fell off the hen-house roof? What was the old bugger doing *on* the hen-house roof? She must be eighty-three if she's a day. Knowing her, I'd say she was up there with the binoculars. (*Pause.*) Broken hip? I expect they'll give her an aluminium ball-and-socket. (*Long pause.*) I just thought I'd drop in. I'm lecturing in Harrogate tomorrow. (*Pause.*) Yes. I know. (*Pause.*) Harrogate ought to be shitten on by a fleet of airborne rhinoceri. (*Long pause.*) I was in the Soviet Union last week. (*Long pause.*) Dad – how can you make the long and tortuous jump from the Soviet Union to me Cousin Donald in two sentences? (*Pause.*) Well, he's getting on then, isn't he? Cousin Donald. Climbing up. Yes. (*Pause.*) Got all his *degrees* for Customs Officer, has he? Well, that's grand. Fine. Let's hope they post him to London Airport. I'm always having scenes there. (*Pause.*) He was an awful little bastard. Used to sit in the woods of a summer's day catching flies with his foreskin. (*Pause.*) By God, you don't half go granite-faced when I say something blue. (*Pause.*) Now I know why it is I'm an intellectual bigot. Me mother had all the so-called 'native' intelligence and you had all the dumb prejudice. (*Pause.*) You're as thick as a post. (*Long pause.*) Been mulling over the Twentieth Party Congress, have you? (*Pause.*)

Of *course* I didn't bloody think you had. (*Long pause.*) I have scenes at London Airport because I have this tendency to arrive there drunk, you know. From here and there. Coming and going. Globe-trotting Bernard. (*Pause.*) I can't wait to see me Cousin Donald's face should we confront each other on the official level, so to speak, one day. (*Pause.*) They're all sadists, but wait till they get him in the ranks. (*Pause.*) Nepotism is a word that's probably not in Donald's vocabulary. But if it is, he won't shove much of it my way. Not at London Airport he won't. (*Pause.*) Dad. What's more interesting about that pig-nosed little turd becoming a Customs Officer than me going to the Soviet Union? I ask you that in your full capacity as a working man. (*Long pause.*) Dad, I *don't* hate you. I really don't. It's just that since me mother died I've begun to *register* you in a different way. That's all.

Fade out and fade in to

Scene Five

BERNARD'S *room as before, but* CHRIS *is preparing to build some shelves. He is planing a long plank on two wooden trestles. It is night. A single bright standard lamp sheds light where* CHRIS *is working.* CLAIRE *is sewing. We hear a distant train, the howl of an ambulance. A long silence. The gentle swish of the plane along the wood.*

CLAIRE. You're working late, Chris.

CHRIS. Working? It's a bloody holiday when Rodge isn't here. Wriggling his arse. Cooing. (*Pause.*) See where there's all white paint spattered on the parquet? That's Rodge. (*Pause.*) Bernard's all right, though. Take these shelves. Well, it isn't part of the job, see. But Bernard, he'll ask you to do a bit extra and stick a tenner in your fist as well as pay for the job. (*Pause.*) And I don't screw him, neither. I take the bread. I do him a good job. (*Pause.*) How's the kid?

CLAIRE. Oh, he's O.K.

Pause.

CHRIS. I wouldn't have thought sewing was in your line.

CLAIRE. I'm not sewing. What my hands are doing, it's a kind of mini-wrestling. The result will be grotesque. (*Pause.*) You should grasp the idea that ineptitude has its uses in life.

CHRIS. I don't get you.

CLAIRE. I mean this: my mental picture of walking the kid out, you know. In his carriage. My vision is that he should look like he was a demented Lap. The son of a demented Lap. The grandchild of a demented Lap. And so on, backwards into the dark mists of ancestral time.

Pause.

CHRIS. I thought you was rich –

CLAIRE. There is no contradiction between the possession of money and the desire for your kid to look like something the reindeer brought in.

Pause.

CHRIS. He'll have to move down here, when we're doing his room.

Pause.

CLAIRE. Rass?

CHRIS. No, I mean Bernard. (*Pause.*) Or *you* will and he can have yours. (*Pause.*) Then we shall be doing yours, and –

CLAIRE. You think *I* should get on to some goddam truckle bed down here whilst he –

CHRIS. It isn't what I think. It's just you'll have to work it out between the two of you. (*Pause.*) If you're staying.

CLAIRE. Listen. I'm taking advantage of Bernard whilst I've got him. It's no secret. So I'm rich and I could stay in a hotel. Or anywhere. But here's where I lived with Haggerty and here's where I stay for a while. Till I've carried out a few investigations. Like, if Bernard was *capable* of getting me out I'd be out. Wouldn't I? There'd be no problem.

Pause.

CHRIS. You hurt Bernard.

Pause.

CLAIRE. So I hurt Bernard. That's like saying I breathe! If he put his boot in my can I'd whizz out like any other sonofabitch. Bam! Down the stairs. Rass dangling from my nerveless fingers. (*Pause.*) *Could* he dangle though? With *that* amount of hair? You seen Rass's hair? What nature proposes turpentine disposes?

CHRIS *has finished the plank, taken it off the trestle, and now he leans it against the wall. He takes a broom and begins to sweep up the wood-shavings.*

CHRIS. I wish you'd lay off Rodge, as well.

CLAIRE. Lay *off* Roger? I'm the first time the concepts 'lay' and 'female' have been brought together in the poor little bastard's life!

Pause.

CHRIS. He's not bad. Underneath. (*Pause.*) *I* needle him all day as well.

Pause.

CLAIRE. Chris, you choke me. I mean, you really do.

Pause.

CHRIS. Let it drop about the turps. That's all. (*Pause.*) Then Rodge won't rib you so much either. (*Pause.*) He's like that.

CLAIRE. Thank God he isn't American! Think what the little twink could do with *napalm*!

Pause.

CHRIS. Bernard's very good with Rodge.

Pause.

CLAIRE. OK. So the scalp defoliation incident shall never more be referred to. I submit. You raped me into a state of grace.

Pause.

CHRIS. Bernard tell you I knew Haggerty?

CLAIRE. Yeah. (*Pause.*) Haggerty in depth? Or just once-a-week-therapy?

Pause.

CHRIS. For about half an hour. (*Pause.*) I once came here to – see,

I was working for a builder's then. We was rung up and Haggerty said he had this roof fallen in.

CLAIRE. Which roof?

CHRIS. Well, it's Rass's, now.

Pause.

CLAIRE. If only the man himself had been underneath it!

Pause.

CHRIS. So me and my mate, we come round to have a look at the damage. Sort of estimate it. (*Pause.*) And when he answered the door, your husband's crying.

CLAIRE. Haggerty *crying*?

CHRIS. You could tell he'd *been* crying. From his face –

CLAIRE. I didn't assume even he would greet you with his ass! Though it's not entirely out of the question.

CHRIS. Mrs Haggerty –

CLAIRE. You think I was *married* to him?

Pause.

CHRIS. That's none of my business. I mean, what you and he was in your relationship, and –

CLAIRE. It wasn't a relationship. It was a labyrinth.

Pause.

CHRIS. Frank and me. We have a look at the ceiling, and that. Then your . . . Haggerty brings out the drinks and we have a chat and we tell him the score with the ceiling. And we leave. (*Pause.*) I never did the ceiling meself. I was bloody fed up with my firm anyway. So I starts this with Rely-On.

Pause.

CLAIRE. And so what was it about Haggerty? That hit you so hard? In your guts. In half an hour.

Pause.

CHRIS *has the shavings in a neat pile. With a brush and pan, he gathers them in.*

Shall we talk about something else? I can be garrulous on a fantastic variety of subjects.

Pause.

CHRIS. Ask yourself. What was you to Haggerty? And him to you? (*Pause.*) When you split up. (*Pause.*) Why. (*Pause.*) All that. (*Pause.*) It's time I was off.

CLAIRE. You got a bird?

CHRIS. Not just now.

Pause.

CLAIRE. Live with your parents?

CHRIS. No. I've got a room. Paddington way.

He empties the shavings into a large, empty paint tin. BERNARD *enters, looking tired. He is wearing an old short raincoat, open. He takes a notebook from the pocket and throws it down on his desk.*

CLAIRE. Hi –

CHRIS. I was just going, Bernard.

BERNARD (*notes the beginning of the shelves*). You shouldn't have stayed so late.

CHRIS. No odds to me.

CLAIRE. A drink?

BERNARD. Yes. I'd like one. Why don't you have one before you go, Chris?

CHRIS. Thanks.

CLAIRE *goes into the kitchen.* BERNARD *sinks into a chair, rubbing his face with his hands. He takes out a packet of cigarettes, offers one to* CHRIS, *who shakes his head, and lights one for himself.*

Been at the theatre?

BERNARD. Yes.

CHRIS. Crap?

BERNARD. Crap.

Pause.

CHRIS. It'd drive me up the wall.

BERNARD (*points up at the ceiling*). That's exactly where I am.

CHRIS *looks towards the kitchen, then back at* BERNARD. *Pulls a telegram from his trouser pocket.*

CHRIS. This come this afternoon.

BERNARD. Why the secrecy? (*He takes it, opens it.*)

CHRIS. It's International.

BERNARD (*just beginning to read*). So?

CHRIS. I sort of thought it might be from Him.

BERNARD. Do I hear a capital 'H' on the Him? As, for example, when referring to some deity?

    Pause.

CHRIS. But it is, though. Isn't it?

BERNARD. Correct.

    Pause.

CHRIS. None of my business.

BERNARD. I get your drift entirely. Therefore listen. It says: WHEN BITCH ARRIVES WILL BE VIOLENT AND EXPLOIT YOU STOP. DISSIMULATE SUBMISSION STOP. REMEMBER J. JOYCE: SILENCE, EXILE AND CUNNING STOP. HAGGERTY.

    CLAIRE *enters with a tray : ice, whisky, glasses. As she comes in,* BERNARD *stuffs the telegram in his pocket. She puts the tray on the desk. Pours three drinks. Gives one each to* BERNARD *and* CHRIS. *Takes one herself.*

    BERNARD *and* CHRIS *sip their drinks in silence.*

CLAIRE. You need a new ice-box.

BERNARD. I know.

    There is a long silence. CLAIRE *looks from* CHRIS *to* BERNARD.

CLAIRE. What's with what?

    Pause.

BERNARD. Nothing.

    CHRIS *finishes his drink quickly and makes for the door.*

CHRIS. Time I was off. See you tomorrow.

BERNARD. 'Night, Chris –

CLAIRE (*as the door closes*). G'night, Chris –

    She moves to a chair and sits with her drink. BERNARD *takes off his raincoat and goes with his drink to the typewriter.*

You writing your piece tonight?

BERNARD (*looking at his notebook*). Yes.

Pause.

CLAIRE. I guess I'll just finish my drink.

BERNARD. What time does Rass get *his* drink?

Pause.

CLAIRE. You know, when I came in just now –

BERNARD. Yes?

CLAIRE. With the drinks –

BERNARD. Yes?

CLAIRE. There was an 'atmosphere'. Between you and Chris. A real atmosphere.

BERNARD. Oh, I don't think so.

CLAIRE. Digging round for a good word for the atmosphere. I'd say it was *palpable*.

Pause.

BERNARD. D'you know what tonight's play was like?

CLAIRE. What?

BERNARD. I really mean – what it *was*.

CLAIRE. What was it?

BERNARD. A third-rate misfiring farce, written by an unconscious reactionary who thinks he's a combination of Strindberg and Lenin.

Pause.

CLAIRE. Well, at least –

BERNARD. At least what?

CLAIRE. You got the opening blast of your review in one sentence.

Pause.

BERNARD. I think I probably have.

Pause.

CLAIRE. Type away, Bernard. Ignore me. I need a couple of drinks, though.

Pause.

BERNARD. I always hate this bit. (*Pause.*) When I've got in. And it's late. And quiet. And I've got to commit myself to a few paragraphs.

Pause.

CLAIRE. Don't you ever see either of your wives? Or ex-mistresses? Or mistress or something, dammit?

BERNARD. First wife won't see me. Hasn't for ten years. (*Pause.*) I ring her once a year. Husband answers. (*Pause.*) When it's only once a year – why do I always get *him*?

CLAIRE. I'd say the problem defies statistical analysis.
    Pause.

BERNARD. And my second wife. Is in Australia. (*Pause.*) Lives with a professor of philosophy.

CLAIRE. They have philosophy in *Australia*?

BERNARD. Must have. (*Pause.*) I expect they have it everywhere. In one way or another.

CLAIRE. Yeah. I expect he wrote a brilliant thesis for his doctorate entitled: Baaaaaaaaa.
    Pause.

BERNARD. She owes me a hundred pounds. (*Pause.*) Left, owing me a hundred. (*Pause.*) That was their first two months' rent when they shacked up together in London.
    Pause.

CLAIRE. You miss the hundred?
    Pause.

BERNARD. No. But before he got the job in Australia, I used to think. Used to imagine them in their flat. In their bedroom. (*Pause.*) Banging away. (*Pause.*) And I'd hear myself suddenly yell, as I reflected: AND IT'S MY BLOODY HUNDRED. (*Pause.*) Once I was very pissed about three in the morning and I rang them to shout down the phone: IT'S MY BLOODY HUNDRED.
    Pause.

CLAIRE. What happened?

BERNARD. Well, *he* answered. He was rather forthright, considering who owed whom and how much. He said: Get stuffed – *bourgeois*!

CLAIRE. And you said?

BERNARD. He rang off. I fell asleep.

CLAIRE. Bernard. I think you better work. And I'll just sit here and be quiet. Or I shall start tearing you limb from limb.

Pause.

BERNARD. I know what you mean. But you see apart from the question of guilt. Of which I think he was incapable. He *did* have some cause for resentment.

CLAIRE. Being?

BERNARD. I paid them for their abortion. Her abortion. Just after she left me.

CLAIRE. Jesus Christ almighty!

Pause.

BERNARD. That was another hundred.

Pause.

CLAIRE. I can see you really brutalized this guy!

BERNARD. Yes. That's what I mean.

CLAIRE. *Mean* is the word. *Mean*-escalating-to-*sadistic*. (*Pause.*) You wicked Link!

BERNARD. I know. That's why the second hundred comes in a special category. Sort of psychic equivalent of tax-relief. I call it: THE AGGRESSIVE HUNDRED. (*Pause.*) Sounds like one of those Crimean Battles. Doesn't it?

CLAIRE. I gather you don't crave for the second hundred then?

BERNARD. No. That was money well spent. (*Pause.*) Only the first hundred. (*Pause.*) I'm not only bourgeois. I'm liberal, with it. (*Pause.*) And secretly, turbulent with hatred. (*Pause.*) Ho ho.

CLAIRE. We better not send you to my place in Amagansett. (*Pause.*) I think definitely not.

There is a long silence. Then BERNARD *switches on his desk lamp and begins to type.* CLAIRE *sits with her glass held to her lips.*

Fade out and fade in to

Scene Six

The stage is dark. An illuminated sign is lowered saying : HAVANA.
A single spot picks out BERNARD *standing in his shirt sleeves. A
second spot picks out an* INTERPRETER *standing just behind him,
left.*

BERNARD. The delegate from the United Arabic Republic said –
I believe I quote him correctly – 'If we are to take bread from
the people to buy a spotlight in a theatre: then the people must
have some control over what happens beneath that spotlight.' I
wish to propose a special discussion of the implications of that
statement.

The INTERPRETER *steps forward and repeats what he has said
in Spanish.*

The spots on BERNARD *and the* INTERPRETER *fade as he
continues.*

I am aware that the Assembly may consider this proposal an
unwelcome digression from the actual contents of today's agenda.
None the less –

Fade out spots on BERNARD *and* INTERPRETER. *Darkness
whilst* BERNARD *puts on a jacket.*

Fade up BERNARD *pulling forward a chair and sitting down to
face the audience.*

Dad – who can resist you? Who can resist a man who writes:
'Your Uncle Charlie's had his other leg off. A finer man never
wore a pair of boots'? (*Pause.*) Look, I'm only trying to say the
statement has its comic side. (*Pause.*) I *know* there's nothing
funny about losing both your legs. For God's sake! (*Pause.*)
Look. I was in the bloody blasted war, you know! (*Pause.*)
What? (*Pause.*) I've told you before. I got that wound in the
arse when I was climbing out of a burning tank! It's not,
cowardice-wise, a question of which way I was pointing, dad.
(*Pause.*) How could I be running away from the Germans when

the sods had us encircled? Go on! Tell me! And tell me, whilst we're at it, why you have to bring it up about three times a year? (*Pause.*) You've given me more scars talking about it than the actual piece of bloody shrapnel! (*Pause.*) I *know* it's not the same as Uncle Charlie. So he gets one chopped off down the pit, and one sawn off years later in hospital. I mean, I suppose the surgeon knew what he was doing. I just – (*Long pause.*) All right. I'll accept that. We'll try to stay off 'controversial topics'. Jesus. (*Long pause.*) Dad, you don't believe in God either so why get worked up about me saying Jesus? (*Long pause.*) Yes. I expect I am a bit tanned. I've been in Cuba. I wrote and told you I was *going*. All I can say is your memory for anything to do with me has *gone*. It simply doesn't function. (*Long pause.*) Well, I was a bit frightened of sharks. Sea's boiling with sharks round there. *And* barracuda. (*Long pause.*) Three and a half pounds, was it? A perch? Down at Crawston Dam. (*Pause.*) Dad. Don't say things like: 'From the sublime to the ridiculous'! Please. There is *no* contest on between my sharks and your perch. None whatsoever. (*Long pause.*) What? You thought Cuba was part of America and it's been and gone and gone communist?

BERNARD *stands, looking in front of him woodenly. Long pause.* Dad. Your mind doesn't have ideas. It has enigmatically related confusions. (*Pause.*) Sorry. (*Pause.*) I was about to say there *was* a sense in which Cuba was part of the USA. But it bloody well isn't any more! (*Long pause.*) Why are you crying? (*Pause.*) All my life I thought you were something like a mute. (*Pause.*) *She* did all the talking. (*Pause.*) Now *you* do the talking. (*Pause.*) And when you revert. When you go mute. Which is to say: when I begin to think I recognize you again – dammit, you cry! (*Long pause.*) Padre o muerte! Venceremos!

Fade out and fade in to

Scene Seven

*The same as Scene 5, but later in the small hours. The room is dark,
lit only by a street lamp outside.* CLAIRE *is asleep in her chair.*
BERNARD *enters from the upstairs exit. He stands watching her a
moment. Then he goes to her and gently shakes her.*

BERNARD. Claire –

> *She is instantly awake, reaching beside her for her glass.*
> BERNARD *goes to the desk and switches on the lamp, pulling it
> down so that the room is only softly lit.*

CLAIRE. What time is it?

BERNARD. Just after four.

CLAIRE. Oh, my God! The kid –

BERNARD. It's all right. He started howling. I went up and fed him
and he went back to sleep.

> *She rubs her face with her hands.*

CLAIRE. Seems like I drank the whole damn bottle.

BERNARD. Most of it.

CLAIRE. You manage to finish your piece?

BERNARD. Yes.

CLAIRE. I hope it was a good old stinger-roo.

BERNARD. The tone was one of stylish malice.

> *Pause.*

CLAIRE. I'm sorry about the kid.

> BERNARD *goes to the desk and gets his glass. He pours a drink
> from the whisky bottle beside* CLAIRE'S *chair.*

BERNARD. How d'you feel?

> *Pause.*

CLAIRE. Muzzy. And vicious.

> *Pause.*

BERNARD. I'll just have one drink. Then I'll get out of the firing
line.

CLAIRE. I mean generalized vicious, Bernard. Not you.

Pause.

BERNARD. Long time since I mixed and administered a feed.

CLAIRE. You take a good look at him?

BERNARD. Not much point in looking elsewhere. What with having the teat rammed into his little mouth. And the trickling, and so on.

Pause.

CLAIRE. Cross your mind he looks like Mao Tse Tung?

BERNARD. Looks like any baby. To my mind they always do. (*Pause.*) Shouldn't you get some sleep?

CLAIRE. I just had some, didn't I?

BERNARD. In bed, I meant.

CLAIRE. Sleep is sleep.

Pause.

BERNARD. Aren't you a bit pissed, though?

CLAIRE. My mouth tastes like a weasel's foreskin. Otherwise – compos mentis.

BERNARD *sits opposite her.*

BERNARD. I'm a bit of an insomniac. Usually about this time I have a few last drinks and play some nostalgic record or other.

Pause.

CLAIRE. Times of love.

BERNARD. I expect so. Yes. Records are better than milestones. What with them being round and flat. And when you stick a needle on them they induce sensations. Which can be carefully regulated according to mood. (*Pause.*) It's my favourite time. In one eye a tear, in the other a glint. When I think of my lacerating comments on the theatre of this-that-or-the-other. (*Pause.*) A harmless form of omnipotence.

CLAIRE. Except for the poor sod who wrote the play.

Pause.

BERNARD. Most of the best playwrights don't give a damn about the notices. Quite rightly, I and my fellow criticism-grubbers are simply unreal to them. (*Pause.*) I like that, since the notion that I am unreal coincides with my own self-evaluations.

(*Pause.*) Also, I might add. If it's a good play — I give it a thorough analysis and unstinting praise. Needless to say, that is a rare enough strain on my feeble reserves of generosity. (*Pause.*) All these things combined, well ... they concede me a certain grudging respect.

He drinks. CLARE *takes a small drink.*

CLAIRE. You going to play one of your milestones, then?
 Pause.

BERNARD. I think: a touch of the Leonard Cohen's. But this one, I assure you, is emotionally neutral. (*Pause.*) Partly because I discover these singers about two years after everyone's been at them for at least a year. (*Pause.*) And the last year has been ... from the woman point of view, shall we say? Pretty arid.

 As BERNARD *goes to the Hi-Fi, which is a jumble of gear on the floor in one corner :*

CLAIRE. I *told* you. The idea of laying me *did* flicker across your — dare I say it after so much unjust irony? — across your mind?

 BERNARD *starts the Leonard Cohen record. Resumes his seat.*

BERNARD. Must get a new typewriter. It seemed to make an awful clatter when you were sitting there asleep behind me.

CLAIRE. And a new ice-box.

BERNARD. We've already agreed that.
 Pause.

CLAIRE. That's Haggerty's ice-box.
 Pause.

BERNARD. He left a few things.
 Pause.

CLAIRE. Haggerty was always unlucky with artefacts. Anything man-made: walls, floors, windows, electronic stuff. You know what I mean? You had the impression when Haggerty moved in somewhere, the gadgetry of civilization went on strike. He is the only man I know who actually did get his penis trapped by the lid on the lavatory bowl. (*Pause.*) For example. The lid was in the up position one moment, as for standard male-usage. The next it was pinning his poor old prick to the porcelain. (*Pause.*) It was like he took poltergeists with him. Everywhere.

BERNARD. If we take your description as correct, he must have been something of an acrobat.

CLAIRE. Use your head, Bernard! He was kneeling. He had it over the goddam side of the bowl.

BERNARD. Kneeling to pee? Was he a kind of micturitional evangelist?

CLAIRE. Haggerty was often drunk. And when in the john liked to keep his head low in case he should throw up.

BERNARD *reflects, drinking.*

BERNARD. Then he must quite often have been belted across the head by the lavatory lid. (*Pause.*) Therefore, I suppose on the occasion you describe, he was also leaning backwards? His head backwards? (*Pause.*) Or else the genital would never have been struck. (*Pause.*) I think.

Pause.

CLAIRE. I never worked it out, Bernard. I haven't got the academic twist of mind, like you.

Pause.

BERNARD. Talking of academic matters. I'm lecturing in Paris tomorrow evening. To some of those students, you know? Who are a trifle iconoclastic these days. About art.

CLAIRE. They'll pull your guts out and hang them over the Sorbonne.

Pause.

BERNARD. Curious. At forty-five, one has to face the fact that one is a mere relic. (*Pause.*) Culturally, a relic.

CLAIRE. There are plenty of guys facing that problem in New York at thirty!

Pause.

BERNARD. Do you like the Leonard Cohen, Claire?

CLAIRE. I don't like any kind of music. Especially emotional milestone music.

BERNARD. Which I said it wasn't.

CLAIRE (*rising*). I'm going up. You finish your drink and enjoy what you enjoy, Bernard. Rass's id – I think they only have id at this stage, don't they? His id will be in full voice between six and seven. (*Pause.*) What time's your plane?

BERNARD. About one p.m. Air France. I always go Air France, Orly being nearer the city than Le Bour –

CLAIRE (*cutting in*). Sleep late and I'll call you around eleven. OK?

BERNARD. Fine.

She goes to the door. At the door, turning:

CLAIRE. The Mormons were here this morning.

BERNARD. *What?*

CLAIRE. Yeah. Mormons. At your door. My door. Haggerty's door. You know? Mormons?

BERNARD. I know what they *are*.

CLAIRE. They looked like they were fresh out of some CIA training establishment. Mormons, I said? Don't give me that, fellers. You get back to the good old USA and piss into the files. That, I said, might guarantee you a place beside the Lord.

BERNARD. Oh dear.

CLAIRE. Why oh dear?

Pause.

BERNARD. It's just . . . I've had a certain amount of attention from the Special Branch. In my time. Here in London. And –

CLAIRE. Don't lose your cool, Bernard. I told them I was your cleaning woman and you're a Roman Catholic. I figured it this way: Mormons or CIA, how will they push *this* conversation?

BERNARD. And how did they?

CLAIRE. They bowed their nice all-American cropped heads and withdrew. For your further edification, quite by accident I had a long sharp carving knife in my hand. Carving knife, huh? You *do* remember we had roast lamb for lunch?

BERNARD (*distractedly*). Oh, yes. Very nice it was. Yes. Roast lamb. (*Pause.*) And string beans.

CLAIRE. I warn you, Bernard. From now on it's out with the carbohydrates and in with the proteins. Huh?

    BERNARD is still abstracted, but looks down at his paunch.

BERNARD. It never works, you know. Not with me.

CLAIRE. I'm gonna starve that paunch to within an inch of its life. (*Pause.*) Before I go.

BERNARD. I see.

CLAIRE. So you either collaborate. Or you've got me for an even longer stretch than you had in mind.

    Pause.

BERNARD. Starvation it is, then!

CLAIRE. G'night, Bernard –

BERNARD. Good night, Claire.

    She goes out. BERNARD goes to the record and changes it. He goes back to his chair and his drink. Softly, a Mozart BASSOON CONCERTO wells up. BERNARD goes and switches off the desk light. Returns to his seat – once more the room is lit by the street lamp.

    Fade out and fade in to

Scene Eight

The stage is dark. An illuminated sign is lowered saying: PRAGUE. A spot picks out BERNARD, in his jacket. A second spot picks out an INTERPRETER standing just behind him, left.

Above and behind them, suspended, there is the effect of a human figure slowly burning. This continues throughout.

BERNARD. I can hardly speak.

    The INTERPRETER translates this immediately in Czech.

(*More aloofly and formally.*) You know. And I know. That it is impossible for me to give the proposed lecture on contemporary English Drama. Or for you to listen.

    The INTERPRETER translates this.

I have no doubt that many of you . . . share . . . my disgust . . .

with the hypocritical indignation of the Western countries.
(*Pause.*) Even in your anguish. (*Pause.*) Your isolation. (*Pause.*)
Someone said to me yesterday: don't come here from your comfortable house in London to tell us what a Marxist you are.
(*Pause.*) I had no such intention, of course. (*Pause.*) There are
many ways of burning. (*Pause.*) But let each way, each fire, con-
sume whatever is destroying our humanity. (*Pause.*) I can say no
more.

BERNARD *stands expressionless, whilst the* INTERPRETER
translates in Czech. As she finishes, a slow clapping begins. The
INTERPRETER *comes forward, her back to the audience, facing*
BERNARD. *She takes up the clapping rhythm herself. This con-
tinues for a few seconds.*
The spots on BERNARD *and the* INTERPRETER *fade. The clap-
ping stops. The burning human figure fades into darkness.*
Darkness for a few seconds.
Fade up BERNARD *pulling forward a chair. He sits. There is a
long pause.*

I see. (*Pause.*) You were ill. You were alone. Nobody came to
see you. Nobody even popped in and offered to do you a bit of
shopping. (*Pause.*) Mrs Lambert next door's what? Been taken
into mental hospital? (*Long pause: he stands pointing.*) The
bloody telephone's still there, isn't it? (*He sits.*) Why did I . . . ?
(*His voice fades away wearily.*) Why do you think I had the sod-
ding phone put *in*? (*Long pause.*) I see. I should have telephoned *you*, dad. (*Long pause.*) I'm telepathic. I'm clairvoyant.
I *know* you're ill without being told. Eh? (*Pause.*) Oh. (*Pause.*)
Yes, I see. When I was in Jugoslavia. But it was Czechoslovakia.
(*Pause.*) That's right. (*Pause.*) So why didn't you ring the
doctor? The Old People's Welfare? Downing Street? (*Long
pause.*) Dad, I only use sarcasm to your actual face because I
can usually rely on it not penetrating your skull. And that is
therapeutic. Yes, for me, I mean. It normally relieves my ten-
sions without damaging *you*. (*Long pause.*) What? It was Mr
Lambert's sarcasm sent Mrs Lambert round the bend? (*Pause.*)

You and I have conflicting views on mental illness, dad. (*Long pause.*) Yes. I know. On everything. (*Long pause.*) I feel like getting down on my knees and pleading your forgiveness for not being a Customs Officer. (*Pause.*) Your scale of what constitutes human achievement is one I comprehend – but reject. See? What's more, I roll in from Prague and me Cousin Donald *is* at London Airport. What does he do? Carves me up for having three bottles of slivotiz instead of one. You should have seen the smarmy expression on his face. I said – I was high, I'll admit – I said: Donald, let me take the two offending bottles and pour them down the lav. What did he say? By all means, he said. But you'll still have to pay the tax because you brought them *in*. (*Pause.*) I turned to his – what do they call it? Colleague? And yelled: that man used to catch flies under his – (*Pause.*) OK, OK, I'll wash me dirty mouth out. (*Pause.*) Dad I am forty-five. (*Pause.*) Drink? What's drinking got to do with it? (*Pause.*) You're ashamed to have me Cousin Donald see me pissed at the airport? I am ashamed of your shame.

    Fade out and fade in to

Scene Nine

As the previous night, except the drinks have been cleared and the typewriter is covered. It is afternoon.

An old man enters – at least, he is over seventy. A big man in an old but well-brushed and pressed suit, a checked shirt with a large bulging knot on his tie, and a trilby hat. He carries a brown paper carrier.

He looks round : the room is empty. He takes off his raincoat, folds it and puts it over a chair back. He removes his hat and places it carefully on the desk.

He sits in the middle of the room, his back straight, his hands on his knees. Physically, he is a formidable size and shape. He looks awkward but dignified.

ROGER *enters, wearing denim shirt and trousers, and a flowered kerchief. He is carrying a large paint tin. Looks wretched. The old man* – BERNARD'S FATHER – *has his back to the hall door and doesn't turn.* ROGER *crosses the room and into the kitchen with the paint tin. The* FATHER *takes out a flat tin of tobacco, papers, and begins to roll a cigarette.*

ROGER *comes a few steps out of the kitchen.*

ROGER. Hello.

FATHER. How d'ye do.

    Pause.

ROGER. It's . . . er . . . I think it's in the kitchen. Under the sink.

    Pause.

FATHER. What is?

ROGER. The (*failing*) – the meter. Mmmm?

FATHER. Well, I'm very interested to hear that. I always like to know where t'meter is.

    Pause.

ROGER. Not Gas Board? London Electricity?

    FATHER *looks up from rolling his cigarette.*

FATHER. Young man. I bought this suit off t'peg in Doncaster in nineteen fifty-two. (*Pause.*) Now. To you it might very well make me look like t'gas man. To me it were a bloody bargain.

    ROGER *hovers, as always wary of instantaneous attack.*

ROGER. Then –?

FATHER. Then I had Mother take up t'cuffs an inch. And after that it were champion. (*Holds one arm out.*) Feel that material.

ROGER. Might one ask how you got *in*?

FATHER. One might. One found t'door open. (*Pause.*) And while we're about it. Might *one* ask you who the bloody hell you are?

ROGER (*pertly*). I was going to ask you the very same thing!

    Pause.

FATHER. I'm Mister Link's father

    Pause.

ROGER. *Oh*, dear me! I *am* sorry!

FATHER. Don't let it put thy nose out of joint.

ROGER. Terrible brick dropper! I'm *awful*.

    Pause.

FATHER. Be that as it may.

    Pause.

ROGER. You see, Bernard's in Paris. Doing his talkie-talkie bit.

FATHER. Eh?

ROGER. He's giving a lecture in Paris. Would you like a cup of tea?

FATHER. I wouldn't say no. I've just come off t'train.

ROGER. Was it ghastly? From where was it?

FATHER. You wouldn't know it. Little place near Doncaster. Heard of Doncaster, 'ave you?

ROGER. Look, I'm devastated, you know? With shame? I mean about the Gas Board.

FATHER. Nay, lad. Sometimes when I go into a pub in Doncaster, they take me for a detective. What does't think on that? Eh?

ROGER. I don't really know, Mr Link.

FATHER. It's me feet, tha sees. An' me raincoat. And t'way I *hold* meself, if you get me. I *hold* meself like a detective. I've been told so. (*Pause : he chuckles.*) I've seen some faces drop when I've gone in one or two places after closin' time. (*Pause.*) Our Bernard, he – are you a friend on his, then?

    Pause.

ROGER. Well, not exactly a friend –

FATHER. Not from t'Gas Board, are you?

    ROGER *greets this with a sickly smile.*

I like a feller as can take a joke.

ROGER (*muted*). I'm in this firm that's doing his flat up. Rely-On.

FATHER. *Rely-On*, is it? Now there's a name for a firm. Somebody's got their head on their shoulders.

ROGER. Yes. Well. It isn't me. I'm just one of their wretched serfs.

FATHER. Serfs? I thought them was abolished in the nineteenth century. (*Pause.*) Tolstoy's time, round about. Wasn't it?

Pause.

ROGER. It was a manner of speaking, Mr Link.

FATHER. Nay, I've read a thing or two about serfs. In me time. Mind you. I'm only a self-educated man, Mr –

ROGER. Call me Roger.

FATHER. Call you anything you like, lad. But between you and me. I haven't read a book for nigh twenty years. Haven't found one that caught me interest, you know. (*Pause.*) When's he due back, then?

ROGER. Well, you never know. With Bernard.

Pause.

FATHER. I'll give you that one! Straight away.

ROGER. I mean. *Quite* a will-o'-the-wisp! Isn't he?

FATHER. I'll tell thee what, lad.

ROGER. What?

FATHER. I'm gagging for that cup o' tea. I don't want to trouble you. I'd get it meself. Only I've never been here before.

ROGER. Milk and shug?

FATHER. If it's no trouble.

> ROGER *starts for the kitchen, then comes back to the* FATHER *confidingly.* MR LINK *sits, as always, with his hands on his knees.*

ROGER. Er –

FATHER. Go on, lad. Go on!

ROGER. I don't know whether I ought to say. *Warn*, I was *going* to say –

Pause.

FATHER. What's up?

Pause.

ROGER. 'Course, the place is in an awful mess to start with. But apart from that. (*Pause: semi-whisper.*) There's an L-A-D-Y living here. (*Pause.*) If that's the word for her.

FATHER. Eh, that's nowt new! He's 'ad more than one companion since his last divorce. Does't think I'm narrow minded or sum-at?

ROGER. She's got a baby as well.

> *Pause.*

FATHER. Oh, aye? That *will* take a minute to sink in, I'll admit. First he's had out of wedlock as far as I know.

> *Pause.*

ROGER. Oh, it's not *Bernard's*, Mr Link! Oh dear me, no!

> CLAIRE *enters with a polythene bag crammed with laundry, from the door leading upstairs.*

CLAIRE. Roger, I –

> *She stops and registers the scene.* MR LINK *sits impassively.*

(*sharply to* ROGER.) I was about to say I shall be at the launderette for the next half-hour. I thought Chris might keep an eye on Rass.

ROGER. Mr Link. This is the lady I was telling you about. Claire dear, Bernard's father. All the way from Doncaster.

> MR LINK *gets up and holds his hand out.* CLAIRE *drops the bag and shakes hands with him.*

FATHER. How d'you do, love –

CLAIRE. Glad to meet you, Mr Link. And surprised too, because Bernard's –

FATHER. In Paris. Aye. T'young man told me. (*Pause.*) If I've caught you at an inconvenient moment –

ROGER. I was just going to make a cuppa –

> ROGER *flits off into the kitchen.* MR LINK *sits down.*

FATHER. I hope I'm not putting nobody about –

CLAIRE. Of course you aren't. Only, I'm sure Bernard wasn't expecting –

FATHER. Well, he wouldn't be, would he? I hadn't told him I was coming. When I were sitting in t'train: I thowt – wait till I see yon one's face. (*Pause.*) When you come to think about it, I'm bloody lucky if I see his face at *all*. (*Pause.*) Since his mother passed on. (*Pause.*) You know what our Bernard does?

CLAIRE. He never mentioned his parents.

FATHER. Aye. Well, tha sees, he's nobbut *one*. That's me.

CLAIRE. I'm sorry –

FATHER. Nay. Claire – can I call you Claire, is it?

CLAIRE. Sure.

FATHER. Are you his young lady?

Pause.

CLAIRE. I'm more a kind of visitor, Mr Link.

Pause.

FATHER. I take it you are from America. By the sound of your voice.

CLAIRE. That's right –

FATHER. I was going to say. What our Bernard does. He sends me ten quid a week to top up me pension. Then when it comes to setting *eyes* on him. Well, I can go and whistle, can't I? (*Pause.*) Not that he isn't a good lad. One of the best.

ROGER *enters with tea things on a tray. He sets it on a desk.*

ROGER. Can't we *phone* Bernard or something?

CLAIRE. Suppose you keep your cute little muzzle out of it, Roger?

ROGER (*mincing out*). See what I mean, Mr Link? Serf! And nothing in the Rely-On terms says we have to bend over hot kettles, either!

He exits.

FATHER. I say! That were a bit sharp, weren't it?

CLAIRE. Don't worry, Mr Link. If you went for Roger with a road drill it'd slide right off him.

Pause.

FATHER. I saw a programme about them on television.

CLAIRE. I beg your pardon?

FATHER. On telly. There's more about than you'd think. 'Omo-sexuals. Yer know? Omo. Like t'soap powder. Bit too much sex in them adverts, an' all. If you ask me. Which nobody does. Sex everywhere, it is. And as for *London* –

CLAIRE. Mr Link. Did you come down to see Bernard about anything special? Is it urgent, I mean?

Pause.

FATHER. Floods.

Pause.

CLAIRE. I'm sorry?

FATHER. Me house is flooded. Three feet o' water in t'back
kitchen. And the way them houses is built, it isn't no bloody
Noah's Ark neither. I can tell you. Talk about t'animals two be
two! I'd like to march yon council into my *house* two be two.
They'd need more than wellington boots. They'd need to be
bloody frogmen.

> ROGER *comes busily in with the teapot. Set it down with the rest*
> *of the things. Turns to* CLAIRE.

ROGER. There we are, ducky. I won't say you be mum! We'd all
be in fear of our lives, wouldn't we? So *I'll* pour.

CLAIRE. Where *is* Chris?

ROGER. Clearing up the shmatters in the back yard.

CLAIRE. You got a cup there for him?

ROGER. I have indeed. Chris has been very sunny of disposition
today and has been awarded the Gnome. First class.

> ROGER *is pouring the tea.* FATHER *stares heavily at* CLAIRE.

FATHER. So there's two on them, is there?

ROGER. What's she been saying about me? (*Peering round.*)
I don't see any luggage. Haven't you got any luggage, Mr
Link?

FATHER. I have that.

ROGER. Must be invisible.

FATHER (*holds up his carrier*). It's in me carrier. Pyjamas. Two
shirts. An' me razor. (*Pause.*) When Mother were alive, o'
course, it were different. Two bloody big cases at least. Grand,
staggering up and down them escilators on t'underground wi'
two cases, eh? (*Pause.*) So now I always travel light, like.

> ROGER *gives him a cup of tea, and one to* CLAIRE. *He goes out*
> *to the kitchen and we hear him calling:*

ROGER (*off*), Chrissy! Chrissy!

> *He comes back, as* MR LINK *is clumsily holding his cup and*
> *saucer and looking at the room.*

FATHER. He's always shifting round, is our Bernard. Don't ask *me* what for. What were wrong wi' his last place? Up Hampstead. Now that had a reight bit o' garden, I put fifty daffodils on yon garden. (*Pause.*) He won't have brought them with him, I suppose?

ROGER *is peering archly at* CLAIRE *over the rim of his mug.*

ROGER. Seen Bernard's daffies anywhere?

FATHER. Nay, he'd not bother wi' flowers, wouldn't Bernard. Nature to him, it's either summat God made or his dad planted. And he doesn't give a bugger for neither on us.

ROGER. All we've got here's a weeny back yard, I'm afraid. Well, it's got three manky old trees and a border. Not much to get your teeth into, Mr Link. Chrissy – that's your other man from Rely-On. Chrissy's out there clearing it up a bit. I mean, we shoved all the empty paint tins and things out there.

CHRIS *enters, dirty and hot.* ROGER *immediately pours him his tea and offers him the Gnome.* CHRIS *stands looking at* MR LINK.

CLAIRE. Mr Link – Chris. Chris, this is Bernard's father.

FATHER. How d'ye do, Chris.

CHRIS (*comes forward and shakes* LINK'S *hand*). Pleased to meet you.

Long silence.

FATHER. I don't know why you three's got mugs an' I've got a cup and saucer. I never use a cup and saucer.

CLAIRE. Roger's a very refined person, Mr Link.

FATHER. Well, there's something in that. When *we* had visitors Mother always put out t'cups and saucers.

ROGER *puts his tongue out at* CLAIRE.

ROGER. See!

CHRIS (*to* ROGER). I thought you were going to paint that hall door –

ROGER. I *was*, sweetheart.

A long silence.

FATHER. Well. It's quite a bit on a tea party. Isn't it?

ROGER. Goodness knows *where* we're going to put you, Mr Link.

FATHER. Tha can peg me out on t'clothes line if tha likes, lad. I'm none fussy.

CHRIS (*sharply*). You get that paint, Rodge?

ROGER. Yes, I did! And for Bernard's room as well. *And* I got those hessian wallpaper samples he was talking about. (*Sniffs.*) Hessian! A bit camp for Bernard, don't you think?

    CHRIS *drains his mug and puts it down.*

CHRIS. Let's get on with it, then.

ROGER. I'm just going to take a couple of Disprins. I feel *awful.*

FATHER. I were just thinking. You don't look in very fine fettle. Not to me you don't.

    ROGER *goes to a mirror.* CHRIS, *with an angry expression, goes out.*

ROGER. It's my eyes. No?

FATHER. Aye. They look like summat staring out at you from a cat's backside. Don't they?

ROGER. *Charming!*

FATHER. Nay. Don't take on, lad.

    ROGER *turns from the mirror. He is crying.*

    Eh, lad. I didn't mean nowt. (*To* CLAIRE.) He's crying.

ROGER. It's not what you said, Mr Link. It's last night. A black man hit me. In Portobello Road.

FATHER. You want to watch out wi' them blackies.

ROGER. I do hope you aren't a racist, Mr Link.

FATHER. Where did he hit thee?

ROGER. On the ear. With his *knuckles!*

FATHER. Had tha done owt to offend him, then?

    Pause.

ROGER. I asked him for a light. That's all.

    Pause.

CLAIRE. For Jesus Christ's sake, Roger! Get the paint and start the hall door, will you? On the *hall* side.

    ROGER *glumly goes into the kitchen and emerges with a paint tin and brush. Goes out through the hall door, casting a venomous glance at* CLAIRE.

I guess it's all kind of bewildering, Mr Link. Would you like me to explain?

FATHER. I don't want nobody to put theirselves about. Not for me I don't. (*Pause.*) I can get t'evening train at King's Cross and stop at his Auntie Bertha's, you know. *They* not flooded. They live up by t'colliery. It's high ground, where they are.

CLAIRE. When did you last see Bernard?

FATHER. Oh, it'll be a bit, now. I don't know who invented family ties; but any road, our Bernard must've come into t'world wi' a pair of scissors. You know, to cut t'family ties?

CLAIRE. I'm right with you, Mr Link.

Pause.

FATHER. It's funny how you can say things to a stranger. (*Pause.*) Don't mind me calling you a stranger, love. I mean nowt wrong by it. (*Pause.*) But I *do* get lonely. (*Pause.*) You'll not know t'north of England, I suppose?

CLAIRE. I've been to Lincoln –

Pause.

FATHER. Aye. Lincoln. You see, *that* – it's not exactly what *we* call t'north. If you take me meaning. Up our way, we more like call it t'south. (*Pause.*) That's if anybody were to bring it up, like.

CLAIRE. Supposing you wash up, or whatever? And I'll kind of put you in the Bernard picture –

FATHER (*startled*). Wash up?

Pause.

CLAIRE. I meant: your hands? Or maybe you –

FATHER. My mistake love, *my* mistake. I assume you are using an American expression. Wash up. For a minute I thought you meant t'tea things! We say 'wash up' when it's t'plates, you know. Dirty cutlery and that. But I – well, if you'll pardon the expression, I *am* bursting. (*Pause.*) I don't like going, on trains.

CLAIRE *smiles. She goes to the door leading upstairs.*

CLAIRE. It's upstairs. First landing, facing you.

FATHER gets up and goes to the door.

FATHER. Maybe I'd best go back. I shall only be in the way. (*Pause.*) And I am a bit confused, young lady.

CLAIRE. Mr Link – you'll stay. And see Bernard. And you'll be in nobody's way.

He smiles back at her, embarrassed. Then goes out. She comes downstage, sees the brown paper carrier. Picks it up. Puts her hand in. Comes out with a rolled pair of blue and white striped pyjamas. She stands looking at them, then replaces them in the carrier. Puts the carrier back exactly where he left it. She stands thinking, her face expressionless.

MR LINK reappears at the upstairs door. She jumps as he speaks.

FATHER. Why does it say Haggerty outside?

Pause.

CLAIRE. Outside?

FATHER. Beside t'door bell. Haggerty, it says. I thowt I'd come to t'wrong house.

Pause.

CLAIRE. It's a long story, Mr Link.

Pause.

FATHER. Oh. (*Pause.*) He'll have to get it changed, though, won't he? You can't have Haggerty when it's Link. Now can you?

CLAIRE. That's true –

Pause.

FATHER. Typical of our Bernard.

CLAIRE. Why?

FATHER. All you need is take that little card out. And put another one in saying Bernard Link. (*Pause.*) He's got no regard for the little things, hasn't Bernard. Me, I'd have had Link in that card slot afore I'd been in ten minutes. But that's me, isn't it? (*Pause.*) I've heard the name Haggerty. It's Irish.

CLAIRE. He isn't Irish.

FATHER. I don't like the Irish. They talk too much, and they'd rob a blind hen on a worm any day on t'week. (*Pause.*) He wants to get some cards *printed*, you know. He's not short o' brass. Printed. *LINK*. Nice big black letters. (*Pause.*) Don't want yon Haggerty's *bills* comin' here – now do we?

He vanishes upstairs again. CLAIRE *stands very still.*

CLAIRE. Get back quick, Haggerty. You're being *Linked*.

Curtain.

ACT TWO

Scene One

There have been small changes to the set since ACT ONE – *the decorating is nearly finished, and the shelves. Touches here and there demonstrating* CLAIRE'S *presence – perhaps a couple of pictures, flowers, rugs on the floor. Darkness, and sign lowered saying:* LONDON.

Fade up on BERNARD *sitting hunched on a chair with his raincoat on his knees. He is spotlit, the rest in darkness. He is scribbling in a small notebook balanced on his raincoat.*

The INTERPRETERS *from* ACT ONE *now double as* ACTORS – *three women and a man – dressed in the style of the Living Theatre. They circle* BERNARD'S *chair, whispering, the whispers becoming louder and louder.*

MAN. I am not allowed to travel without a passport.

1ST WOMAN. I cannot live without money.

2ND WOMAN. I am not allowed to take off my clothes.

3RD WOMAN. I am not allowed to smoke marijuana.

> BERNARD *scribbles away, as they circle, stop, address him and move on.*

3RD WOMAN. I cannot travel without a passport.

2ND WOMAN. I cannot live without money.

1ST WOMAN. I am not allowed to smoke marijuana.

MAN. I am not allowed to take my clothes off.

> *The last sequence is repeated in a loud shout, and* BERNARD *looks up furtively from his notes. The* THREE WOMEN *and the* MAN *break out in a rising cry of despair.*

> BERNARD *stuffs his notebook in his pocket, takes his raincoat*

*and comes downstage. The spot moves on him, leaving the chair
and the rest in darkness.*

BERNARD *stands a moment, looking shiftily from side to side
and clearing his throat. The* MAN *follows him and touches*
BERNARD'S *hand.*

MAN. Holy hands –

BERNARD. Er –

The MAN *touches his mouth.*

MAN. Holy mouth –

BERNARD. Well, I –

The MAN *touches his eyes.*

MAN. Holy eyes –

And by now thoroughly persecuted BERNARD *shifts his folded
raincoat in front of his genitals. But the* MAN *touches his head.*
Holy hair –

The MAN *exits.* BERNARD *is petrified, but a cynical jauntiness is
defensively pushing its way through. He stands very still for a
moment.*

BERNARD. Holy smoke!

Pause.

I'll bet they leave this country fully dressed. Passports firmly
gripped in paws. Cakes of hash in their tooth-paste tubes.
AND A LOT OF OUR MONEY!

Fade out and fade into

Scene Two

BERNARD'S FATHER *is sitting centre, in his characteristic position –
back straight, hands on knees. He stares expressionlessly in front of
himself. After a moment we hear a child howling upstairs. This fades
away. The hall door opens and* BERNARD *enters, fairly drunk.*

MR LINK *doesn't move a muscle.* BERNARD *stands swaying just
inside the room. Finally he circles unsteadily until he is front and
just left of his* FATHER.

BERNARD. I beg you not to lay formal charges until we reach the station. (*Pause.*) Even the long arm of the archetype must have its human side. What's more, I shall require the presence of my lawyer. (*Pause.*) I shall ring him before we leave this very room. And I warn you, he is no ordinary man. Any time of the night and day I can ring this lawyer and he will rush – through the night or day – to my rescue. The man is going mad from lack of sleep due to a surfeit of clients like me. And do you know why? Because he would rather be relied on than find the necessary and I might add wholly justifiable, violence within his gentle soul . . . he would rather be relied *on* than say, piss *off*.

By this time BERNARD *is at the telephone with his hand on the receiver. His* FATHER, *still without moving, utters at last:*

FATHER. Drunk again!

BERNARD, *struggling to co-ordinate, makes his way back across the room. He stands looking down at his* FATHER *for a long time. The old man now meets* BERNARD'S *eyes fair and square.*

BERNARD. I am holy. (*Pause.*) I am holy all over. (*Pause.*) I have been told so tonight. So don't have the *audacity* to start nagging a holy man.

BERNARD *pulls forward a chair, sits down.*

FATHER. I thought you was supposed to be in Paris.

Pause.

BERNARD. In Paris, I was, dad. And quick as a flash from the air-port to earn my bread, being persecuted by a bunch of actors into a higher state of cynicism than ever before. (*Pause.*) No sign of Donald at the airport. New system now. Red sign for those with something to declare. Green sign for those whose avarice is properly confined within the area circumscribed by the law.

FATHER. Nay. In Paris, they said you was.

BERNARD. Would Donald be red – or green? Which colour would you say, in the circumstances, would offer most scope? After all, even when you go through the green they still have the right to pounce on you. Yes. Green for Donald. He's a pouncer.

(*Pause.*) No fun waiting on the red side for those who announce by the very direction of their tired feet that they have an excess of this-that-or-the-other in their suitcases.

Pause.

FATHER. I knew I shouldn't have stopped.

Pause.

BERNARD. Dad, it's four in the morning. I must admit that at least one other critic and I scuttled from the theatre to the nearest boozer. There to anaesthetise . . . even inhibit, as the saying goes . . . our shifty if complicated reactions to the evening's entertainment.

Pause.

FATHER. Pubs closes at eleven.

Pause.

BERNARD. Yes, indeed! But we made merry at my colleague's nearby house. Yea, until three and four in the morning. We drank all the way from holy to howly. What I mean is, I think one of us – possibly both – cried. We cried like men. America's messianic if cranky message . . . it got us, dad. It got us in the end. Poor weary tired sceptical old us. (*Pause.*) And speaking of America.

FATHER. It's just been yawlin' its head off.

BERNARD. America has?

FATHER. Well, I suppose he *is* American? In't he? T'baby? What with his mother being American, I had presumed that the father –

BERNARD. Hold on! Hang on! The question of the father will have to be gone into some other time. (*Pause.*) I just wanted to say, dad: how much it makes me feel at home to stagger in at four a.m. and find you sitting there with your hands on your knees. Waiting. Waiting waiting waiting. Time no object. We know, do we not, that sooner or later the door must open and the monster will come slithering across the room. Do we not? Know? Don't we?

Pause.

FATHER. Eh, Bernard! T'house is flooded.

BERNARD *lifts up one foot and then the other*.

BERNARD. Maybe I *am* holy! Maybe I've been walking upon the water! But I don't see it.

Pause.

FATHER. *My* house, lad.

Pause.

BERNARD. Oh, damn and bugger it!

FATHER. There's no cause to go on like that.

BERNARD. Take no notice. It's a cry of rage against so much iniquity visited upon so much innocence.

Pause.

FATHER. You what?

Pause.

BERNARD. Dad. Has she taken care of you? Looked after you?

FATHER. The young lady?

BERNARD. Yes. Has she?

FATHER. By, I'll tell you. I've nowt but respect for that young woman. She's treated me like a king. (*Pause.*) We had summat called pumpkin pie for afters last night. I thought it were a bit queer at first, but I got to like it after a couple of spoonfuls.

BERNARD. Pumpkin pie, dad, is to America what Yorkshire pudding is to the West Riding. (*Pause.*) How many times do you have to get flooded before you shift out of that house?

Pause.

FATHER. I'm stopping in yon house. (*Pause.*) Your mother wouldn't like it. Me going. Not after all those years.

Pause.

BERNARD. Funny.

FATHER. What is?

BERNARD. Well, I mean, with me mother being dead. I mean, can a dead person continue to like or dislike . . . I mean –

FATHER. I *know* what you mean. I've heard it before. (*Pause.*) And *you* know what *I* mean.

Pause.

BERNARD. True.

>Pause.

FATHER. Well, you've got a reight going on here. Haven't you? (*Pause: leans forward.*) I don't know what you doing wi' a 'omosexual prancing round t'place. (*Pause.*) Mind. Chris seems a straightforward young feller. (*Pause: looking round.*) I liked it better in Hampstead. More air in Hampstead. Higher. More green. (*Pause.*) But it's a lovely baby. (*Pause.*) Bit of a yawler. (*Pause.*) *You* were a bit on a yawler. (*Pause.*) It's not a bad thing in a baby. (*Pause.*) Gets t'oxygen into their lungs, you know.

BERNARD. Does it?

>Pause.

FATHER. There's more *oxygen*, up Hampstead way.

>Pause.

BERNARD. You ever come across the name Raskolnikov before?

FATHER. Can't say I have, lad.

BERNARD. Well, that's its name. The baby's name.

>Pause.

FATHER. That certainly clears up one mystery.

BERNARD. Does it?

FATHER. Well, I take it that Rass is short for Rask-whatever-you-said. (*Pause.*) And I had wondered what sort of a name Rass might be. Her referring to the child by that name. And I didn't wish to intrude by inquiring any further. (*Pause.*) She's a fine young woman. She is entitled to name her bairn according to her wishes. (*Pause.*) Or the father's.

>*There is a really piercing, long howl upstairs. They both listen. After a few moments the cries fade, then* CLAIRE *enters in a housecoat.* BERNARD'S FATHER *smiles at her.*

Making a reight din tonight, in't he?

>CLAIRE *crosses to* BERNARD, *as she answers,* MR LINK.

CLAIRE (*to* FATHER). He's eaten some of the fur off his monkey.

FATHER. The little devil!

CLAIRE. Welcome home stranger!

They confront each other in silence for a few seconds. MR LINK *sits, looking ahead.*

FATHER. Aye. He's back. And none too sober.

BERNARD *crosses slowly to* CLAIRE. *Kisses her gently on the cheek. He turns, spreading his arms wide.*

BERNARD. Here we are at last. Our heterogeneous little family. All under one roof. At last. (*Pause.*) Leaping from the taxi outside, I ached for solitude. But that was selfish. Welcome home, *all* you strangers!

FATHER. It's not one over the eight wi' him! It's eight over the bloody twenty.

CLAIRE. Mr Link! I said not to wait up –

FATHER. What I often think to mesen is: if he'd just think on his dad when he 'as that one too many – he wouldn't. If he'd just think on t'effect on his father.

BERNARD. If I thought of you when drinking, dad, I'd be dead from cirrhosis of the liver.

CLAIRE *looks stonily at* BERNARD *and goes into the kitchen.*

CLAIRE (*exiting*). Rass's spewing it at both ends.

Pause.

FATHER. I'll get meself upstairs, then. 'Appen you'll be in a more fit state in the morning. (*He stands up, hesitating.*)

BERNARD. I'll drive you up to Yorkshire, dad. We'll get the house fixed. Only I wish you'd *move*!

FATHER. Get it fixed? Does't think I've lost t'use on me own two hands, then?

Pause.

BERNARD. Dad – I'm pleased to see you.

FATHER. Aye. I've no doubt. Wi' a skinful o' whisky inside thee!

BERNARD. Ah, dad! War, famine, pestilence, murder, injustice, capitalism in crisis, Stalinism tightening the screws harder and harder. And on top of it all, being a bloody theatre critic! If you'd gone through what I went through tonight –

FATHER. I fired engines nigh on fifteen year. I drove expresses thirty-five year, wi'all them people's lives behind me. And I never took a drop. As for t'theatre I've none gotten further than seeing Mother Duck at Leeds pantomine. Don't look at me for no sympathy!

BERNARD. I agree. It would be futile.

Pause.

FATHER. I'll say goodnight, then.

Pause.

BERNARD. Goodnight, dad. Throttle up those expresses in the old roaring dreams.

FATHER. When I dream. Which is not very often. I dream on thy mother.

He goes out, upstairs. CLAIRE *enters with nappies over her arm.* BERNARD *sits staring belligerently after his father.*

BERNARD. Imagine living with her forty years then dreaming with her for the rest of your life! Nobody could say my mother was one to let a little thing like dying stand in the way. In the way of. Of her.

CLAIRE *sits down tiredly with the nappies.*

CLAIRE. He sure brings out another side of you, Bernard!

BERNARD. I've got my facets. I have got my facets. (*Pause.*) Lurking.

Pause.

CLAIRE. Rass's quiet. (*Pause.*) Jesus, I'm screwed! (*Pause.*) So how was Paris? I made some coffee in the kitchen. You want some?

BERNARD. I wouldn't mind. Yes, please.

She goes into the kitchen and comes back with coffee. BERNARD *sits sipping his. She stretches out exhausted in her chair, the coffee on her lap.*

Floods! He's got floods! I've got floods. My sanity needs a bleeding Noah's Ark. (*Long pause.*) I found a few things out about Haggerty in Paris. Quite by accident, really.

CLAIRE (*sitting up straight, alert*). Well, come *on*, then –

Pause.

BERNARD. First of all, there were these telegrams from Paris. From him.

CLAIRE. Yeah. Chris told me after you left. Sounded authentic Haggerty all right.

Pause.

BERNARD. Well, in Paris, I met a lecturer who'd known him a week or two. It seems Haggerty . . . did he have any money by the way?

CLAIRE. A few thousand dollars when he left New York for London. (*Pause.*) My money, needless to say. (*Pause.*) What the hell! *My* money was my father's money. And any way of using it to besmirch his dear old memory suits me. I mean, any way subversively disposing of that graceful Republican hypocrite's cash! Both Haggerty and I are well qualified.

Pause.

BERNARD. It seems . . . Haggerty left Paris. And he left a man acting for him as a kind of agent. With some money, and a peculiar list of instructions – which included the telegrams.

Pause.

CLAIRE. What are we to live in fear and trembling of besides the telegrams?

BERNARD. That he wouldn't say. (*Pause.*) Scrutinizing me in relation to the whole arrangement, he looked . . . smug. (*Pause.*) Vulpine. (*Pause.*) He kept on wiping his mouth with a handkerchief and looking at me pityingly. Some kind of lawyer. Nothing illegal was involved, he archly informed me.

CLAIRE. And the fiendish Haggerty disappeared to *where*?

BERNARD. I do not know, Monsieur. It is not of my business. The man said. (*Pause.*) Who is now sleeping where, by the way?

CLAIRE. Unless you have a kind of yen to sleep with your father – (*Points at a divan.*) I made up a bed there.

Pause.

BERNARD. I don't know why I don't just move out. For a while. For ever. (*Pause.*) What if Haggerty's fixer-man in Paris sent us a bomb?

CLAIRE. Nothing illegal, remember?

BERNARD. Oh, yes. Still. You and I haven't exactly worked out a modus vivendi yet. Have we? (*Pause.*) You had me in a state of shock for days! (*Pause.*) Of course, I realize coming here and finding the flat –

CLAIRE. Oh, for Christ's sake, Bernard! I'm going to bed. (*She goes to the door, with the nappies.*)

Want to bed down in Rass's room? Got a supply of ear plugs and nose filters?

Pause.

BERNARD. *Good night!*

> CLAIRE *exits.* BERNARD *finishes his coffee. Wanders over to the divan. Kicks it. Turns back the covers. He sits down and takes his shoes off. Then his trousers. Half fills a glass of whisky. Takes the desk lamp to the divan side. Climbs into bed. Raises his glass.*

Thus we launch our frail coracle into the night! (*He drains the whisky. Puts out the light.*)

Scene Three

Sign lowered saying : CHICAGO.

> *A spot picks out* CLAIRE, *the rest of the stage in darkness. Her hair is tied back. She looks much younger. Her dress is in a fashion of fourteen years ago. She calls out :*

CLAIRE. James –

> *She pulls up a chair and sits down. She is fiddling with her hair. She looks up.*

James Mawnan Haggerty, *I'm* going to call you 'Haggerty' from now on. (*Pause.*) Look. OK. You take the newspaper into the john. OK. D'you have to bring it out? (*Pause.*) I mean, we just ran away together. We arrive. I mean, we haven't un-packed and you vanish into the john. With a *newspaper*! (*Pause.*) Haggerty, I will not have you sit in front of me reading. I wouldn't

care if it was . . . if it was *anything* else. But *reading*! (*Pause.*)
It's not a passionate thing to do. Budapest? (*Long pause.*)
Geography I am weak on. (*Pause.*) They're doing what? (*Pause.*)
Haggerty I am *seventeen* and I do not even grasp America.
James Mawnan! Huh! Was it your mammy or your daddy
stuck you with those two pins. (*Pause.*) When you raise your
eyeballs over the top of the paper you know what you look like?
Two large plonks of bird shit rolling on a wire! (*Pause.*) I dig
you are conveying antagonism. (*Pause.*) Already. (*Looks at her
watch.*) We have been alone together in our new life for sixteen
and one quarter minutes. (*Pause.*) I *know* my vernacular is not
that of rich daddy's background and status. (*Pause.*) I mix my
vernaculars because I am an adolescent in a condition of revolt.
(*Pause.*) Is what is going on in Budapest passionate, I want to
know? I mean screw the political angle, I just want to have a
kind of guideline whose side I'm on. (*Pause.*) *Both* sides are
communist? (*Pause.*) I am reduced to awed silence. (*Pause.*)
Who'd elope to *Chicago*? (*Pause.*) Yeah! But *I* wasn't born here!
And what did it do for you? (*Pause.*) I know I've a lot to learn.
(*Pause.*) And you'll have to do the educating, won't you? I
mean, being here with you isn't exactly a passport to Vassar –
is it? (*Pause.*) Haggerty, I *told* you. I *invented* the way I talk.
It is calculated to negate my background and suggest whorish
undertones. (*Pause.*) If I take all my clothes off will you put that
goddam paper down? (*Pause.*) Russians? Tanks? Christ, I've
hardly gotten over the English knocking hell out of the Arabs!
(*Pause.*) How is one to *orientate*, man? (*Pause.*) Haggerty, I
am going to remove my clothes and lie on that crummy stinking
bed and open my legs. Should you continue to ingest foreign
news so stubbornly. I shall then hit you with a chair. (*Pause.*)
Haggerty, I love you. I want you. (*Pause.*) I think I am going to
cry.

   Fade out and fade in to

Scene Four

The following day. Afternoon. CHRIS *is wiring a new socket for the hi-fi equipment.* ROGER, *precarious on a three-step aluminium ladder is ronsealing the new shelves.* MR LINK *sits centre, his nose tipped with a pair of glasses, a newspaper on his knees. But he is staring into space.* CLAIRE *enters, switches on the vacuum already plugged in and starts cleaning. There is a definite atmosphere in the room. She comes to* MR LINK *– he lifts his feet. She vacuums under his chair and he puts his feet down again. She stops working and goes into the kitchen : comes out with a beer.*

CLAIRE. Want a beer Mr Link?

FATHER. No thanks, love.

CLAIRE (*negligently*). Beer, anybody?

CHRIS. I will when I've got this wired up. It's tricky.

CLAIRE (*looking up at* ROGER). Tinkerbell?

ROGER (*brushing and not looking at her*). If you mean *me* dear, I'm not a beer person at all. (*Turns, and looks down at her.*) I don't like beer, twinklecrutch dearie –

CLAIRE. God, that stuff you're putting on stinks!

ROGER (*busy*). If Bernard wants his shelves ronsealed – ronsealed they shall be. And you may have noticed, though I doubt it, I seem to come in for the stinky jobs. Nobody has to tell *me* I'm not a genius with the carpentry. These hands were meant for finer things.

CLAIRE. Yeah! Like –

ROGER (*quickly and firmly, looking at* MR LINK). Pas devant les pères, s'il vous plaît, dear!

  Pause.

FATHER. Always beats me why they don't never seem to get on –

CLAIRE. Who doesn't?

FATHER. Women and 'omosexuals. They'd 'ave summat in common, you'd think. Always biting each other's noses, you two are,

(*Pause.*) I've been thinking it over. I suppose we 'ave them up north. Have 'omos, I mean. But you never seem to come across it. I've never come across it, not up north. (*Pause.*) And another thing. Considering Bernard's comfortably off and you're well set up yourself, young lady, why not 'ave somebody in to clean? (*Pause.*) I have one, you know. Home help. Every Wednesday. (*Pause.*) Pinched one on his mother's hats. I nearly went up t-Town Hall about it, but I can't prove nothing. Wait till I see her wearing that hat in t'town one on these Fridays when I'm doing me shopping. (*Pause.*) I'll rip it off her bloody head. (*Pause.*) She's one on them as cleans *round* things. Never thinks on going underneath. You'd think there wasn't no such thing as underneath. (*Pause.*) But that's where all t'fluff is.

CLAIRE. You kept Mrs Link's hats ever since she died?

FATHER. I kept *that* 'at.

ROGER. Was it a gorgeous one?

Pause.

FATHER. It was round. And all made on fur. (*Pause.*) Our Bernard brought it back from Moscow for her. His first trip that were. (*Pause.*) Best thing 'at come out on Moscow, if you ask me. (*Pause.*) She was a bonny woman. (*Pause.*) A bit over-weight. (*Pause.*) Sixteen stone. (*Pause.*) But she looked a treat in that Russian 'at. (*Pause.*) You be surprised how many women on my generation was overweight. Now why would that be? (*Pause.*) Ate nowt but bread and bugger all else for many a long year, for one thing. (*Pause.*) Joint on a Sunday. Then rissoles from t'joint on a Monday. (*Pause.*) Course, railwaymen was better off than a lot. (*Pause.*) The aristocracy of the working class, my father used to say. And he was a miner. (*Pause.*) It was the railwaymen broke the general strike, you know. (*Pause.*) Union solidarity's one thing. To watch your bairns go 'ungry and listen to the wife nagging – that's another. (*Pause.*) Three things buggered the strikes: hungry bairns, shame, and nagging bloody women! (*Pause.*) There wasn't a woman with a 'at from Moscow in our village! No. And I shouldn't think in Doncaster either. (*Pause.*)

That's always our Bernard's way: hand out a few quid, buy summat useless from Roumania or somewhere. And goodbye to owt else! (*Pause.*) A lot had their wombs taken away, an' all. Summat 'appens to a woman that's had her womb taken away.

ROGER. Hormones.

FATHER. Eh?

ROGER. Sort of chemicals in the body, Mr Link. We're all at the mercy of these nasty little molecules. (*Pause: tartly.*) Including 'omos!

CLAIRE *deliberately starts vacuuming again.* MR LINK *lifts up his paper.*

FATHER (*shouting*). I brought him t'Gazette, an' all –

CLAIRE *stops vacuuming.* CHRIS *goes into the kitchen for a beer, returning.*

CLAIRE. I beg your pardon?

FATHER. Last week's local Gazette. I brought it down for him. Might as well bring a bicycle for a bloke wi' no legs! Listen to this: Gordon Carghill was remanded on bail after police investigations at Stanhill Mental Hospital. (*Pause.*) I should bloody think he was, an' all. (*Pause.*) Him and our Bernard was at Junior School together and their Gordon – well, he was a bad-un from t'start. (*Pause.*) Wonder what he was getting up to at mental hospital? Charge nurse, an' all. (*Pause.*) He used to pinch rhubarb out on my allotment. You can always tell the way they going to go. (*Pause.*) Rhubarb an' custard. (*Pause.*) I don't suppose that would be a national dish in your country, young lady? I mean, like t'pumpkin pie?

CLAIRE. I guess not, Mr Link.

There is a long silence. MR LINK *studies the paper.*

FATHER. Floods expected to subside within a few days! We've heard that one before! (*Pause.*) Floods goes but rats doesn't. (*Pause.*) I used to 'ave a little terrier could snap a rat's neck like a twig! (*Pause.*) Lots of whippets round our way. (*Pause.*) I never liked whippets. (*Pause.*) 'Course, it *is* a miner's dog.

(*Pause.*) Them and greyhounds. (*Pause.*) I can't bide greyhounds either. Ribs sticking through. Wrap theirsens round your legs like a mucky wet rag. (*Pause.*) A terrier's a reliable dog, though. Hardy. (*Pause.*) It's the *gambling* gets me, wi' greyhounds and whippets! (*Pause.*) I wouldn't never gamble. Summat for nowt. That's what they all want. (*Pause.*) Now a pigeon's a different thing. They gamble as well on pigeons. But it's the bird itself. (*Pause.*) A lovely bird.

> CLAIRE, ROGER *and* CHRIS *are transfixed by the old man's monologue. Helpless, not wanting to stop him or hurt him – he simply represents a world stubbornly impervious to their experience.*
>
> BERNARD *enters, holding a small yellow telegram envelope. He stands looking at the little group.* MR LINK *is quite unaware of his effect on the people around him.*

Did you get my bacca?

BERNARD (*looking at the others*). Yes, I got your bacca. (*Pause.*) You all seem a bit subdued –

> CHRIS *goes back to working on the socket, his beer beside him.*
> ROGER *brushes away at his shelves.*

ROGER. Mr Link's been telling us all about whippets and pigeons. (*Pause.*) And hats. (*Pause.*) Ever so absorbing.

> MR LINK *opens his tobacco tin.*

FATHER. I'm down to a couple o' dog ends. (*Pause.*) What I do, I put me dog ends in me tin. Then when I've got enough I make them up into cigs.

BERNARD (*coming forward*). Here's your tobacco, dad. (*Pause.*) What hats?

FATHER. That one on your mother's t'home help pinched.
> *Pause.*

BERNARD. You don't know whether she pinched it or not. And I'm sure she didn't.

FATHER. Ah, they'd fiddle owt off you when you're on your own. Think you're daft in t'head or summat. Can't see a hat when it's missing! (*Pause.*) I liked home help I had afore her. Now *she* went underneath! (*Pause.*) Dropped dead in Woolworth's it'll be eight month now. (*Pause.*) I don't like to see Claire vacuuming round, neither. What happened to that woman you had in Hampstead?

BERNARD. They . . . they, you know, come and go. In London.

CLAIRE *has been watching and listening to all this impassively.* MR LINK *peers at her over his glasses.*

FATHER. Caught *that* one smoking when she were frying his bacon and eggs one morning. (*Pause.*) Up Hampstead. (*Pause.*) That's southerners for you! Smoking when they cooking. (*Pause.*) Cig dangling out on her mouth whenever you looked at her. (*Pause.*) It's disgusting in a woman. (*Pause.*) At all times.

Pause.

CLAIRE. I smoke, Mr Link –

FATHER (*to* BERNARD). You'll not have bothered to look at Gazette?

BERNARD. No, dad.

FATHER. Police is investigating Gordon Carghill for summat.

BERNARD. Never heard of him.

FATHER. No. You wouldn't have. He just sat next to you at same desk at Junior School.

Pause.

BERNARD. Thirty-five years ago.

FATHER. What difference does that make? You. You remember nowt and nobody. And care neither! Well, it's all here in t'-Gazette.

CLAIRE. Bernard –

BERNARD. What?

CLAIRE. I think you're holding a telegram.

He looks down at it as if he's never seen it.

BERNARD. Oh, yes. (*Pause.*) Yes. (*He opens the telegram and stands looking at it.*)

CLAIRE. Haggerty?

BERNARD *makes for the door to the stairs.*

Read it, Bernard –

BERNARD *stops, turns, hesitating.*

FATHER. Waste o' good money, telegrams. Catch me sending one. It all goes to t'Government. (*Pause.*) Then there's the little matter of it being our Bernard's own business no doubt. If you'll pardon me. I don't like to interfere.

BERNARD. You once opened a letter of mine and read it!

Pause.

FATHER(*flatly*). You was under twenty-one. (*Pause.*) Your mother and me was deeply shocked. (To CLAIRE.) He 'ad a young girl pregnant. That one! That one over there! I've never seen such a letter in all my life. (*Pause.*) Straight into t'fire wi' *that* letter!

Pause.

CLAIRE. And the girl?

FATHER. She'd borrowed some money and had a abortion. (*To* BERNARD.) Dirty young devil! (*Pause.*) It grieves me to think about it now, even after all this time. (*Pause.*) We didn't know the *half* on what *he* did when he left home.

He lifts his paper, emanating his twenty-four-year-old grief.

BERNARD *holds up the telegram, reading it out to* CLAIRE.

BERNARD. Yes, it's Haggerty. It says: PREDICT THE BITCH WILL NOW BE DUG IN STOP (*Pause.*) HOPE YOU CARRIED OUT STRATEGY OF SUBMISSION BECAUSE NOW IS TIME EJECT THE NEUROTIC BUNDLE FROM YOUR FOXHOLE STOP (*Pause.*) REMEMBER JUNG VERSUS J. JOYCE RE JOYCE'S DAUGHTER STOP (*Pause.*) YOU ARE A DEEP SEA DIVER MISTER JOYCE BUT YOUR DAUGHTER IS DROWN-ING STOP (*Pause.*) WISH HAD KNOWN YOU BERNARD STOP (*Pause.*) READ SOME OF YOUR ACID THEATRE RE-VIEWS STOP (*Pause.*) RESEARCHED YOU FULLY STOP FACT IS I SYMPATHISE WITH YOU RE CLAIRE STOP (*Pause.*) REGARD HER NOW WITH CLINICAL DETACHMENT AS A MERE SPECIMEN STOP (*Pause.*) YOU WILL NOT UNDER-STAND AMERICA BUT NEITHER DOES SHE STOP (*Pause.*) PULL RASS'S NOSE FOR ME STOP (*Pause.*) HERE ON DE-ESCALATION OF TELEGRAMS STOP (*Pause.*) HAGGERTY.

Long pause.

ROGER. Cheek!

FATHER. Brazen, I'd call it. Not that I can make head nor tail on it. But it gives off a sort on a brazen impression, like.

Pause.

CLAIRE. Mr Link. The substance of the impression is true. But about me not Haggerty. I mean so far as Bernard is concerned. (*Pause.*) All your son did was lease a flat. And who brought Rely-On into Bernard's life? Well, that *was* Haggerty. Then me, Rass, and –

FATHER. *I* come on me own accord. I always do.

Pause.

BERNARD. It says in this morning's paper the floods went down yesterday.

Pause.

FATHER. I can take a hint.

BERNARD. I didn't mean that.

Pause.

FATHER (*staring in front*). He's always been on his own before. (*Pause.*) Bit of a hermit, like. (*Pause.*) Never managed to make a right home. Keep a good woman. (*Pause.*) *I* think there's summat up wi' our Bernard. (*Laughs to himself.*) Owt to put him in Stanhill Asylum and let Gordon Carghill knock a bit o' sense into him! (*He turns to* BERNARD.) Tha lets people tread all over thee! (*Turns to* CLAIRE.) And I'm not speaking on you, love.

CHRIS *stands up from his work, finishing his beer.*

CHRIS. Haggerty recommended Bernard to Rely-On because of me. (*Pause.*) I'm not boasting. (*Pause.*) He knew I was leaving the other firm, and he knew I'd see Bernard right with the work. (*Pause.*) I told him I was a drifter. (*Pause.*) I like to move about a bit. Always do a good job. Painting, wiring, plumbing. You name it, I can do it.

BERNARD. Why should Haggerty *care*? About whether I get good workmanship or not?

Pause.

CHRIS. He liked good workmanship. (*Pause.*) I expect he'd knocked about a bit in America before he met Claire. (*Turns to look up at* ROGER *on the ladder.*) 'Course I've no idea if he knew the sort o' talent they *get* at Rely-On.

    Pause.

FATHER. I think I'll take mesen out a bit. (*Pause.*) Have a bit of a walk. (*Pause.*) Not that it isn't muggy down here compared with Hampstead.

    They all watch him get up in silence, acknowledging the old man's rough tact. He puts his jacket on and takes his hat.

(*To* BERNARD, *nodding at* CLAIRE.) I told her. You want to shift yon one's name off t'door.

CLAIRE. Mr Link, I only came here because I thought Haggerty'd *be* here. We *lived* here before I went back to New York and had Rass –

FATHER. By – you fell over yoursen to get back after t'little lad were born, didn't you? (*Pause.*) But it's none on my affair, young lady.

    He goes out. BERNARD *still stands weakly by the door leading upstairs.*

    We hear the baby start howling. BERNARD *goes out and upstairs followed by* CLAIRE. ROGER *comes down off the ladder to* CHRIS.

ROGER (*menacingly, for him*). I think it's time we cleared the air, dear. You and me.

    Pause.

CHRIS. Take a bit o' clearing, the air round here!

ROGER. *You* know what I mean!

    Pause.

CHRIS. Do I carry you on my back on these jobs or not?

    Pause.

ROGER (*sulkily*). Well. What if you do?

    Pause.

CHRIS. Bernard's not interested, you know.

    ROGER *puts the ronseal tin down. Lays the brush across the top.*

ROGER. I know. (*He starts crying.*) Jimmy threw me out last night. (*Pause.*) Said he was going away for two days. (*Pause.*) Well, it's been quite unpleasant between us for a week or two. Anyway, he came back a day early. And who's upstairs with a *divine* spade?

CHRIS (*drily*). Little old Rodge.

ROGER. Yes. Little old Rodge. D'you know Jimmy actually *kicked* me? Down the stairs? And threw all my things down as well. (*Pause.*) I mean I thought if *she* went. I thought Bernard might –

> *Pause.*

CHRIS. She'll go before long. She's not here to squeeze Bernard. (*Pause.*) And *you're* not going to squeeze him either –

> *Pause.*

ROGER. God! One might think you were a bit Bernard inclined yourself the way you talk!

> *Pause.*

CHRIS (*quietly*). Put the ronseal brush in the tin of white spirits in the kitchen. And we'll knock off for today. (*Pause.*) It's Bernard's old man that gets me. (*Pause.*) I mean, sitting there like he does. And coming out with all that ramble. (*Pause.*) He upsets me, you know?

> ROGER *takes the brush into the kitchen.* CHRIS *tidies the corner where he's been working and puts some tools into an open leather bag.* ROGER *comes in, looking a little brighter.*

There's a room going where I live. Paddington way. (*Pause.*) Four quid a week. (*He grins.*) House full of spades –

ROGER. Oh, Chrissy! (*Pause.*) One can't *think* how it's all going to end up here.

CHRIS. I don't know. (*Pause.*) You never know. (*Pause.*) For my money, Haggerty'll walk in through that door one of these days.

ROGER. And *then* what?

CHRIS. Work it out. Look at her. Listen to her. (*Pause.*) That bird'll walk out the door with Haggerty and the kid.

Pause.

ROGER. Poor old Bernard!

    ROGER *pulls on a sweater.* CHRIS *gets his old reefer jacket. They exit.*

    Fade out and fade in to

Scene Five

Darkness. A sign is lowered saying : NEW YORK.

    An empty chair is spotlit. CLAIRE *enters, wearing a light raincoat. She looks round. Takes off the raincoat : underneath, a white summer dress, bloodstained.* CLAIRE *has blood on one side of her face. She curls up in the chair, hugging herself in her arms. After a moment, she sits up and turns towards the audience.*

CLAIRE. Don't say it, Haggerty! Yes. OK. The demonstrations are shit. The marches are shit. (*Pause.*) The sit-ins were a start. Then *you* get all high and mighty. And we end up you studying guerrilla warfare in the pad and me getting beaten to hell in the streets. (*Pause.*) Well, *look* at me, will you? (*Pause.*) I'm lucky I wasn't busted! (*Pause.*) No, I *don't* want you to clean me up, and kiss me, and screw me into submission. I want to just sit here, man, and be *bloody*. (*Long pause.*) God, it's been rough with you! And I go on and on and on and on! (*Pause.*) Well, I did get tougher, didn't I? And less stupid? And read a million books? (*Pause.*) Sure. Leaves Vassar standing. I sometimes dream that's *where* I'm standing: in Vassar. And *loving* it. (*Pause.*) And I wish you were in Cuba, or on goddam Mars or somewhere. (*Pause.*) Haggerty, you don't stir a *toe* any more. You preparing for civil war out of a book? (*Pause.*) Listen, after all you said it first: America'll rook you or cook you. And in the meantime we sit on our fannys? (*Pause.*) Honey, no! Don't touch me. I'll get in the bath and stick me up with a band-aid. (*Pause.*) Jesus, it's hot! And I bounced out of that tangle like a kangaroo. (*Pause.*) I am *not* crying – it's tear gas. (*Pause.*) Hell,

I'm crying as well. Tear gas tears and me tears. Because I feel like I'm going to crack. Split. Wham! Right down the middle. (*Pause.*) Yeah. I know. Half the kids at school with me are on the shrink's couch by now. So who needs a shrink when there's life with you? (*Pause.*) *Life!* (*Pause.*) Next summer Oakland. Next summer somewhere else. (*Pause.*) Any sonofabitch calls me a white liberal after all this, I'm gonna carve his goddam eyes out. (*Pause.*) Just give me a couple months and I'll be a black fascist. (*Pause.*) Whilst you brood!

CLAIRE *gets up from the chair and comes downstage, followed by the spot.*

Can we just go to my place at Amagansett? For a week-end, or something? And just swim. And lie in the sun? (*Pause.*) Do you need me at all? (*Pause.*) Have I, in trying to become something for you and then seeing it for myself . . . have I become a kind of *joke*? (*Pause.*) Not that you ever laugh. (*Pause.*) You used to. (*Pause.*) I mean, are we still human? As well as humanity? (*Pause.*) Do you know that now I can see with your eyes? Hear with your ears? Spit with your tongue? (*Pause.*) That I am inside your *head*, Haggerty? (*Pause.*) Does it *corrupt* you or something? (*Pause.*) But I am as separate, and hard, and knowledgeable as you could wish. (*Pause.*) Will you hold me? (*Pause.*) Will you lick this blood off my face? (*Pause.*) Will you permit me one hour's *peace*?

Fade out and fade in to

Scene Six

BERNARD'S *room.* MR LINK *sits in his chair, a paper on his knees, his head thrown back. He is asleep and snoring gently. To one side of him :* BERNARD, *smoking and staring into space. To the other side :* CLAIRE, *with a drink, also staring ahead, over* BERNARD'S *shoulder. It is after lunch.*

CLAIRE. Thank God he sleeps plenty.

BERNARD. Yeh.

Pause.

CLAIRE. You know the steak?

BERNARD. What steak?

CLAIRE. We had *steak* for lunch. You remember? That kind of brown triangle with black grill marks on it you ate? That was steak.

Pause.

BERNARD. Oh. (*Pause.*) Yes.

CLAIRE. He bought it.

BERNARD. I know.

CLAIRE. How d'you know?

BERNARD. It's like a sort of perverse gift. I can always recognise steak me dad bought.

CLAIRE. He spends an awful lot of time talking about meat.

BERNARD. Yes. He's a butcher manqué. Shove him out in the fields, he doesn't see animals. He sees cuts.

Pause.

CLAIRE. Does he make a habit of visiting you when he's *not* flooded?

Pause.

BERNARD. It started about two years ago. He just turns up. And sits. And watches. (*Pause.*) If I'm drunk, I mock him. (*Pause.*) If I'm sober I spend half the time lying and the other half apologising for having turned out badly. (*Pause.*) He's only got to walk in through the door and I can make regression look like progress compared with my bloody performance.

MR LINK *wakes up with a twitch and sits straight.*

FATHER. Insects.

BERNARD. Who? Us?

Pause.

FATHER. I were thinking.

BERNARD. You were sleeping.

FATHER. Do you think I don't know t'difference in mesen?

BERNARD. I could imagine you having genuine difficulties in making a distinction.

FATHER. Does t'ever understand what he's on about, Claire?

CLAIRE (*laughing*). Oh, I don't know. I guess so.

    Pause.

FATHER. I was *thinking*. On a summer evening many a long year ago. (*Pause.*) Were only a fireman then. (*Pause.*) We was taking this goods train up a long gradient, right out in t'country. (*Pause.*) I had t'firebox door open and we went through a great cloud on them little gnats. They got caught up in the hot air. And it consumed them. (*Pause.*) Thousands on tiny little bodies going up in the air, like sparks, you know. (*Pause.*) By, they do bring me out in bumps if they get me when I'm fishing.

    Pause.

BERNARD. Nice piece of steak, dad.

FATHER. I thought you'd appreciate it.

BERNARD. Plenty of nice fat and gristle.

FATHER. Meat's nowt wi'out a bit of fat.

BERNARD. That's right. And what's more, I still can't spit it out.

FATHER. You what?

BERNARD. When I was a kid, you used to make me sit and chew it till I was crying and spewing at the same time. Get it down thee! It's what puts t'muscles on. (*Holds up his arm.*) Look at that arm nearly forty years later. If you can find a muscle I'll give you ten quid.

FATHER. That's because tha spends thy time on thy backside. Tchah! Theatre critic! (*Pause.*) Now if folks like George Formby an' Gracie Fields was still going! That *was* entertainment. (*Pause.*) I suppose they was well known in America as well. (*To* CLAIRE.) But you'd be too young, love. It's all jitterbugging now over there. In't it?

BERNARD. Dad –

FATHER. What, lad?

BERNARD. Have you noticed –

    Pause.

FATHER. What?

BERNARD. You spend quite a bit of time on *your* backside. In that chair, for example.

> *Pause.*

FATHER (*shouts*). I'm retired!

BERNARD. You don't sit because you're retired. Or old. Or ill or weak. (*Stands up, speaking wickedly.*) You sit because nothing moves or stirs within! Nothing triggers off the old vaso-motor system, does it? A leg here, an arm there. A meaningful rotation of the eyeballs. Eh? Not a bloody quiver!

> MR LINK *has probably heard a lot of this kind of thing before – but not in front of a third person. He folds his paper. Slowly gets up. Lumbers to the stairs door. Looks at* BERNARD, *then* CLAIRE.

FATHER. What it is, young lady. Our Bernard doesn't like me, you see. He doesn't even *like* me –

> *He goes out.* BERNARD *flops back into his chair.* CLAIRE, *angry, goes to the window.*

CLAIRE. You wouldn't even talk to that little fag actor like that.

> *Pause.*

BERNARD. Everything in its proper place. Including spleen. (*Pause.*) And be careful. Don't go for me. (*Pause.*) You know a thousand times less about him and me than I do about Harlem!

CLAIRE (*acidly*). Does it all go back to the dark satanic mills, honey?

BERNARD. Oh, piss off –

> *Pause.*

CLAIRE. I *am* going, soon.

> *Pause.*

BERNARD. *Right.*

> *Pause.*

CLAIRE. Bernard –

> *Pause.*

BERNARD (*quietly*). Do you think he doesn't nearly make me bloody *cry*?

> *Pause.*

CLAIRE. Bernard, once I moved in here – I never did a damn thing about tracing Haggerty. (*Points.*) I arrived at that door fuming. And you caught it. And I'm sorry. (*She sits in the chair vacated by* MR LINK.)

BERNARD. Did you really think he was still in London?

    Pause.

CLAIRE. I thought he might be.

BERNARD. And if he had been?

    Pause.

CLAIRE. I guess I'd have tried to force the usual things on him. (*Pause.*) Fourteen years of me stuck in my groove. (*Grimacing.*) Very *un*groovy! (*Pause.*) Me yelling, whining, loving. And that man so still. So quiet. So . . . secret. (*Pause.*) But he could slice my head off with one word. And me? I'd stand up spouting blood and show him my head on a platter and bawl: look what you *done* to me, Haggerty –

BERNARD (*not ungently*). It's what they call being a slow developer. I haven't developed at all. Still the same chubby little lad Mam packed off to school. (*Pause.*) After threatening to put me in the orphanage for being bad. (*Pause.*) If I'd been bright, I'd have realized she might have a problem with the orphanage. I mean, proving she and me dad were dead. (*Pause.*) Well, at least you stuck out fourteen years with Haggerty. I split my stint into two sevens with two women. (*Pause.*) Didn't seem to dilute my sheer inadequacy for either of them. (*He gets up. Goes to her.*) *I* thought I took your melodramatic descent with a . . . with a certain lugubriousness. Considering.

CLAIRE. Yeah. That was very deceitful of you.

BERNARD. Why?

    Pause.

CLAIRE. It kind of deflated me. In the end. (*Pause.*) You don't resist, Bernard. You absorb. That's highly dangerous. (*Pause.*) Your old man isn't so dumb! *He* said you'd – God give me the dialect – he said you'd 'niver kept a good wooooman'.

    Pause.

BERNARD. Aside from the irrelevance of dadda's ethics, it's true. (*Pause.*) He's a trifle behind on quaint contemporary issues like your autonomy, your independence, your self-liberation and your women in society and all that.

CLAIRE. *All that!* Man, I've kicked it!

Pause.

BERNARD. I don't think I'm very far in front of him, either.

Pause.

CLAIRE. *God,* what a hunk of fly-blown little nothing England *is*!

Pause.

BERNARD. I'd like you to stay. In this flat, I mean.

CLAIRE. Look. All that stuff I dished you about wanting to lay me. I was *needling*, Bernard –

BERNARD. Well, I'm not talking about 'laying'. (*Pause.*) I'm worn out.

CLAIRE. By *what*, for Christ's sake?

Pause.

BERNARD. By feeling barren.

CLAIRE. And do I make you feel less barren, Bernard?

Pause.

BERNARD. Yes. I think you do.

CLAIRE. And what about the small noise shit and spit machine upstairs?

Pause.

BERNARD. I don't mind Rass –

CLAIRE. You don't *mind* him?

BERNARD. I mean –

CLAIRE. *I* mind him! I resent every subatomic particle *in* the little bastard.

Pause.

BERNARD (*quietly*). You *are* married to Haggerty? Aren't you?

Pause.

CLAIRE. Yes. Only I don't call it being married. I call it being shredded. Cell by goddam cell. (*Pause.*) So I usually deny the mind-stopping fact. A passion so aberrated and inexplicable as I had for Haggerty . . . I mean, the *scale* of the outrage to self-interest . . . it still surprises me. It's the only *surprise* . . . of which I am still capable.

BERNARD. Passion you had – or have for Haggerty?

He touches her face. She shakes away his hand. She is crying.

CLAIRE. I don't *know* Bernard –

Pause.

BERNARD. I've no passion (*Pause.*) You touch me.

Pause.

CLAIRE. Like your father touches you?

Pause.

BERNARD (*stiffly*). We'll leave it all alone then. (*He goes and sits down.*) Let it be.

Pause.

CLAIRE. What do you think *I* need? (*She gets up, walking up and down.*) I mean, *I've* had enough! (*Pause.*) The American *experience* they call it! Guys like you sitting round some studio table on British TV – *opining*, Bernard. *Pontificating*. Specialists in American affairs and God knows what. Washington, Chicago, Oakland, Detroit, Haarlem. Haggerty slipped through it all like some big bombed-out cat. Never a public figure, or a face. No pushing the Haggerty charisma, not on your life. Guts I don't need to prove, says he. Strategy. Tactics. Let the black-brained whites and the white-brained blacks boil it up, man. (*Pause.*) Weapons. Organization. (*Pause.*) And books and more books. Whilst little orphan white-fanny me! (*Pause.*) Exactly what are you implying that you are proposing, Bernard? I live here till we sink into some sort of tender stagnation? Waiting for the apocalypse? (*Pause.*) I've got money, energy. I've got fury, intelligence. I am *informed* out of my mind! I am warped beyond recognition, when I recall the infatuated buffoon slipped out father's ludicrous apartment overlooking Central Park. (*Pause.*) The way he fought it was pretty good. No nonsense with attorneys and the law and the fuzz. No. Just an emanating centre of *hurt*. Of *pain*. Just a quiet unremitting bombardment of *feeling* over there on Central Park. That I had killed him long before he died. (*Pause.*) And to ram home the point. When he *did* die. He left me pretty rich. (*Pause.*) The machiavellian bastard! (*Pause.*) Knowing of course that living with Haggerty it was a point of doctrine to live poor. I mean on my part. Haggerty himself was as unaffected by the availability of money as he was by the absence of it. (*Pause.*) You want *me*, Bernard?

Pause.

BERNARD. Living here. (*Pause.*) And then. You never know.

Pause.

CLAIRE. I guess the first thing is to sit it out until Haggerty's guy in Paris has carried out all his instructions. Huh?

Pause.

How can *you* make *me* cry?

Pause.

BERNARD. Just do as you like.

She looks at her watch.

CLAIRE. It's nearly four. Where do you suppose Sawdust and Tinsel have got to? I offered them lunch. No, said Chris. We'll go round to the pub. (*Pause.*) *I* think that boy's a killer lost his vocation!

Pause.

BERNARD. The work's finished. (*Pause.*) I asked them round for a drink about six. (*Pause.*) Have a drink. Give them a few quid bonus in cash. (*Pause.*) Have a few drinks –

Pause.

CLAIRE. I'm going up and talk to your father. You stabbed at him good and hard, Bernard –

Pause.

BERNARD. Do you feel anything about me?

CLAIRE. Yeah. You make me feel you've decided to be old. Which makes me feel *older*.

CLAIRE *exits. The outside doorbell rings.* BERNARD *goes to*

answer it. After a moment he comes back carrying a wreath.
There is an envelope pinned to it, with a card inside. He takes
out the card and reads:

BERNARD (*reading*). Bernard, man – I am not dead yet. I guess I
imagined that out of either depression or apoplexy, you might
now be ready to drape this round some cat's neck. (*Pause.*)
Your well-wisher: Haggerty.

    BERNARD *picks up the wreath, sets it down on a chair in a*
corner. Goes out.

    Fade out and fade in to

Scene Seven

Darkness. Two signs are lowered, one saying: AMAGANSETT, LONG
ISLAND; *the other –* CRANTHORPE, YORKSHIRE.

Two chairs: in one, BERNARD. *In the other,* CLAIRE.

A moving, dappled green and yellow light shifts across CLAIRE.
BERNARD *is in a glaring white spot.*

Before she speaks, we hear sea sounds: Before he speaks, we hear the
rattle and clatter of a pit.

CLAIRE. I don't care what you say, Haggerty. I shall hang on to
this place till the day I die. (*Pause.*) I spent my summers here.
(*Pause.*) I would like to have my baby here. (*Pause.*) Yes. And
we'll go to Europe because we go where you say.

    Pause.

BERNARD. You've said everything you think about drinking to
me, dad, except *why*. For which thank God because the problem
has had me and my psycho-analyst ruminating for a number of
years. (*Pause.*) No, dad, I am *not* an out-patient at a mental
hospital. I am *not* in danger of what you would call insanity.
(*Pause.*) I lie on this man's couch in his consulting room and I
talk. (*Pause.*) Or I'm silent. (*Pause.*) Or I go to sleep. (*Pause.*)
What? Three guineas a session. (*Pause.*) Five days a week.
(*Pause.*) Yes. I am well aware that that adds up to three times

your pension. (*Pause.*) The idea, dad, is to penetrate the enigma that is Bernard. (*Pause.*) What's that? (*Pause.*) And bloody good luck to you too!

Pause.

CLAIRE. In my seventh month, Haggerty, I shall come back to America and have your child here.

Pause.

BERNARD. Well. I send you ten quid a week, don't I? And I live on forty. (*Pause.*) So I suppose I must make sixty-odd quid a week. (*Pause.*) Nothing, dad. You fell asleep. I was just mumbling to myself, having failed to notice that you had withdrawn that minimal animation which passes for unconsciousness in you.

Pause.

CLAIRE. It seems like I cannot remember the pre-Haggerty universe.

Pause.

BERNARD. Yes, I remember. God, I remember. The first slum. The second slum. (*Pause.*) Then the first council house. (*Pause.*) Hitler, Mussolini, Len Hutton. (*Pause.*) Yes, I remember you used to take me up on the footplate. (*Pause.*) And let me press the button on the coal hopper at the sheds on wage days. (*Pause.*) Yes. Considering the historical conditions of the period, as the comrades used to put it . . . yes, I had a happy childhood. (*Pause.*) I *did* love my mother. (*Pause.*) But I only discovered that when she was dead. (*Pause.*) I believe that is not uncommon dad.

CLAIRE. I know you'll leave me, Haggerty. Yes, I know. (*Pause.*) Sometime. (*Pause.*) I have known this from the beginning. (*Pause.*) That's a lot of years of wanting it in one way and fearing it in another.

Pause.

BERNARD. Somehow, I didn't know *you* till she died.

CLAIRE. I know one day you will simply disappear. (*Pause.*) You will have planned it.

Pause.

BERNARD. And now – it's too late.

CLAIRE. I should think it will be after the child is born. (*Pause.*) You'll want to be sure I have the real live thing kicking in my arms.

BERNARD. Blame? Blame you? (*Pause.*) For what?

CLAIRE. I'm going down by the sea, Haggerty. Walk by the sea. (*Pause.*) Watch the rollers.

    Pause.

BERNARD. I'm moving again. (*Pause.*) To Hampstead. There's a bit of garden. A garden flat. (*Pause.*) Come down –

    Pause.

CLAIRE. Out of this house. Through the woods. (*Pause.*) Only for a couple of hours. (*Pause.*) I don't want you to see one single more tear on my face! (*She stands.*)

BERNARD (*standing*). You could plant me a few flowers. (*Pause.*) Yes. Daffodils, if you like. (*Pause.*) Will the time come when it doesn't end up with you crying? (*Pause.*) Did you never want to cry when she was *alive?*

    The spots go out. The signs raised.

Scene Eight

Fade up on: MR LINK in his chair. BERNARD sitting on his swivel chair by the desk. CLAIRE right of MR LINK. CHRIS left of MR LINK – both seated. ROGER standing. They all have drinks and there is a trolley with bottles, glasses, ice, etc. MR LINK has a glass of Guinness. The others whisky or vodka. There is an uncomfortable silence for some time.

FATHER. You'll be moving on to another job, then. Chris and Roger. (*Raises his glass.*) Good health –

    Pause.

ROGER. Not me I won't. I've got the sack.

FATHER. I'm sorry about that, young man. But it isn't as if it was your trade. Now, is it?

ROGER. Oh, absolutely! Just a question of body and soul being kept together, that's all.

Long pause. FATHER *looks round.*

FATHER. There in't nobody gives you a good job for your money nowdays. No pride in what they do. Chuck it together, grab your brass and off.

CHRIS *stands, goes to* MR LINK.

CHRIS. You dissatisfied with what we done with Bernard's place?

Pause.

FATHER. I was speaking generally, young man. Don't take it personal.

CHRIS. Right. (*He turns and moves away a little.*)

FATHER. Mind. When you come to look round. When you take a *close* look. It's cheap paint. And where there's wood – cheap wood. (*Pause.*) Don't reckon much to t'grouting on them bathroom tiles, neither.

CHRIS *rounds on him.*

CHRIS. We done a thorough job! And listened to *you* drivellin' on for hours into the bargain –

Pause.

FATHER. Bernard. Are you going to let this one speak like this to me in your own house?

BERNARD. Chris –

CHRIS. I run away from one like you, Mr Link. Just like you, an' a dirty southerner *into the bargain*. With you it's all up north and pre-war and this and that and the other. With him it was Dunkirk. El Alamein to Rome! But you're all the same. You're all bloody fossils! And we different and you don't like it. You sneer and mumble at what we wear, what we do, how we feel, how we screw. (*Pause.*) Well, I'll say to you what I said to him: *screw you!* (*He drains his glass and puts it down.*) Sorry, Bernard –

FATHER. Now that's a bit on a mystery, that is –

Pause.

ROGER. No mystery about it, dear! Just try not to get upset, that's all. What's Chrissy to *you*?

Pause.

FATHER. He 'ad *me* deceived at first. I thowt he were t'best on the two of you. (*Pause.*) You being like, an *amateur* Roger –

ROGER. Thanks ever so!

BERNARD. Dad, you don't know a thing about interior decorating, or carpentry, or any of it.

ROGER. And I suppose you think *I'm* inferior because I'm queer! Don't you worry, Father Bear – the *'omo* is *off*. Not going to hang round listening to –

FATHER (*cutting in*). I know *quality* when I see it, Bernard. Quality of *workmanship*.

ROGER. I only stuck it out for Bernard's sake –

FATHER. Aye. I'm not surprised to 'ear that, neither.

BERNARD *gets up and goes to his father.*

BERNARD. And what do you mean by *that*?

Pause.

FATHER. Manly is as manly does.

ROGER. God, he's awful! I mean I thought he was lovely and primitive and quaint when he arrived. (*Going to* FATHER.) My Link, you're a nasty destructive old man. And your Bernard's *'etero* – though I don't suppose you'll get that because it isn't a soap powder, is it?

ROGER *slams down his drink and flounces out.* BERNARD *takes the chair occupied by* CHRIS. ROGER *pops his head back round the door.*

ROGER. More's the pity, Bernard – (*And withdraws again, closing the door.*)

Long pause.

BERNARD. Thanks very much, father.

FATHER. No point in bottling owt up.

Pause.

BERNARD. We were supposed to be having a friendly drink before they left!

FATHER. *Friendly drink!* Have you seen yon ceiling in t'baby's room? (*Pause.*) It could come down, that ceiling could. Aye. An' wi' a bairn underneath. I give it a prod, an' all flakes come down. What they've done, they've licked a bit of paint over rotten plaster. (*Pause.*) It's the modern way, in't it? (*Pause.*) That doesn't mean you've got to keep your mouth shut.

CLAIRE. Mr Link. Chris went over the place and made a list of everything needed doing. Then he did what Bernard said he could afford. What he did seems pretty good to me. D'you think *I* don't know the condition of this apartment? I lived here long enough!

Pause.

FATHER. Our Bernard. He won't speak up for his own good –

BERNARD. No. He's not manly enough, isn't our Bernard.

FATHER. Well, I'm right, aren't I? You've never been what I'd call a man. And if I see summat wrong when I'm down in London, well, I try to put it right. You won't speak up for yoursen. You'd let 'em rob t'shirt off your back. Is *that* manly?

Pause.

BERNARD. No, dad.

Pause.

FATHER. *Always* been a weakling. (*Pause: to* CLAIRE.) He run away from t'Germans, you know. In t'war. Got a scar on his backside the size of a bakin' tin. (*Pause.*) His mother was a fine woman, but I always thought there was summat wrong on her side on t'family. More than one bad 'un. Who handed out t'half-crown pieces every time when her brothers were locked out on t'pit? Me. Muggins. (*Pause.*) He's picked summat up from her side, Bernard has. (*Pause.*) She had all the good on her side on t'family in *her*, his mother did. God rest her.

Pause.

CLAIRE (*standing*). I guess I'm moving over the other side of the barricade from you, Mr Link. Reluctantly, but you sure do provoke! I thought it was just Bernard needled *you*. (*Pause.*) What's the matter with you, Mr Link?

FATHER. Nothing's wrong wi' me, love. (*Drains his glass.*) I'm
fine. Fit as a lop. (*Pause.*) I'm used to people taking against
me. We very blunt you know, in Yorkshire. Blunt but straight.
Straight as a die.

CLAIRE. Anybody in Yorkshire take against you?

MR LINK *slowly swivels his head, to where he can see the wreath
standing in a corner.*

FATHER. Might I ask what a wreath's doing in the house?
Pause.

CLAIRE. My husband sent it.

FATHER. Oh. He did, did he? Somebody kicked t'bucket, like?

CLAIRE. No, Mr Link. He has a kind of morbid sense of humour.
Pause.

FATHER (*slowly*). Is there owt funny goin' on, then?

CLAIRE. Not a thing.
Pause.

FATHER. There's another one wasting his brass then. In't there?
(*Pause.*) I was hoping we'd have a bit on a talk one of these
days. About your husband. (*Pause.*) I'd have that baby's name
changed by deed poll if I was you. You can do it, you know. It
might be a quid or two. But he can't go to school wi' that name
– can he? Bernard said it come out on some book or other.

CLAIRE. That's right. (*Pause.*) A book called 'Crime and Punishment'.
Pause.

FATHER. That in't a morbid sense of 'umour! More like a screw
loose, in't it?

CLAIRE (*drily*). Haggerty is as Haggerty does, Mr Link –
Pause.

FATHER. Aye. Everyman's the right to be master in his own
house. (*Pause.*) Except o' course, he's nowhere to be seen.
(*Pause.*) The way they split up nowadays! What do they get
married *for*?
Pause.

CLAIRE (*quietly and deliberately*). Well, you see, Mr Link. I married Haggerty when I was very young. And I had absorbed the beliefs of my parents –

FATHER (*cutting in*). That's right an' all. It's in the Commandments. Honour thy father and thy mother that thy days shall be long in the land which the Lord thy God giveth thee.
Pause.

CLAIRE. Yes. (*Pause.*) Very well put, Mr Link. Only I came unstuck because you see I sort of had the Commandments on the one hand, and the desire to fuck Haggerty day and night on the other.

BERNARD'S *father is stunned. His glass drops out of his hand.*

FATHER. Bernard – I'm not stopping here another minute!
Long pause.

BERNARD. I don't see you moving, dad.

FATHER. Did you hear what she *said*?

BERNARD. Yes. *Isn't* she a dirty-mouthed bitch! After all?

FATHER (*to* CLAIRE). I'm afraid that that is what I think you are, young woman! I've never heard the like –
Pause.

BERNARD. Still sitting there, dad –
Long pause.

FATHER. I'll shift when *I'm* ready. And it'll be for good, I can tell thee!

BERNARD *goes to the wreath, picks it up. Holds it, looking at it.*

BERNARD. What size do you take dad? Shirt collar?

FATHER (*caught off balance*). Eh?

BERNARD. Size of shirt collar?

FATHER. Seventeen an' a half. But –

BERNARD (*cutting in*). Yes. Well, I think it might fit.
He walks to his father, holds the wreath over his head and slowly places it down over his shoulders.

FATHER (*half rising*). What the bloody hell –

BERNARD *puts his hands on his father's shoulders and firmly presses him back into the chair.*

BERNARD. No. Don't move, dad. Too old to change your habits now. (*Pause.*) It looks well on you.

CLAIRE *can't take this, she turns away. Slowly* MR LINK *rises to his feet – dazed, clutching at the wreath but holding it in position.*

FATHER (*almost crying*). Eh, Bernard –

Pause.

BERNARD. Cruel?

FATHER. *Bernard –*

BERNARD. Not comical?

Pause.

FATHER. *Bernard –*

BERNARD. Bear up. Remember one of your many hundreds of banal remarks. Oft repeated. (*Pause.*) A nod's as good as a wink to a blind donkey –

MR LINK, *trance-like, pulls the wreath off and throws it down. He looks at his feet.*

FATHER. I'm an old man. And your father.

Pause.

BERNARD. Yes. You are.

Pause.

FATHER. I should be respected.

BERNARD. Yes. You should be respected.

Pause.

FATHER. I'll have no more on thee!

Pause.

BERNARD. I've had enough of you.

Pause.

FATHER. You should be ashamed.

BERNARD. I *am* ashamed.

FATHER (*shouting*). I'll strike thee down!

Pause.

BERNARD. Strike me –

Pause.

FATHER. I'll not touch thee. I'll not mucky my hands.

Pause.

BERNARD. You never *have touched* me.

Pause.

FATHER (*now crying*). I've loved my son.

BERNARD. Undetectably.

Pause.

FATHER. I've failed thee? Some road?

Pause.

BERNARD. No, father.

Pause.

FATHER. So . . . tha loved only thy mother!

BERNARD. No, father. I loved you as well.

Pause.

FATHER. What did I do to harm thee? I worked mesen dead. Come home nearly too tired to eat. Fell into t'chair by the fire. (*Pause.*) And went to bed when I woke up.

He stands a moment, rubbing his eyes.

You an' your mother was always chattering away. (*Shouts.*) I know I niver had nowt to say!

Pause.

BERNARD. Shall we say, father . . . that after your fashion, you became eloquent once she was dead? (*Pause.*) It was high time somebody flung a wreath on you.

Pause.

FATHER. I can't make nowt on any on this.

BERNARD. There's nowhere to begin. Is there?

Pause.

FATHER. You've broken my pride this day.

BERNARD *simply stands staring at him. His* FATHER *looks pleadingly towards* CLAIRE, *but her back is turned.*

MR LINK *slowly shuffles to the stairs door and goes out, closing it quietly behind him.* CLAIRE *goes to* BERNARD.

CLAIRE. *Are* you ashamed?

BERNARD. Yes.

Pause.

CLAIRE. But you could go through with that –

BERNARD. You didn't make a bad start yourself.

> *Pause.*

CLAIRE. I'm more ashamed than you are.

> *She sinks into one of the chairs, her face in her hands.* BERNARD *remains standing. The doorbell rings.* CLAIRE *takes no notice. After a moment,* BERNARD *goes out to answer it. There is a mumble of voices in the hall. Two men walk in through the hall door carrying a coffin.* BERNARD *follows them helplessly.*

BERNARD. I tell you you've come to the wrong place –

FIRST MAN. No, we 'aven't, sir.

SECOND MAN (*holds out a piece of paper*). It's your address, sir. And the order was from the agent of a Mr Haggerty in Paris –

FIRST MAN. Nobody dead in the house? Well, it's an *empty* one, sir. Must be a joke –

> *He laughs half-heartedly.* CLAIRE *is sitting up staring horrified at the coffin. The two men go out.*

SECOND MAN (*leaving*). There's a plaque and some writing on it, Mr Link. (*Exits.*)

CLAIRE (*sharply*). Read it out, Bernard –

> *Pause.*

BERNARD. You read it. (*Pause.*) It's none of my affair.

> BERNARD *goes out through the hall door, pulling his jacket off a chair as he goes.* CLAIRE *slowly approaches the coffin. She kneels beside it and reads out slowly :*

CLAIRE (*reading*). There's more to this box
>> Than macabre wit.
>> Haggerty's dead
>> But he's not in it.

> *Pause.*

>> Bury it some place
>> If you have a mind.
>> The rightful contents
>> Would be hard to find.

> *Pause.*

James Mawnan Haggerty. Guerrilla. Killed during a skirmish between Government Forces and a rebel unit. Africa. Nineteen seventy.

> CLAIRE *stays beside the coffin for some moments. She gets up. Looks round. Sees the wreath on the floor. She picks it up and drops it on the coffin. Exits through the door to the stairs. Curtain.*
> *The coffin remains downstage of the curtain.*